Decolonisation of Materialities or Materialisation of (Re-)Colonisation?

Symbolisms, Languages, Ecocriticism and (Non)Representationalism in 21st Century Africa

Edited by

Artwell Nhemachena, Jairos Kangira &Nelson Mlambo

Langaa Research & Publishing CIG
Mankon, Bamenda

Publisher
Langaa RPCIG
Langaa Research & Publishing Common Initiative Group
P.O. Box 902 Mankon
Bamenda
North West Region
Cameroon
Langaagrp@gmail.com
www.langaa-rpcig.net

Distributed in and outside N. America by African Books Collective
orders@africanbookscollective.com
www.africanbookscollective.com

ISBN-10: 9956-763-94-2

ISBN-13: 978-9956-763-94-8

© Artwell Nhemachena, Jairos Kangira &Nelson Mlamboe 2018

About the Contributors

Dr Artwell Nhemachena holds a PhD in Social Anthropology; MSc in Sociology and Social Anthropology; BSc Honours Degree in Sociology and a Certificate in Law. He lectures in Sociology at the University of Namibia. His current areas of research interest are Knowledge Studies; Development Studies; Environment; Resilience; Food Security and Food Sovereignty; Industrial Sociology; Conflict and Peace; Transformation; Science and Technology Studies, Democracy and Governance; Relational Ontologies; Decoloniality and Anthropological Jurisprudence. He has published in the areas of social theory, research methods, democracy and governance; conflict and peace; relational ontologies; industrial sociology; development; science and technology studies; anthropological jurisprudence, environment, mining, biotechnology and knowledge studies; transformation and decoloniality.

Professor Jairos Kangira earned his PhD in Rhetoric Studies from the University of Cape Town, South Africa. He is an international scholar of rhetoric, particularly presidential rhetoric. Prof Kangira has travelled the length and breadth of the world delivering conference papers, guest-lecturing and conducting workshops in universities - the latest workshop being the International Rhetoric Workshop that was held at Uppsala University, Sweden. The workshop was attended by 50 PhD students in rhetoric from across the world. He has published extensively in the field of rhetoric and language. He is the Dean of the Faculty of Humanities and Social Sciences at the University of Namibia (UNAM). Previously, he was the Head of the Department of Language and Literature Studies at UNAM. He was the Deputy Dean of the Faculty of Arts at the University of Zimbabwe before he relocated to Namibia in 2006, joining the then Polytechnic of Namibia (now Namibia University of Science and Technology). Having great interest in research and publication, Prof Kangira successfully established two international journals in Namibia, *Nawa Journal of Language and Communication* at

NUST in 2007, and the *Journal for Studies in Humanities and Social Sciences* at UNAM in 2012, and became the founding editor of both publications. He is also the founding board member of the UNAM Press where he has played a leading role in the publication of many academic books. Prof Kangira's other qualifications are: a Master of Philosophy in Linguistics, a Special Honours in Linguistics degree and a Certificate in Education from the University of Zimbabwe; a Bachelor of Arts from the University of South Africa; and a Postgraduate Certificate in Tertiary Education Management and a Master of Tertiary Education Management from the University of Melbourne, Australia. Prof Kangira has made a great impact in the development of the English language in Namibia.

Dr Nelson Mlambo holds degrees from the University of Zimbabwe, University of Namibia and Stellenbosch University. He is currently a Lecturer in the Department of Language and Literature Studies at the University of Namibia. An author of three books and more than twenty refereed journal articles, Dr Mlambo has also supervised more than fifteen Masters and PhD students. Dr Mlambo's research interests are in the area of literary studies, particularly focusing on recent theorisations which are of relevance to Africa's present challenges. Of late Dr Mlambo has been researching on the value of health communication in multilingual societies as well as the significance of postcolonial ecocriticism in genocidal literature, with a specific focus on the Herero/Germany fiction about the genocide.

Professor Ruby Magosvongwe is an Associate Professor in the Department of English, Faculty of Arts, University of Zimbabwe. Professor Magosvongwe holds a DPhil from the University of Cape Town, Master of Arts Degree in English, Bachelor of Arts Special Honours in English Degree, Bachelor of Arts Degree and Graduate Certificate in Education, all from the University of Zimbabwe. Professor Magosvongwe is also a Research Fellow with the English Department, University of the Free State, South Africa. With effect from March 2017, she was appointed the interim **Editor-in-Chief,** of *Zambezia* University of Zimbabwe's Journal of the Humanities. Professor Magosvongwe is the current Chairperson of the

Department of English, University of Zimbabwe where she currently lectures English Literature and African Literature. She has co-edited and published *African Womanhood: Emerging Perspectives on Zimbabwean Women's Writing in Indigenous Languages* (2006), College Press, with Zifikile Mguni; *Rediscoursing African Womanhood in the Search for Sustainable Renaissance: Africana Womanism in Multi-disciplinary Approaches,* College Press (2012), with Zifikile Mguni, Itai Muhwati and Tavengwa Gwekwerere; *Dialoguing Land and Identity in Zimbabwe and other Developing Countries: Emerging Perspectives* (2015), with Zifikile Makwavarara and Obed Mlambo; *Africa's Intangible Heritage and Land: Emerging Perspectives* (2016), with Obed Mlambo and Even though Ndlovu. She has also widely published in Literature and Gender, African Literature and Comparative Literature. She is the current Chairperson of the Zimbabwe International Book Fair Association General Council and has also been recently appointed a Board Member of the National Arts Council of Zimbabwe.

Lázaro Pedro Chissano is an English-Portuguese Translator. In 2016, he graduated from the University of Namibia, where he obtained the degree of Master of Arts in English Studies. He also holds BA (Honours) in Translation and Interpretation from Eduardo Mondlane University in Mozambique. He is currently employed as Translator (Portuguese) at the Southern African Development Community (SADC) at its Headquarters in Gaborone, Botswana. Before joining the Secretariat, he worked for four years as a legal translator (Portuguese) at the SADC Tribunal in Windhoek, Namibia. His research interests have been focused on political rhetoric in Southern African countries.

Dr Tapiwa Victor Warikandwa holds a Doctor of Laws. He is a Senior Lecturer in the Faculty of Law at the University of Namibia. He specializes in International Trade Law, Labour Law, Indigenisation Laws, Mining Law and Constitutional Law amongst other disciplines. Prior to coming to Namibia, Dr. Warikandwa worked as a legal officer and later legal advisor in the Ministry of Public Service Labour and Social Welfare in Zimbabwe. Key amongst his duties was legal drafting. Dr Warikandwa worked with the law reviser of the Ministry of Justice in Zimbabwe in reviewing laws administered by the Ministry of Public Service Labour and Social Welfare. Dr Warikandwa also completed an ordinary and advanced training in Labour Law Making at the International Labour Organization's International Training Centre in Turin Italy. On numerous occasions, Dr. Warikandwa was actively involved in the activities of the Cabinet Committee on Legislation on behalf of the Ministry of Public Service Labour and Social Welfare. Dr. Warikandwa has since written books on labour law and women's rights in South Africa and Namibia amongst others, as well as publishing articles in accredited peer reviewed journals such as Law, Development and Democracy, Speculum Juris, Potchefstroom Electronic Law Journal, Comparative International Law Journal for Southern Africa and the African Journal of International and Comparative Law, amongst others. Dr. Warikandwa has also been awarded a number of merit based scholarships and has served as a Post-doctoral Fellow with the University of Fort Hare in South Africa. He has also worked as a senior lecturer at the University of Fort Hare and presented papers at conferences in and outside South Africa. Dr Warikandwa studied for his Bachelor of Laws, Master's degree and Doctoral degree at the University of Fort Hare in South Africa.

Dr Munetsi Ruzivo holds a PhD in Religious Studies. He is a Senior Lecturer for Christian History and Thought, and Christianity in Africa. He is based in the Department of Religious Studies, Classics and Philosophy at the University of Zimbabwe.

Juliet Sylvia Pasi is a lecturer in the Department of Communication at the Namibia University of Science and Technology. She teaches linguistics, communication and literature courses to Undergraduate, Honours and Masters Degree students. She holds a Masters in English Degree, an Honours Degree in English, a Graduate Certificate in Education from the University of Zimbabwe and an on-line Certificate on Building Teaching Skills through the Interactive Web from the University of Oregon. Her research interests are in gendered identities, ecocriticism and ecofeminism and children's literature. A number of her articles in these areas have been published in academic journals. She is currently pursuing Doctoral studies at the University of South Africa.

Njabulo Chipangura is employed by the National Museums and Monuments of Zimbabwe as an archaeologist and is based in Eastern Zimbabwe at Mutare Museum. His research interests include looking at the configuration and reconfiguration of museum collection and exhibition practices within colonial and post-colonial settings. He has also carried out research on the hosting of cultural festivals at heritage sites specifically looking at the dissemination of public culture at these festivals and how they give communities a sense of heritage ownership. His other research focus is on the different classifications of heritage in Zimbabwe with an interest on the category of colonial historic buildings and he has looked at how it has lost relevancy in the present conservation discourse. This research saw him critically analysing the emergence of the category of liberation war heritage in the country and how it has seemingly supplanted all the other forms of heritage in terms of conservation priority. This research was extended to take an inside look at liberation war heritage and he analysed the narratives that have emerged from exhumation exercises of liberation war fighters which he has been involved in as an archaeologist. He is currently a Wenner Gren PhD Fellow in the Anthropology Department at the University of Witwatersrand in South Africa. His PhD research looks at the archaeological, ethnographic and historical characteristics of artisanal and small scale mining of gold in the Eastern Highlands of Zimbabwe. In this research, he intends to establish the historical connection between ancient gold mining and contemporary artisanal mining by 'illegal miners' who are presently exploiting the gold reef around Mutanda cultural landscape.

Pauline Chiripanhura holds a BA Honours Degree in Archaeology and a Master's Degree in Heritage studies from the University of Zimbabwe. In 2014, she began full-time study towards a PhD in Archaeology with the University of Cape Town. She recently submitted her PhD thesis for examination. She works as a Curator of Archaeology at Mutare museum which is administered by the National Museums and Monuments of Zimbabwe (hereafter

NMMZ), since 2012. She has researched a lot on legacy collections housed in Zimbabwe museums and is working on publishing her findings. She also researched and mounted a permanent exhibition at Mutare museum, the first post-independence permanent exhibition within NMMZ.

Martin Uadiale is an academic, scholar, and researcher. He has held fellowships, won laureateships and grants. He was an international researcher at the Center for Trans-Atlantic Relations, Paul H. Nitze's School of Advanced International Studies at Johns Hopkins University in Washington, D.C., United States of America; Leading to the completion of a book chapter in a recently published book: *Dark Networks in the Atlantic Basin: Emerging Trends and Implications for Human Security*, published by Johns Hopkins University and The Brookings Institution, Washington, D.C. He is also a scholar-in-residence, at the Minerva Center for the Study of the Rule of Law under Extreme Conditions, at the University of Haifa, Israel. He has since 2014 being a Scholar at The Democratic Governance Institute, of the Council for the Development of Social Science Research in Africa (CODESRIA), Dakar, Senegal. He was at the Harvard Law School, Institute of Global Law and Policy (IGLP), New England, Massachusetts, United States. He is currently completing a thesis on: *Neo-liberal Spatial Dynamics and Applied Agrarian Political Economy*, at the Nigerian Defence Academy, Kaduna, Nigeria. His most recent published works includes; *Boko Haram; A Concoction of State Failure, Elite-Class Competition and Alienation in Nigeria*, published by Cambridge Scholars Publishing, United Kingdom, 2017;, *Land Grabs, Food Sovereignty and Sustainable Development, in, Agenda 2030 and Africa`s Development in the Twenty-First Century*, published by the United Nations University, International Institute of Global Health, Kuala-Lumpur, Malaysia, 2017.

Awala-Ale Anirejuoritse attended Benson Idahosa University for undergraduate studies. He graduated with second-class honours, upper division (2:1) in International Studies and Diplomacy. His postgraduate studies were based at Coventry University where he was awarded the degree of Master of Arts, with distinction in International Relations.

Dolphin Mabale obtained her Master of Arts degree in Anthropology at the University of Venda, South Africa. She also graduated with the Postgraduate Diploma in Arts specialising in Heritage Studies from the University of the Witwatersrand, South Africa. Her areas of specialisation are Anthropology and Heritage Studies, with a focus on Public Culture and Politics of Identity. Mabale is currently employed by her alma mater, the University of Venda, as a junior lecturer in Anthropology and Archaeology at the E'skia Mphahlele Centre for African Studies, since 2008.

Coletta M. Kandemiri is currently a student at the University of Namibia in the Faculty of Humanities and Social Sciences. She is completing Master of Arts in English Studies. Her main interest is in literature that relates to social life, and her passion for literature is driven by the fact that literature is all about "creatures" called human beings. Kandemiri has the following publications which are mainly in literature: *Interrogating the Literary Representations of an Exceptional Group in Society - Old eople; Articulating the Unsayables; Multifaceted Didacticism of Ba's So Long a Letter; Healing approaches: African versus Western Approaches in Chinodya's Strife.* She has five newspaper publications, in a local Namibian newspaper, on different topics from the courses that were offered in her master studies. Also, forthcoming are her two book chapters in literature and one paper on academic writing. She obtained her first degree at the University of Zimbabwe after which she joined the University of Namibia to complete a B.A (Hons.) degree before enrolling for a Master of Arts in English Studies degree. She sees literature as a point from which all other life affairs stem from.

Okom Emmanuel Otegwu is a Nigerian and a PhD student with the Department of French and Francophone Studies, School of Language, Literature and Media Studies, Faculty of Humanities, University of the Witwatersrand, Johannesburg, South Africa. His area of study is on translation and mediation in the teaching of French as a Foreign Language. He has lectured, in Federal College of Education, Yola, Nigeria, for a decade before transferring to Nigeria French Language Village, Inter-University Centre, Ajara – Badagry, Lagos, Nigeria. He holds a B.A Education/French from

University of Ife, Ile-Ife, Nigeria and M. A. (Translation Studies) from Abia State University, Uturu, Nigeria. He attended summer schools in Besancon, France and had his year abroad programme in Lomé, Togo. Besides the articles published in some Nigerian dailies, he has published several scholarly articles in both local and international journals. He has also published a book in the area of French language didactics and translation. In addition he is a freelance conference interpreter and translator.

Asteria N. Nauta grew up in the northern part of Namibia in a small village Onekukumo-Ombaanhu Omusati region. She attended her primary school-education at Onelago Combined School (Anamulenge Circuit, Omusati) and she completed her high school education at Canisianum Roman Catholic High School (Anamulenge circuit, Omusati). After completing her high school education, she was admitted at the University of Namibia in the multidisciplinary course BART of which she enrolled for Psychology, Sociology, History and Professional Communications. In 2016, she was awarded an Honours Degree, double major in Sociology and Industrial Psychology. During her studies at the University of Namibia, she participated in some extramural activities and she was also a member of two societies, Sociology Society and Psychology Society. Asteria is looking forward to studying for an MA degree.

Paulus Mwetulundila is a Staff Development Fellow in the Social Science Division of the Multidisciplinary Research Centre (MRC) of the University of Namibia. He holds a double major BA degree in Industrial Psychology and Sociology from the University of Namibia. Currently he is studying for an MA in Gender and Development Studies degree with the same institution. His primary research orientation focuses on gender and labour with an emphasis on gender inequalities in the labour force. His current research interests are guided by Goal 5 of the Sustainable Development Goals (SDG) which advocates for providing women and girls with equal access to education, health care, decent work, and representation in political and economic decision-making processes so as to generate sustainable economies that benefit humanity.

Table of Contents

Foreword

Debates about (de-)coloniality have gripped the contemporary world like frenzy. Recently, South African universities have witnessed student movements around matters of "decolonising" the university curricula. Such "decolonisation" of the curricula cannot possibly take place without attending specifically to "decolonising" languages that constitute the media of instruction in the universities. However, at the core of "decolonising" languages and the broader university curricula is the issue of decolonising materialities of which the languages constitute the symbols. In other words, languages and literary works are closely imbricated with materialities to such an extent that decolonising one necessarily has a domino effect on the nature of the other. The imbrications between languages and materialities constitute an important facet of the contemporary discourses around what are called "new materialities' that are rather hastily considered by some scholars to be a part of decolonisation. While postmodernists and poststructuralists have advanced some theoretical postulates that might be understood to provide the foundations for "decolonising" languages, Africa specific "decolonisation" needs not be confused with postmodernist and poststructuralist deconstructionism. In this sense, decolonisation is not similar to deconstruction: in fact deconstruction of African institutions was part and parcel of the colonisation process. In the contemporary era the ongoing deconstruction and decentring of Africa should be understood in terms of the exigencies of the ongoing global coloniality that is facilitated by postmodernist and poststructuralist theoretical pretensions. Besides, the languages of instruction and [postmodernist] theorisation within universities remain the [central] dominant languages of the former colonial masters, which languages have often historically resulted in mistranslation of African modes of thought and ecological engagements. The continued employment of the languages from the colonial *lingua franca* poses deep and resilient questions about matters of translation particularly in the light of scholarly concerns about "decolonisation" and the accuracy of translation processes as well as the attendant losses and inaccuracies of meanings across linguistic domains.

The contemporary and ongoing efforts at translating African environments, particularly efforts to understand African metaphors in relation to African ecologies have often missed the nuances of African languages [metaphors] that are often erroneously translated literally. Such mistranslations [which often borrow heavily from colonial mistranslations of African ecologies and cosmologies] risk perpetuating misunderstandings of African engagements and thought systems in relation to their ecologies. Early colonial scholars and travellers have for instance mistranslated African ecologies in terms of animism and consequently they have mistranslated Africans as [Godless] worshippers of nature. Such assumptions of animism have underpinned the misrepresentations of Africans as practising the most primitive forms of religion involving the worshipping of nature; they have legitimised the misrepresentations of Africans as indistinct from nature, including animals, hence the misrepresentations have legitimised the dismissal of African languages as incomprehensible blabbering, much like animals would do. In this sense, the marginalisation of African languages is traceable to the colonial misrepresentations of Africans as animists and as indistinct to nature including animals. In the heat of postcolonial critiques about colonial misrepresentation of Africans, some contemporary scholars have shifted discourses to what they call "nonrepresentationalism" in which they capitalise on African metaphors [which are erroneously and conveniently interpreted literally] to effectively carry on with colonial misrepresentations. These misrepresentations and mistranslations are resurging in a context where African [metaphorical] assertions in terms of for instance *mwana wevhu* (Son or daughter of the soil) are being interpreted literally in order to resuscitate colonial caricaturing of Africans as indistinct from nature. The misrepresentations speak to broader scholarly debates on representationalism, postmodernist nonrepresentationalism and the fate of languages and materialities that happen to be understood through postmodernist and poststructuralist questioning of signifiers and signified as well as the attendant antifoundationalism. In other words, the question is about the import of postmodernist antifoundationalism in an African context where materialities often constitute the foundations of languages that provide signifiers which help distinguish different materialities.

The question is about the relevance of postmodernism and poststructuralism [which posit "erosion of binaries" while paradoxically declining to restore and restitute materialities looted in colonial Africa] in explaining African realities including significations, referents, symbolisms, representations and materialities. The question is about the necessity and relevance of the conflation that results from undoing binaries between the literal and metaphorical meanings; the signifier and the signified. The question about the implications of nonrepresentationalism for languages - how might nonrepresentationalism and [African] languages sit together? Would nonrepresentationalism not attack the core of [African] languages premised on referents and on binaries between signified and signifiers? The question is about the implications of the conflation on the structure of languages that are subject to poststructuralist and postmodernist deconstruction. The question is about how Africans might be best understood, using lenses of Pan Africanism, in relation to their ecologies in the postcolonial era?

Artwell Nhemachena; Jairos Kangira and Nelson Mlambo

Chapter One

Materialities and the Resilient Global Frontierisation of Africa: An Introduction

Artwell Nhemachena; Nelson Mlambo & Jairos Kangira

Settler moves to innocence are those strategies or positionings that attempt to relieve the settler of feelings of guilt or responsibility without giving up land or power or privilege, without having to change much at all…a settler move to innocence…it is an attempt to deflect a settler identity, while continuing to enjoy settler privilege and occupying stolen land…land, water, air, animals, and plants are never able to become postcolonial; they remain objects to be exploited by the empowered postcolonial subjects…Vocalising a 'multicultural' approach to oppressions, or remaining silent on settler colonialism while talking about colonialism, or tacking on a gesture towards indigenous people without addressing indigenous sovereignty or rights, or forwarding a thesis on decolonization without regard to unsettling/ deoccupying land, are equivocations. That is they ambiguously avoid engaging with settler colonialism… (Tuck et al, 2012: 10-19).

Political power without economic power is a myth. Land is life. Life is land. Food, houses, farms, herbs for medicines, animal pastures, gold, diamonds, platinum and other mineral wealth are not in the sky or air. They are in the land. Land is the principal means of producing all the necessity of life. That is why colonialists always target the land of other people. When Rhodes said, 'I prefer land to niggers', he was making the crude and barbaric philosophy of imperialism very clear (Pheko, 7 May 2014).

"Animals" seems to have become the new epithet to use to refer to African-Americans: we have gone from being called "niggers", to "predators" in the 90s, "thugs" in the 2000s and now "animals" (The Guardian, 28 April 2015).

The (Neo-)Colonial Frontierisation of Africa

Since the era of enslavement, Africa has been a (neo-)imperial ritual subject pushed to the thresholds, the margins, the frontiers and to the beneath of the world in spite of the continent's apparent riches in material resources. Thus, Africa has for long been constituted as an imperial ritual subject even as (neo-)empire has been posturing as modern and modernising. Even though the national constitutions [and laws] on the continent are often regarded as [clearly] national constitutions, the sad thing is that they are also liminal negotiated constitutions, that is, they have been negotiated to suit the exigencies of rapacious forces beyond the national and continental borders. (Neo-)imperial rituals of dispossession, exploitation and impoverishment have constituted the continent of Africa as a ritual subject occupying a liminal zone – a threshold - constantly in the shadows of starvation, impoverishment and general want. Being a threshold, liminal or twilight zone, nothing is [supposed to be] certain, it is a zone of partial darkness – a zone where victims of robbery and dispossession are ritually modelled such that they cannot readily distinguish between those that are stealing from them and those that are helping them, a zone where the ritual subjects cannot distinguish between those who usher darkness and those who usher light, a zone where ritual subjects [victims] cannot distinguish between police officers and murderers, between lawyers and villainous criminals, between God and the devil. In short, the liminal, threshold or twilight zone into which Africa has been constituted is one where the spellbound ritual subjects often fruitlessly fight their own shadows in the belief that they are fighting the ritual master.

No amount of ideological ritual chanting of "justice', "equality", "freedom", "democracy", "transparency", "accountability" or "rule of law" has helped to undo the historical effects of the material dispossession, enslavement, disinheritance and impoverishment in Africa. While anthropologists and other scholars wrote about liminal ritual subjects in African and other societies (Turner, 1967; 1969; Van Gennep, 1960; Douglas, 2003), the fundamental difference between (neo-)imperial ritual subjects is that, in spite of gargantuan sacrifice on their part (Nhemachena, 2016b), they seldom successfully graduate to their desired states or even to states that the (neo-)imperial ritual "master" professes. The ritual subject remains in the thresholds, in the liminal spaces, in the frontiers, in the interstices while the Janus-faced (neo-)imperial ritual "master" ritually shouts for more change, for more transformation, for more transition and for more becomings which in effect sadly amount to retrogression of the status of the (neo-)imperial ritual subjects. Thus, while African children, who were subjected to traditional rituals or rites of passage, successfully graduated to state of distinct adulthood, (neo-)imperial rituals subjects remain trapped by impoverishment in states of unmarried adulthood – which is according to Douglas (2003) a dangerous threshold state of betwixt and between.

Constituted into (neo-)imperial ritual subjects in which impoverishment and dispossession were the mechanisms, many impoverished Africans live in threshold or liminal states wherein there is absence of clarity of distinction between human beings and animals, between skin and leather, between the dead and the living, between adult and minors, between war time and peace time. While Douglas (2003: 98) aptly captures the condition of ritual subjects as living dangerously in the cast margins, in formlessness, a ritual liminal space of dirt, obscenity, lawlessness, it is necessary to note that [contrary to traditional rituals] (neo-)imperial rituals do not include rituals of aggregation to assign a new position because African ritual subjects have not been aggregated into the centre of (neo-)empire – for centuries they have remained at the margins or thresholds of empire no matter how hard they strive for recognition, inclusion and fellowship with the ritual masters. So, anthropologists like Turner (1967; 1969); Van Gennep (1960) and Douglas (2003) define liminal individuals' identities as neither here nor there, betwixt and between, at thresholds, in the interstices, at the bottom. Liminal ritual subjects are first stripped of the social status which they possessed prior to the rituals, the ritual subjects are inducted into the liminal period of transition which sadly for the majority of (neo-)imperial ritual subjects is an unending period for which graduation out of liminality is seldom experienced. Thus enslaved Africans were deprived of their social statuses when slave "masters" addressed and treated the enslaved as animals or beasts without rights even to marry and to be

3

married, to establish families, without rights to property, without rights to their heritages, without freedom and liberty as provided by their [jurisprudence] societies (Nhemachena, 2016a). Dispossessed and disinherited of African materialities, Africans and *a fortiori* African "youths", many of whom now can't even marry, are trapped in a liminal or threshold state in which they are unsure whether they will ever or have effectively graduated into adulthood, [which Honwana (2015) calls "waithood"]. Dispossessed of their land, minerals, livestock and of their labour power, Africans [youths] are increasingly finding it difficult to graduate into [marriage] adulthood. We argue that, similarly, nations that were dispossessed, exploited and disinherited without restitution are kept in threshold "waithood" periods where there is uncertainty whether or not they are independent, whether or not they have sovereignty and autonomy and whether or not they have graduated out of the (neo-)colonial strictures.

In the light of the above, we take exception to scholars that define and postulate postcoloniality in terms of hybridity which in fact translates to threshold, liminal, betwixt and between, interstitial positions or uncertainties. In this sense, if during the enslavement and colonial eras, Africans were regarded and treated as animals or beasts of burden and forced to live in threshold or liminal states between animality and humanity, postcoloniality does not have to continue to privilege hybridity and the attendant ritual liminality. Thus, postcoloniality, postmodernism and poststructuralism that are defined in terms of hybridisation, creolisation, and syncretisation perpetuate notions of endless (neo-)imperial transition or liminal phases for Africans particularly in so far as hybridity and liminality are relied upon [by (neo-)imperialists] to deny Africans' sovereignty and autonomy over their resources – material and nonmaterial, tangible and intangible resources. In this regard, [African] liminal ritual subjects are lodged into threshold positions that are replete with ambiguity, they are deemed to be polluting and dangerous even by the (neo-)imperial ritual "masters" who are often quick to deny visas and to very swiftly deport those that try to migrate to (neo-)imperial centres that glitter with opulence paradoxically realised on the backs of the animalised Africans (Fanon, 1963; Nhemachena, 2016a;

Nyamnjoh, 2016). Meanwhile, anthropologists like Turner (1967; 1969) observe that liminal individuals have nothing – no status, no insignia, no secular clothing, no ranks, no kinship positions, nothing to meaningfully and hierarchically demarcate them structurally from their fellows. While these aspects are noted by anthropologists, it is imperative to note parallels where Africa as a continent [unlike Europe and North America] is not permitted to have unity with federal continental hierarchies of order; one African state - like the ritual subjects described by the anthropologists - is not different from the others because all of them are ritual subjects in a [postcolonial] liminal threshold without order, with ambiguity and with not much rank orders separating the leaders from the populace. In a context where African leaders are subject to discipline by the (neo-)imperial forces, which have set up international courts specifically to catch and punish African leaders, the distinctions between leaders and populace have been eroded in ways that render both African leaders and the rest of the populace as (neo-)imperial ritual subjects.

In the light of the above, we argue here that when Euro-American states disregard African sovereignty and autonomy, their logic is to ritually destroy African order and push Africans into thresholds or liminality within which as liminal subjects they will not be able to protect their resources and properties. While Euro-American states set up the "International Criminal Court" supposedly to stem impunity, we contend that the logic is much more complex than is presented by the proponents of the court. To effectively demonstrate antipathy to impunity, we would expect Euro-American states to first of all deal with and make good their own centuries old crimes perpetrated on Africans. The logic of the courts, we contend, is to push Africans into liminality, into thresholds so that they are easier for (neo-)empire to control, manipulate and continue to dispossess. The contemporary scramble for Africa and the contemporary transnational land grabs in Africa (Nhemachena, Warikandwa and Mtapuri, 2017; Southall *et al*, 2009) should ordinarily constitute crimes against the humanity of the defenceless African peasants who are being rendered landless. However, because the transnational corporations are part of the extensions of the (neo-)imperial ritual "masters" they cannot be subjected to (neo-)imperial ritual flagellation for crimes against humanity – in any case (neo-)empire continues to regard [contemporary] Africans as indistinct from animals or nature. It is necessary to cognise the fact that in the early colonial period, empire destroyed African states on the pretext that African Kings and Chiefs and Queens had impunity (Nhemachena, 2016c) even if paradoxically the same imperial states and the colonial settlers were busy dispossessing, exploiting and disinheriting Africans with impunity – destroying African kinship and descent systems, cultures and religions that were also pivotal in delimiting and defining African tangible and intangible heritages (Nhemachena and Dhakwa, 2017; Nhemachena and Bankie, 2017).

As ritual sacrificial imperial subjects, pushed to liminality, Africans are and were dispossessed of their sovereignty, autonomy, forms of order, forms of personhood and of their land so as to cushion settlers who had been dispossessed by their Western enclosure system for which they needed an antidote in Africa (Nhemachena, 2017a). Deemed to be and constituted into modes of ambiguity, liminality and marginality, the Africans were and are considered to be indistinct from animals such that their lives were/are not valued as human lives requiring human dignity, ownership of property, freedom and liberty. Much like in the contemporary Black Lives Matter campaigns in which African-Americans are deemed to be "animals" and then killed (Mail and Guardian, 14 July 2016; The Guardian, 28 April 2015; Lebron, 2017), African women and men were/are demonised as anarchic beasts and monsters that cannot govern themselves without the aid of the supposedly more polished and more human Westerners, who sadly arrogate the privileges to [surreptitiously] poke into African governance systems (Morgan 2011: 27-28; Nhemachena, 2016c; Nhemachena, 2017a; Magubane, 2007; Atkinson, 1905; Morgan, 1997). Thus, described as having breasts that hang down below their navels so that when they stooped to do work, Africans [women] were deemed to appear with four legs (Morgan, 1997: 168); the animalised African women were enslaved, treated as chattel to be sold, their marriages and families were disregarded (Atkinson, 1905) much as is happening in the (neo-)imperial contemporary era.

If the term frontier refers to migrating regions, to places of diffusion, places of conversion, places of enculturation and zones of transition with multiple processes marking a fluid zone (Black, 1995: 6-13; Quarleri, 2017; Prado, 2012), we would argue here that African institutions including families, marriages, property ownership and possession regimens, identities, polities, cultures and religions were pushed into interminable frontier zones that were/are defined by (neo-)colonisation and the attendant animalisation of Africans. While some scholars including African ones celebrate theoretical postulations of debordering, fluidity, ambiguity, hybridity, nomadism, permeability, openness, ambivalence and hence liminality, Morris (1992) rightly observes that frontiers and thresholds are 'strategic fields' with interplay of conflicts, dispossession, power and knowledge. Thus for purposes of this book, in the frontiers or liminal zones, the (neo-)imperial ritual "master" is able to exercise power, take advantage of the ambiguity within such threshold zones and dispossess, exploit, divide and rule and further confuse the prostrating [African] ritual subjects. Having been forced to stay in the liminal zone for centuries, some ritual subjects are increasingly becoming unsure whether they are human beings or animals; they are unsure whether there are any distinctions between colonist and indigenous people – they are unsure whether they are becoming indigenous people or there are becoming colonists; they are unsure whether they are staying in houses or in the wilderness. In this vein, Prado, (2012) argues that indigenous peoples' territories [sovereignty, autonomy, jurisdiction and ownership of resources] are constantly and increasingly subjected to (neo-)imperial disputes, deemed to be open fringe areas – wilderness where (neo-)empire can seek resources and cheap labour.

While some contemporary scholars argue that Western science generated and guarantee certitudes, neutrality and objectivity, we argue that both Western science and Western religions were historically used to ambiguate Africans' humanity. From a Western religious point of view, it was argued that if Africans were not sons and daughters of the deviant Adam and Eve then they were supposed to be treated as nonhumans and then colonised and dispossessed. From a Western racial scientific point of view, African humanity has consistently been rendered a subject of intense contestations by natural philosophers, anthropologists, zoologists and other scientists – there were preferences among Westerners to think of Blacks as animals and slaves. Africans have been consigned to similar places as animals and so it was deemed by Westerners to be as natural to possess [African] slaves as it was to own cattle (Quallen, 2016). While these observations may be erroneously considered by some readers to be merely historical narratives, it is necessary to note that when transnational corporations continue to dispossess Africans whose land is currently being grabbed by these corporations in the new scramble for Africa, the (neo-)imperial implication is that Africans are animals and not human enough to own and possess their property or resources. When transnational corporations demand - via concessions, tax holidays - setting up sweatshops in which they exploit cheapened African labour without worries about [African] labour laws, the ultimate logic is to say Africans are still [enslaved as] animals or beasts for transnational corporations and (neo-)imperial profits. Similarly, when Africans continue to name not only their countries, cities, residential areas but also their children after (neo-) imperial personages, we wonder whether these are not signifiers of the materialisation of enslavement (Nhemachena, 2016b). Thus Quallen (2016: 50- 84) notes:

> Slavers absorbed , digested and regurgitated the arguments scientists crafted in support of racial difference with verve-even style...slavery, the argument ran, was an important component of the natural order science had identified. Masters named the children of the black slaves...Naming slaves was one weapon among the complement of animalising practices slavers possessed in their arsenal, but a striking one. Not only does naming slaves sever the connection between the parents and children, it gives the master, now the namer, the ability to say what the child is – who they are. Many masters used the opportunity to say their newest slaves were animals. In an analysis of the names of Virginia slaves...Laversuch, a scholar of names, finds the presence of many slaves named for animals...When she attempted to group the 960 distinct names into categories the first to emerge was plant and animal names, situating the slaves clearly within the natural world.

Slaves named by their masters, bore names including Peach, Lemon and Dolphin. Across the south, they bore pet names; Kitten, Lamb, Honey and Sugar…the vast majority of names given to slaves match names given to mules, pets or domestic animals- as many as seventy percent by one count. One of the fugitive advertisements on which Dr Laversuch relies took the practice of naming and carved it into the flesh, the runaway sought bore the initials of their masters by knife, on their cheek. For the many slaves who worked around cattle, the similarity to branding must have been inescapable.

Although some scholars like Butler *et al* (2013) argue that land and property ownership have been at the heart of onto-epistemologies of subject-formation in the histories of Westerners [which histories are also noted as having originated notions of ownership, sovereignty, human subjects and universal humanity], it is imperative to note that ownership is not necessarily a unique feature of the Westerners. The only distinguishing feature of Western "ownership" is that the Westerners have since the enslavement and colonial eras sought to distinguish themselves in forcefully owning, possessing and exploiting what belonged to other people. Noting that Africans also had notions and practices of ownership and possession (Nhemachena, 2016c; 2017a; 2017b), we argue that the only distinction in the world is that some have historically distinguished themselves in robbing [often politely addressed as conquest] the properties and resources of others. In Africa having and owning was also distinguished as an essential part of being human only that having and owning did not translate to predilections to dispossessing peoples, including those residing in other continents. The fact that Africans had their own technology and industries, which have suffered from the Western myths of inferiority and absence (Schmidt, 2006: 175; Nhemachena, 2016c; Nhemachena and Dhakwa, 2017), underscores the existence of precolonial notions and practices of ownership and possession – African producers of technology [just like African rearers of livestock] obviously possessed and owned what belonged to them. The fact that enslaved and colonised Africans felt pain and fought or fled from the barbarity of enslavers and colonisers also underscores the fact that Africans had notions and practices of ownership of their bodies as well as of their resources. Contemporary Euro-American quibbles that Africans did not have notions of ownership merely replicate ideologies of the enslavers who, while they branded enslaved Africans with red hot iron, justified their brutalities on the pretext that the enslaved did not own their bodies over which the names and symbols of the masters were etched using the red hot iron. Besides, the fact that Africans had scripted books about maths with division, subtraction of fractions, geometric formulars to calculate area and volume and distance and angles and algebraic equations about sizes of floods (Blatch, 2013; Nhemachena, 2017a), indicated that they could own these things which they produced and or inherited from their forebears.

The upshot of the foregoing is that Africans resisted colonial dispossession and disinheritance because they owned and possessed the land of which colonists were illegally and unjustly dispossessing them. So, worrisome are the contemporary popularisations of theories that privilege agency, action and performativity [minus morality and ethics] (Latour, 2005; Deleuze and Guattari, 1987) which theories appear at this time of the new scramble for Africa in which transnational corporations and Euro-American governments cannot care less about morality, ethics and human rights of the Africans whose land is being grabbed by the corporations and their home states (Nhemachena, Warikandwa and Mtapuri, 2017). Thus, also celebrating the agency, actions and performativity of things/objects, colonists who could not directly defeat the resisting Africans and other indigenous people resorted to introducing famines and strange colonial diseases including epidemics of infections and respiratory diseases among the indigenous people.

Thus, belying the contemporary theoretical postulations by proponents of new materialities and relational ontologies, we argue here that colonists did not bring subject-object relations to Africa. Rather colonists relied on manufacturing viruses, bacteria and other agents/actors which they then used against resisting indigenous people. To the extent that colonists manufactured and used viruses, bacteria and other agents to fight with them, we contend that the problem in Africa is not necessarily Cartesian binaries but the fact that colonists [recognised the agency rather than the passivity of objects and things] deployed chemical and biological agents against Africans and other indigenous people. Diseases such as smallpox, meningitis, bubonic plague, mumps, chickenpox, cholera, diphtheria, typhus, leprosy, yellow fever tuberculosis, influenza and measles were introduced to decimate the resisting indigenous people (Dowling, 1997; Tukur, 2016; Nhemachena, 2016a; Mear, 2008; Martin *et al*, 2002). So, the indigenous people, who were deemed to be less than animals and whose sovereignty was ignored by the colonial invaders, were tormented via the introduction of strange diseases and famines. In this sense, celebrations of theories that privilege the agency, action, vibrancy of matter and performativity of things [without much regard to ethics, morality, humanness and law] including what are called nonhumans (Latour, 2005; Bennett, 2010; Butler, 1988) are in fact counterproductive particularly in the age of the new scramble for Africa. In this sense, theoretical postulations to the effect that colonists conceived matter or objects as passive are not correct because they in fact manufactured biological and chemical agents which they deployed to kill resisting indigenous people [while pretending that the diseases were natural]. In this regard, Warren (2014) notes that:

An outbreak of smallpox in Sydney in 1789 killed thousands of Aborigines and weakened resistance to white settlement. Chris Warren argues that the pandemic was no accident, but rather a deliberate act of biological warfare against Australia's first inhabitants...In April 1789, a sudden, unusual, epidemic of smallpox was reported amongst the Port Jackson Aboriginal tribes who were actively resisting settlers from the First Fleet. This outbreak may have killed over 90 per cent of nearby native families....The strength of the Aboriginal opposition was much greater than anticipated...We also need to notice that flint lock muskets were not effective against Aboriginal weapons. They were inaccurate at moderate ranges or against moving targets. They misfired and needed reloading after every shot. They had no rearsight and only a rudimentary foresight that was obscured when a bayonet was attached...In the 18th century, the use of smallpox by British forces was not unprecedented. This tactic was promoted by major Robert Donkin and used by General Jeffery Amherst in 1763, when smallpox-laden blankets and handkerchiefs were distributed to Native Americans from Fort Pitt near the Great lakes...At the time when smallpox was released, native people outside the United Kingdom were often seen merely as goods and chattles...What is certain is that if smallpox had not been used, the history of Australia might have been very different.

While some scholars have celebrated the [brute] agency, action, performativity and vibrancy of matter (Latour, 2005; Bennett, 2010), other scholars have noted that (neo-)colonists often covertly destroyed the means of livelihood of indigenous people (Kruer, 2009: 3) and such destruction of the means of livelihoods of indigenous people include surreptitious manipulation and weaponisation of weather and climate. In this regard, assuming that human beings and nonhumans [all matter] are on the same plane of immanence or are symmetrical (Latour, 2004; 2005; Loayza, 2016; May, 1997) would be to equivocate – it is to ambiguate things to hide them and to constitute liminality which, we argue here, is a *conditio sine qua non* of coloniality, in this sense the ongoing (neo-)colonialism. In the contemporary era, the global media which is itself funded and owned by transnational corporations is noted as silencing voices attempting to expose secret programmes designed to secretly modify and weaponise the weather and climate so as to coerce the world to accept consuming genetically modified crops which are produce by corporations like Monsanto and Syngeta (Freeland *et al*, 2014; Nhemachena and Mawere, 2017; Nhemachena, Warikandwa and Mtapuri, 2017). In this regard, it is noted that transnational corporations' projects to force the world to accept GMOs is at the centre of contemporary discourses on climate change; and so people who expose the deliberate manipulation of weather and climate through the [nomadic] High-Frequency Active Auoral Research Program (HAARP) are victimised (Freeland *et al*, 2014; Nhemachena and Mawere, 2017; Nhemachena, Warikandwa and Mtapuri, 2017). So, critical scholars should be able to note the connections between the transnational corporations that are on one hand producing GMOs, owning and controlling global media and other institutions, and on the other hand the emergence of climate change discourses at a time when huge efforts are being made to legitimise GMOs in the world. In this sense, the disaster capitalists [who both create and generate moral panics around disasters] who are angling to control and monopolise global food production [and thus control the consuming world population] are behind the contemporary weaponisation of weather and climate for purposes of controlling the materialties of the world in the context of **full-spectrum dominance** of the oncoming New World Order or One World Government (Nhemachena and Warikandwa, 2017; Nhemachena, 2017c).

Hiding Behind the "Actions" and "Agency" of Nature? The Obfuscatory Functions of Theories

If Euro-Americans are geoengineering weather and climate changes including floods, hurricanes, tornados, droughts, storms, and so on for purposes of realising and exercising full spectrum dominance over the entire planet (Freeland *et al*, 2014; Nhemachena, Warikandwa and Mtapuri, 2017; Elder, 2014), then much of the discourses about climate change are not faithful to what is happening. To present the effects of Euro-American geoengineering as materialisations of weather and climate change is to equivocate and of course such equivocation is premised on contemporary theorisations that make efforts to legitimise and popularise liminality and the associated ambiguities of residing intellectually and physically in thresholds or interstices of things and matters. In this sense, the (neo-)empire that has in the recent past morphed into [a supposedly inclusive] globalisation is now morphing into weather and climate – using Deleuze and Guattari (1987) - (neo-)empire is **becoming** weather and climate such that when (neo-)empire changes this is simplistically interpreted as weather and climate changes. For this reason, Freeland *et al* (2014) argue that we are faced with a tanshumanist future that erases lines between humans and nonhumans, humans and machines and Nano biological hybrids and with microprocesses that infest and haunt human bodies. Programmed into uncritically following (neo-)imperial discourses, some academics [who also fear being labelled as "conspiracy theorists"] and even officials within NGOs blame the public for "climate change" instead of blaming those that are weaponising the weather and climate.

Thus, exposing the geoengineering Olsen (2013) observes that the CIA uses technology to cause earthquakes, storm systems, hurricanes, floods, and the sky is being streaked with chemicals by planes; they can also use HAARP to modify weather by selectively destabilising agricultural and ecological systems of entire regions. Olsen (*ibid*) further notes that this manipulation of the weather is realised through The High-Frequency Active Auroral Research Program, or HAARP which is owned and operated by the U.S. Airforce. Apart from weaponising the weather and climate, HAARP is also designed to cause worldwide brainwave pattern changes in the [world] population with the flick of a switch (Olsen, 2013). Besides HAARP, the struggles to dominate and monopolise the control and ownership over the Earth is aided by some scientists who, in their laboratories, are trying to design certain types of [actors/agents] pathogens that would be ethnic-specific so that they could just eliminate certain ethnic groups and races; other scientists are producing laboratory insects that can destroy specific crops in specific regions of the world. Still others are engaging even in an ecotype of terrorism whereby they can alter the climate, and set off earthquakes and volcanoes, remotely through the use of electromagnetic waves (Olsen, 2013: 133).

One way to preempt the contemporary demands for restoration by indigenous people yearning for their materialities [land, minerals and artefacts] has been to design ideologies about animism and animalisations in which the stolen land, mineral resources, artefact and skulls are portrayed as subjects independent of [indigenous] human ownership, possession and control (Nhemachena, 2016a; The Telegraph, 7 April 2010; Independent, 2 August 2008; The Guardian, 21 October 2015; The Herald, 14 August 2015; BBC News, 13 May 2005; Shyllon, 2009; Independent, 26 January 2002; BBC News, 29 January 2013; Cornu *et al*, 2010; Marttin, 2010). Once [indigenous] human beings are put on the same plane of immanence with their land, minerals and artefacts [also considered by the theorists to be subjects] then the indigenous people will not be able to claim ownership of otherwise "independent" or "autonomous" nonhuman subjects, actors or agents. Thus, some Euro-American states that are resisting repatriation of indigenous peoples' artefacts argue, in ways that animate their Western markets, that some of the artefacts were bought on the market [erroneously and conveniently deemed therein to be independent of colonial machinations and dispossession] (The Guardian, 21 October 2015). Although Africans are not granted visas to freely enter the Euro-American cities where their artefacts are lodged in museums, some Euro-American countries that are resisting repatriation of the artefacts paradoxically argue that the museums in which the artefacts are lodged are in fact [independent] "world museums". Such arguments erroneously presuppose that Euro-American museums are amply accessible to the dispossessed indigenous people [some of whom are paradoxically slammed with sanctions and travel bans by the European and American states] and that they are not (neo-)colonial and have nothing to do with colonial dispossession of indigenous people (The Guardian, 21 October 2015; Opoku, 2015; Mawere *et al*, 2015). Arguments about the emergence of a "global village", the supposed demise of the [African] nation state, the postulations of implicate-order-metaphysics and the postulations about Deleuzian affects (Deleuze and Guattari, 1987; Nhemachena, 2017a) constitute frantic Euro-American efforts to convince the dispossessed, disinherited and exploited indigenous people to think that the supposed shrinking of the world into a global village compensates [sufficiently] for denial of restitution and restoration of looted resources, including land and artefacts. However, the sad thing is that borders, physical distances and financial distances continue to separate the [indigenous] dispossessed from the Euro-American museums wherein their material artefacts are lodged.

To circumvent the challenges of theft which has come to be erroneously but conveniently addressed as mere "separation" or "alienation", (neo-)empire is busy designing modes of virtualities that are intended to bridge gaps between the looted and the looters. Looters and the looted are supposed, in the postmodern theories, to harmoniously live together [but without restitution and restoration] in the envisaged global village. Through discourses and practices of posthuman virtual bodies and virtual environments [which we will dwell on more closely below] (Hayles, 1999; Bishop, 2001; Diodato *et al*, 2012; Waterworth *et al*, 2014), efforts are made to console the robbed and looted via enhance virtual presence, virtual bodies and virtual environments which are being portrayed as not distinct or separable from the real bodies, real environments and so on. Thus, Bishop (2001) notes that the widespread use of cyberspace and large scale multi-user virtual realities illustrate public spaces beyond physical reality. With respect to virtual bodies, Diodato *et al* (2012) observe that the virtual body [which is ghostly - like a ghost, angel, like a shadow, like a beam of light and which is not reducible to representation] sustains itself through its changes of position, dimension, form, and colour – the human body endowed with technological prostheses and an electronic processor. Such virtual bodies are noted as enabling mediated presence or the feeling of being experientially present in a virtual or mixed reality – or distributed embodiment (Waterworth *et al*, 2014). In this virtual theories and practices, reality [looted] is traded for virtualities, in an envisaged post-Cartesian world where, according to the theories, reality and virtuality are not supposed to be distinguished or separated. In other words, Waterworth *et al* (2012) observe:

> Distributed presence describes how our sense of being present in the world is becoming separated from our sense of ownership of a particular body, through the development of new approaches to deploy the technologies of virtualisation that give rise to what is known as "mediated presence", or "telepresence"…We move from a sense of presence in the physical world, through a mediated sense of presence in virtuality, to the mediated sense of being in the physical-virtual world in another body than our own.

Designing forms of virtual realities [that will be conflated, in a supposedly post Cartesian world, with physical realities], emergent virtual bodies as well as emergent virtual environments [including in museums] are not the only ways that assists in evading and circumventing the repatriation of materialities that were looted and robbed from indigenous people. Some Western theorists evasively claim that such looted African material artefacts are not representable, have no fixed meanings, they claim that meanings are fluid, in flux, multiperspectival and that objects and subjects are in processes of becoming, as opposed to being static and representable (Opoku, 2015; O'Sullivan, 2010; Appadurai, 2006; Feldhusen, 2015; Sarvers, 1994; Coole and frost, 2010; Protevi, 2008; Brown, 2001; Bjerregaard, 2006; Dolphijn *et al*, 2012; Frost, 2010; Connolly, 2013; Latham *et al*, 2004; Barret, 2012; Singh, 2017). In this sense, the contemporary theoretical terrain is dominated by postulations on [new materiality] fluidity, flux, becomings, vitality, multiplicity of meanings, agency, action and so on – but it is agency, action, vitality, becomings that are silent about restitution and restoration. Thus, it is often argued equivocally that the art work is not an object [to be recovered by the indigenous people] but has acquired its own history, sociology or political economy, an excess, a raptive, a social life of things, potential of association through affect, action and agency (O'Sullivan, 2010). It has been argued that [indigenous] human beings and things are not radically distinct categories because slaves were once sold as chattel but were infused gradually with personhood and humanity but they can also be recommodified, turned once again into mere bodies or tools, put back in the market place, available for a price, dumped into the world of mere things- it is contended that things move to some new states in their "social lives" (Appadurai, 2006: 16).

Building on colonial era theories of fetishism which assume that objects are irreducibly material and have the capacity of embodying religious, commercial, aesthetic and sexual values as well establish intense relationships such as in the form of amulets (MacGaffey, 1994); some theorists of new materialities posit that matter has agency or vitality. They argue that matter is capable of independent action and has affect that warrants it being considered as subjects and not mere objects to be owned and controlled by [indigenous] human beings. Deriving from the Latin word *fasticious* meaning manufactured or artificial - fetish connotes superstition, unreality, falsehood, derogation, belief, irrational devotion, **pathological** displacement of libidinal interest and satisfaction with a fetish (Bates *et al*, 1993). While some of the theorists on new materialities advocate for logics of fetishism in the ontology of the new materialities, other scholars like Graeber (2005) argue that Africans were portrayed as fetishists, and hence like children who became attached to objects, treated objects as if they had personalities, adoring them and giving them names.

Although Africans may have worn some devices, it does not appear accurate to describe African devices as fetishists for a number of reasons. Firstly to focus on material objects and ignore the spiritual hierarchies in African religions is to labour under intellectual error. In African contexts where there are beliefs in God [the Heavenly Supreme Being] and ancestral spirits as well as evil spirits, the focus is not on objects but on the hierarchy of manifestations of spiritual beings that are understood to make the objects effective. So to describe the effectiveness of an African artefact or medical device on the basis of the visible tangible matter is also to labour under errors of apprehension. While other scholars have argued that objects or the new materialities have their "own embodied vitalities", African devices or artefacts that have been erroneously defined as fetishes are not necessarily understood to embody their own agency, action or vitality (Nhemachena, 2015). Thus, while some amulets were worn on necks, or apparel, to protect people from sickness and disease, preserve and increase natural strength and virility, to protect people from lightning, plague, pestilence, attacks by wildbeasts, scorpion stings, snake bites, drowning etc. (Budge, 1930; Varner, 2008; Adamo, 2011), it is erroneous to focus entirely on the artefacts or devices and ignore the manifestations of hierarchies of spiritual beings that render effectiveness of the artefacts or devices. To privilege the visible material artefacts or devices and ignore the hierarchies of spiritual beings is to succumb to errors of apprehension similar to those of the missionaries and early colonial travellers and scholars who erroneously described Africans as fetishists (Nhemachena, 2017a; Opoku, 1978). In fact, to portray Africans as fetishists is to perpetuate colonial anthropologists and missionaries' caricaturing of Africans as people without religion, without knowledge of and ideas of God when in fact among Africans, God has for long been known and deemed to be the originator of humanity (Adamo, 2011; Nhemachena, 2017a; Wallace, 2015). In other words, African humanity does not originate, as is assumed in Euro-American epistemologies, from the Enlightenment era but it emanates from God and is enunciated via *Ubuntu* or *Unhu* (Zondi, 2014; Nhemachena, 2017a). It is cause for wonder how Africans could be deemed to have no knowledge of God when they have distinctions between good and evil things. Equally it is cause for wonder how Africans could be portrayed as having no religion [but only magic and witchcraft]. Missionaries and colonial scholars' portrayals of Africans as without distinctions between good and evil were merely meant to legitimise and normalise colonial evils of dispossession, disinheritance and exploitation of the indigenous people who were thus conveniently, but erroneously, portrayed as without notions of God, religion and distinctions between good and evil. It is cause for consternation how Africans could be misrepresented as backward and primitive especially by colonialist, missionaries and anthropologists who were themselves engaged in the vilest and most primitive forms of dispossessing, disinheriting and exploiting others.

Missionaries and colonial scholars' misrepresentations of Africans as fetishists, which mirepresentations are evident in the discourses on crises of representation (Ebert, 1987: Nyamnjoh, 2012), raise the question as to why contemporary scholars would want to rely on colonial missionaries and anthropologists' presuppositions of fetishism and animism in understanding Africans religions and materialities? The question is, might this be a case of what Nyamnjoh (2012) calls the resilience of colonial epistemology in Africa? Although postmodernists have avowedly taken the stance of anti-representationalism and nonrepresentationalism (Ebert, 1987), the question is about whether antirepresentationalism and nonrepresentationalism necessarily amend earlier misrepresentations. To resort to antirepresentationalism and nonrepresentationalism without correctly representing the misrepresented is effectively to tolerate and leave unrighted the preceding colonial misrepresentations. In fact the contemporary portrayals of [African] women as indistinct from nature, from the environment from animals etc. are continuations of enslavement and colonial era animalisation of African women – there is nothing postcolonial or decolonial about such misrepresentations. In this sense, theories that privilege vague notions of **connectedness** or **relationality** between human beings and nature are also replicating enslavement and colonial era animalisation of Africans and other indigenous people whose concepts and practices of **ownership** and **possession** of their natural resources are sidestepped by such theorisations (Nhemachena and Warikandwa, 2017).

In the contemporary era, colonial presuppositions of fetishism and animism are being utilised not only to perpetuate colonial misrepresentations but also to buttress transnational corporations that are angling for a New World Order in which there is the rejection of the transcendence of the Heavenly God, even as there is celebration of the transcendence of transnational [institutions] corporations some of which are currently grabbing land from African peasants. In the envisaged New World Order, there is sadly emphasis on transgressions [including bordercrossings, recolonisation, becoming immoral and unethical animals and bodily transgressions] in the absence of a transcendental God. To enhance their surveillance over the emergent New World Order or One World Government, transnational corporations and the global secret society at the helm of the world (Nhemachena and Warikandwa, 2017; Nhemachena, Warikandwa and Mtapuri, 2017), are designing wearable ["intelligent"] tracking devices that monitor the activities of human beings and instantaneously raise alarms about any future rebellions against the emergent One World Government. Wearable tracker devices using sociometric badges are being introduced to control and monitor workers (Mail Online, 15 January 2017; Tsao *et al*, 2017; Ching *et al*, 2016; Schull, 2016; Trindade *et al*, 2016; Chen *et al*, 2017; Ya *et al*, 2014; Ferrando, 2013; Parikka, 2012). Transnational corporations are producing wearable technology comprising devices whose embedded sensors and analytic algorithms can track, analyse and guide wearers' behaviour. Sensor technology and self-care which are called 'data for life' wearables are also being used on telehealth applications, mobile health applications and devices, sensor-based technologies and predictive analytics, chronic management, genomics, and wellness and fitness matters (Schull, 2016). The contemporary popularisations of fetishism and animism are explicable in terms of these emergent innovations that promise not only to yield windfall of profits to capital but also to make the emergent One World Government surveillable and manageable. With human beings wearing T-shirts prototypes that embed textile sensors for the capture of cardio and respiratory signals that can be connected to external monitoring devices (Trindade *et al*, 2016), it will be easier to monitor not only the health condition of the wearers but also their movements and activities – in essence it will be easier also to police humanity even without employing the conventional [African] policemen and women. Thus, other scholars have argued that magic is being realised through technologies that are currently transforming people and material objects into other forms (Kurzweil, 2005).

Technological Materialities: On Theories that Open Up Markets for Emergent Technologies

In the light of the foregoing, we argue herein that the popularisation of fetishism, animism and new materialities discourses is not necessarily motivated by (neo-)imperial affinity for indigenous knowledges which are in any case misrepresented by resilient colonial fetishistic and animist assumptions. The motivation for the contemporary discourses on new materialities and presupposition of fetishism and animism lies in the global capitalists' exigencies that demand popularisation of emergent wearable devices. These wearable devices are electronic devices or computers that are incorporated into clothing and wearable accessories or directly implanted into the environment, into bodies such as electronic skins, as stick-on electronic tattoos, "smart" textile technologies, sensor fusion, and wearable protection units and so on. Without revealing how fusing humans with machines would turn them back to chattel slavery, wearable devices are simply argued to integrate humans with [global capitalists and secret society's] machines (Chen *et al*, 2017). Also, without revealing that transnational corporations are poisoning the [African] environments and proliferating diseases such as cancer, wearable devices are also simply represented as enhancing early prediction and treatment of major diseases by providing health informatics, which deal with the acquisition, transmission, processing, storage, retrieval and use of health information (Ya *et al*, 2014).

The transformation of human beings and objects into other forms is taking place in the context of theorisations about posthumanism, antihumanism, postanthropocentrism (Nhemachena *et al*, 2017; Nhemachena, 2017c). For this reason, it is argued by some scholars that, in the envisaged posthuman future, there will be no distinction between human and machine or between the physical and virtual reality, human and animal, there will be mergers between knowledge in human brains and the knowledge sharing ability of technology (Kurzweil, 2005). It is further argued that intelligence derived from its human biological origins will begin to saturate the matter and energy in the environment. It is contended that the human intelligence will infuse the rest of the universe with its creativity and intelligence such that the dumb matter and mechanisms of the universe are transformed into exquisitely sublime forms of intelligence (Kurzweil, 2005). Although other writers and scholars call such devices 'intelligent multiagent systems' such appliances, systems and environment will derive their intelligence from scientific scanning and uploading of human minds into the matter or substrates constituting the supposedly new materialities (Nhemachena, 2017c; Kurzweil, 2005). The new intelligent systems will include what are called 'intelligent household appliances', which can do laundry, baking, cooking, plan and act autonomously with intelligence in order to achieve requested goals (Steblovnik *et al*, 2011; Jing-Hong *et al*, 2016); also included will be humanoid robots some of which will be sex robots [made from scanning and uploading the human brains into substrates] that human beings will be encouraged to marry in lieu of other human beings (Nhemachena, 2017c).

Scanning and uploading the human mind onto appliances and devices involves scanning all of the human brains' salient details and then reinstating those details into a suitably powerful computational substrate that captures and 'recreates' a person's entire [indistinguishable from original] personality, memory, skills and history with all its subtleties. In the logics of witchcraft and sorcery, particularly the ways in which sorcerers produce goblins (Nhemachena, 2017c), the scanned and uploaded minds are then used for "extensions of human intelligence" (Kurzweil, 2005). Explicating the posthumanistic and transhumanistic era which human beings are supposedly entering, Kurzweil (ibid: 202) argues that human beings will gradually upload themselves without noticing the transfer such that they redesign and rebuild bodies and brains as well as the world with which they interact. Thus, the posthuman world is one where there is reprogramming of human biochemistry and genes in ways that destroy claim to heritages by indigenous people. It is an era in which autonomous weapons [with pattern recognition software] can fly thousands of miles to find specific targets; it is an era in which robotic drones are able to make their own decisions on where to look and find phenomena or targets. For Kurzweil (2005), the posthuman era is one where human beings wear devices in a belt or under shirt; it is also an era in which devices, called 'smart dust', tinier than birds and bumble-bees are used in war; it is an era in which swarms of millions of these devices could be dropped in an enemy territory to provide detailed surveillance and ultimately support offensive warfare missions. Already, massive numbers of essentially invisible spies can monitor enemy territory, identify each person and every weapon and carry out missions to destroy enemy targets. It is noted by Kurzweil (*ibid*) that human commanders will soon be in charge of swarms of "intelligent" weapons but they will also need specialised virtual environments to envision the complex information that these distributed systems/devices are collecting.

Thus, while other scholars like Ferrando (2013) and Asberg *et al* (2015) argue that "human enhancements" [which they argue should not be feared or rebelled against] are essential, the associated posthumanism and transhumanism threaten not only [African] sovereignty but also African autonomy, personhood and privacy. While some writers celebrate new materialism and posthumanism as ushering in postexclusivism, postexceptionalism and postcentralising (Ferrando, 2013), it is imperative to note that the colonisation, dispossession and exploitation of indigenous people were premised on erroneous 16th century Lockean (Parekh, 1995) notions of openness and absence of centralisation in the indigenous [polities] territories. Thus, arrogantly dismissing indigenous exceptionalism and exclusivism, Locke argued that indigenous people were unable to distinguish between insiders and outsiders [hence lacking exclusivism and exceptionalism]; Locke further argued that indigenous people lacked hierarchies and hence centralism. Thus, to the extent that wearable devices are used for surveillance, they are postexclusivist in the sense of infringing otherwise exclusively private spaces; to the extent that wearable devices are used to transcend nation-states, they are postexclusivist in the sense of excluding not only nationalist claims but also indigenous people's reclamations of their resources and property. In this sense wearable devices carry forward Locke's philosophy that indigenous territories and polities are open and waiting for colonisation.

So, the celebrations of new materialities, which are considered to be in emergent processes of materialisation, (Coole and Frost, 2010), are not necessarily justified if looked at from Afrocentric perspectives. Similarly, the celebrations of art as having [deconstructive] autonomous agency, vibrancy and sensations of matter (Wolodzko, 2015; Bennett, 2010); the celebrations of Deleuzian notions of affect, immanence, haecceity or assemblage, singularity, deterritorialisation and reterritorialisation (Protevi, 2008; Deleuze and Guattari, 1987) all negate [African] indigenous peoples' struggles for sovereignty and autonomy. While the Euro-American theorists foreground [supposed] problems of "isolated" or "world transcendent subjects", problems of "rational-calculating subjects", "problems of stasis", "problems of subject-object dichotomies" (Protevi, 2008), it is imperative to note that in Africa the greatest challenge for indigenous people is absence of restitution and reparations for (neo-)colonial dispossession and exploitation. So it is essential to note that the fundamental problem for indigenous people is not necessarily and simplistically "isolation" or "transcendence" but *a fortiori* enslavement and (neo-)colonial dispossession and exploitation that have been raised in recent conferences on reparations (Nhemachena, 2016a).

To attribute subjectivity and agency to objects in ways that put [African] human beings and objects at the same plane of immanence is to equivocate, it is to ambiguate (neo-)colonialism. In this regard, to explain things, including colonialism and coloniality, using notions of univocity, "complexity", immanent agency, and virtuality would amount to exonerating the elusive colonialist and their descendants because as Protevi (2008) argues "complex dynamics" cannot be analysed into a relation of independent and dependent variables – cause and effect. So we argue that in a context where indigenous people are clamouring for compensation as well as restoration of their resources and properties, to theorise existence in terms of the "complexity" would conveniently generate lacunae for the escape of colonialists and their descendants including the marauding transnational corporations that are still grabbing African resources and heritages. Thus, theorisations that attempt to "complicate things theory", to infuse and attribute instability, ambiguity, uncertainty, to relinquish abstraction, to relinquish representation, to consider things as not objects but subjects, to attribute social life to things (Brown, 2001), are also designed to relieve the settlers and their descendants of feelings of guilt. If all things and materialities have [autonomous] agency, the question that the theorists seek to put to indigenous people is, so who or what exactly caused your enslavement, colonisation, dispossession, exploitation and disinheritance? While prematurely absolving colonists and their descendants, the theories also offer lines of escape for the accountability-shy neoimperial machinery currently involved in dispossessing, disinheriting and exploiting African and other indigenous peoples.

Thus, though some scholars have argued for the need to grant voice to objects wherein art objects are [erroneously] deemed to carry intentionality, embody the agency of the collector and of the local community (Bjerregaard, 2006), such theorisations have to be interpreted within the context of the historical juncture where Africans and other indigenous people are increasingly reclaiming their looted artefacts and objects. In this regard, new accounts of materiality that supposedly grant it, "feelings", "desires", "yearnings", "experiences", "sentience", "agency", "relationality" and "affect" (Barret, 2012; Singh, 2017; Dolphijn *et al*, 2012), are in fact meant to circumvent indigenous people's claims of restitution and restoration (Nhemachena, 2016a). Because new materialities are considered to challenge linear models of causation, they are also held to challenge essentialism (Frost, 2011) including challenging [African] human essence which has been the basis of African claims to restitution, reparations and compensation. In this respect, we argue that frontloading Cartesianism as the problematique that supposedly accounted for the "inertness" of matter, for raising humanity to transcendence over matter and for supposedly raising humanity to rationality, hides the real problems that emanate from colonisation in Africa. (Neo-)colonial dispossession, disinheritance and exploitation of Africans cannot be resolved simply by decentring African human institutions, or by decentring African human beings, or by dissolving the Cartesian binaries between nature and culture or by pronouncing "connectivity" and "relationality" (Nhemachena, 2017a). Rather, the (neo-)colonial problems require reparations and restitution as solutions. In this sense, to insist on new materialism that discounts restitution and reparations is to sidestep the areas that really itch on the bodies and existence of Africans and other indigenous people. To sidestep the real problems on the continent is effectively to engage in the social production of ignorance within the academies where false solutions that do not help indigenous people are being proffered each semester (Nhemachena, 2016c). In this regard, Frost (2011) argues that new materialism stresses recursivity and the varied causes and effects as well as the impossibility of knowing which, he holds, is intrinsic to the "complexity" of objects or processes themselves.

Contemporary theorising of existence in terms of complexity of causes and effects is profitable for Euro-America not only because of the need to evade mounting claims for reparations for enslavement and colonial crimes but also to circumvent mounting pressures to account for environmental damage via chemicals that are increasing the incidence of diseases like breast and prostate cancer, homosexuality, hermaphrodism, infertility, weak immune systems and sex reversals (Cadbury, 1997). Thus, noting the effects of chemicals dumped by corporations in the environment, Cadbury (1997: 20) states: "Sometimes hermaphrodism involves not just the external genitalia, but also the internal ones. The testes and ovaries may be modified, forming an intergonad, which has characteristics of both a testis and an ovary". Apart from offering lines of escape from accountability by some human beings and their corporations that are

26

destroying the environment, new materialism also naturalises invasions of African and other territories or polities. Positing that human beings and nonhumans are on the same plane of immanence enables (neo-)empire to engage in invasions while holding that even other natural or nonhuman species do invade spaces. In this regard, Hoffman (2016: 3) notes that already, ecologists accept that people are not disconnected from the environment. Hoffman (ibid) proceeds to argue that scientific understanding of human beings' spread across the globe cannot be isolated from that of other species because in prehistoric times humans' spread was fully compliant with and restricted to the rules of nature which would qualify as a colonisation. For Bennett (2010) new materialities or vibrant matter would mean a politics devoted less to blaming and condemning [(neo-)colonising] individuals than to discovering the webs of forces affecting situations and events.

Other ways in which accountability is being deflected include denials of anthropocentrism and hence denial of human accountability, denials of referentiality and representationalism (Dolphijn *et al*, 2012) and the calls to abandon the primacy of the languages that would otherwise serve to signify the African properties and resources that were stolen. In other words, we argue that if indigenous people are deprived of language and culture as referential grids, one wonders how else they can speak and refer to themselves as the dispossessed, the disinherited, the exploited and the oppressed. Depriving indigenous people of language, which is used as referents, signified and signifiers, is a way to silence them, to make it difficult for them to refer to their materialities and resources that were historically and (neo-)colonially looted and robbed. In other words, we argue here that, while discourses about foregoing referentiality may appear innocent, they serve the (neo-)imperial order by making it difficult for disinherited indigenous people to linguistically refer to their stolen materialities in the age of reclamations.

In this regard, there are ongoing debates about representationalism (Bower, 2017); there are critiques of assumptions of referentiality of literary meaning according to which representations of nature are assumed to have referential accuracy of realistic detail. There are arguments about "referential fallacy" which

27

is held to underscore "misconceptions" of finding faithful recordings of the natural world in literature and in literary texts (Opermann, 2006). While Saussure celebrated image of the sign as a sheet of paper whose indivisible recto and verso represent the material sound of language on one side (the signifier), the thought content (the signified) (Tardiman, 2006), postmodernist scholars hold that representation is always already misrepresentation because for them the relation between representation and prior referent can only be ironic, and deceptive (Oppermann, 2006). However, while language is held to be arbitrary, ambiguous, to be an equivocation, to show the limits of translatability, the limits of comprehensibility and interpretability (Petrilli, 2010), we argue here that in a (neo-)colonial context the problems that are attributed to language are largely a result of equivocations by the (neo-)imperial order that takes the advantage of the equivocations, the thresholds, the liminality into which Africans have been pushed since the enslavement era. In other words, we argue that the limits of [imperial] languages intersect with the limits of the rapacious (neo-) empire; the equivocations of the languages intersect with the equivocations and thresholding on (neo-)empire.

The debates around representationalism, referents, signifiers and signified bear on discourses about ecocriticism – a diffuse critical field that studies nature writing, interplay of human and the nonhuman in literary texts (Branch, 1994; Black, 1994; Sarver, 1994; Cokinos, 1994). Thus, ecocriticism looks at the representation of nature and landscape in cultural texts, paying particular attention to attitudes towards nature and the rhetoric employed when speaking of it (Nayar, 2010). So, material ecocriticism and postcolonial ecocriticism offer ways to analyse language and reality, human and nonhuman life, mind and matter, material forces and substances, the agency of things and processes (Iovino *et al*, 2014; Huggan *et al*, 2009). In this way, ecocriticism reinstates referentiality as a crucial and primary activity of literature – words serve to name, identify, depict and define the material world in which they circulate (Murphy, 2009). However, we argue here that the referentiality needs not be cast in enslavement and colonial era caricaturing of Africans as animals or as indistinguishable from nature. Contemporary referentiality needs to acknowledge Africans and other indigenous people as owners and possessors of their resources, institutions and properties.

While ecocriticism focuses on what "relationships" human beings should have with the world, human and more than human realms (Hoving, 2013), Blacks have for long challenged the enforced description of Africans and their descendants as non-human objects of science; they have challenged police brutality which is premised on the assumption that Black lives do not matter as human bodies and as human lives (Mail and Guardian, 14 July 2016; Lebron, 2017). So, Black lives in USA are being trampled on the premise that Blacks are indistinct from animals or from nonhuman nature. Black African states and nations are also being condemned as "exhausted nationalism" that supposedly needs to be transcended and replaced with cosmopolitanism, universalism and larger purposes of which Euro-American states and peoples are at the helm (Grosfoguel, 2011; Lord, 2012). In such a cosmopolitan world, or cosmopolitical world which is supposedly marked by [equivocative] "relationality", connections, affect, flows, fluxes, becomings, haecceity, associations, (Williams, 2012; Merriman *et al*, 2016; Gosden *et al*, 1999) there is sadly no room or consideration of restoration and reparations for the centuries old victims of (neo-)colonial plunder. In this respect, we argue that the contemporary theoretical equivocative notions of "relations" and "connections", sadly imply that the dispossessed and disinherited indigenous people are supposed to worry more about the supposed "connections" and "relations" than about the overdue restoration and compensation for their plundered materialities (Nhemachena, 2017a).

Thus, while some scholars claim that indigenous people such as in Australia inherited narratives of object mastery and territorial possession from Euro-Americans, we argue here that notions and practices of mastery (Rainforth, n.d), science, subject-object ontologies existed [moderated by the notions of Ubuntu and Unhu] in precolonial societies among indigenous people of Africa. What colonists did was not necessarily to introduce notions and practices of mastery, ownership, possession or subject-object ontologies but they [unlike in Ubuntu and Unhu-informed African practices] performed and introduced massive robbery of land, livestock and minerals – and introducing robbery and theft of land, minerals and territories is different from introducing notions of mastery, possession and ownership (Nhemachena, Warikandwa and Mtapuri, 2017; Nhemachena, 2016a). Apart from introducing widespread robbery and looting, colonists also animalised Africans some of who they have [sought to and] ridden in the colonial animistic logics of the relationships between horse and rider (Owomoyela, 2002: 18; Mungazi, 2010; Nhemachena, 2017a).

In this regard, to argue that nonhuman objects and [African] human beings are indistinct, and should not be separated, is to get Africans back to the colonial logics of horse and rider relationships wherein they were considered to be indistinct from horses or nonhumans, and to be at the disposal of colonial and imperial settlers. To render [African] human beings as indistinct from nonhuman objects and nature is not necessarily to render the "ghostly things-in-themselves"(Harman, 2011), but it is *a fortiori* to conjure the ghostly figure and logics of colonisation in which [African] humans were considered, by colonial settlers as indistinct from nonhuman animals like horses.

While theorists of new materialities and of animism presuppose that all that Africa had was mysticism and magic and preoccupation with [immanent] sacredness of things and objects, it is necessary to note that precolonial Africa had technical sciences and technological feats; it had medical sciences based on empirical rather than magical or mystical evidence (The Guardian, 20 January 2015). In fact it is noted that Europeans, who subsequently plundered Egypt, were astonished to learn that Africans were the first originators of technology; in fact Socrates, Plato, Herodotus, Pythagoras and Aristotle were among the Europeans that learnt much from Africa which at that time had sophisticated sciences, civilisations including engineering and architecture (Chaukura, 2015; Amadiume, 1997: 91; Blatch, 2013; Akpa, 2011; Mail Online, 6 December 2002; Utsua, 2015).

The fact that Africa discovered capsicum, physostigme and reserpine medical procedures, before they were performed in Europe, including vaccination, autopsy, limb traction, broken bone setting, brain surgery, skin grafting, filling in dental cavities,

30

installation of false teeth, caesarean operation, anaesthesis and tissue counterisation (Blatch, 2013), shows that not everything in Africa was about magic and mysticism. In fact Africa had great libraries like the Alexandrian one and universities before Europeans colonised the continent. Al-Azhar University in 970-972, the oldest degree awarding university in Egypt was established in about 961; Philosophy schools existed in Mali around 12th and 16th centuries; Universities of Sankare, Sidi Yahya University, - and Djinguareber University had collections of books on African science, had a capacity of 25 000 students, and had one of the largest libraries in the world with about 1 000 000 manuscripts. Timbuktu was also a major centre for book copying, religious groups, sciences and arts (Utsua, 2015). In spite of all these achievement, it is noted that Africa's scientific epistemologies have for long been discounted by Eurocentric observers (Mail Online, 6 December 2012).

In the light of the foregoing, it is erroneous to assume that scientific epistemologies originated with Rene Descartes or with Euro-America because every society, including African ones, has had both scientific epistemologies and religious beliefs (Harding, 1994; Nhemachena, 2017a; Taiwo, 2010). In this regard, we argue that colonialism was not essentially or fundamentally about introducing science and technology, hierarchies, development, secularism, or political structures – colonialism was essentially about dispossessing Africans of materialities, stealing and destroying African structures and systems of scientific knowledge. It is these aspects that decoloniality should address first and foremost: to avoid fruitless equivocations, other matters pertaining to inequalities can subsequently be address as matters of justice rather than matters of decolonisation.

Writing about the need to avoid equivocations, Tuck et al (2012) argue that decolonisation should bring about repatriation of indigenous land. Like Fanon (1963: 44), Tuck et al (2012) argue for decolonisation, involving restitution, of [African] land and other materialities: Their argument is that the easy option of "decolonising" schools by using methods that "decolonise" student thinking turns decolonisation into a metaphor. In this sense contemporary theoretical privileging of fluidity, becomings, fluxes, hybridity,

31

liminality, multiplicities, multiculturalisms, diversity and new materialities, are in fact the equivocations that Tuck *et al* (2012) are dissuading scholars and practitioners from frontloading. Merely addressing Cartesian binaries does not help in restitution of the land and other materialities (Nhemachena, 2016a). Also, theorising [African] land and other materialities as subjects, or agents, or as assemblages, or as affective and performative subjects does not help in the overdue restitution and compensation. In other words, we argue herein that when Africans seek restitution, repossession and reclamation of ownership of their properties and resources, it is important to note that they are not merely seeking to [nebulously] 'connect' or to establish "relationships" with nature or the environment. In this regard, it is imperative to note that colonialist did **NOT** merely "alienate" or "separate" nature from humans, rather they looted, dispossessed and disinherited Africans as exemplified by the **Loot Committee** [which was not simplistically a "separation", "alienation" or "disconnection" committee] that Cecil John Rhodes set up in early colonial Zimbabwe (Palmer, 1977; Clarke *et al*, 2010; The Patriot, 16 April 2014) – this is what has to be addressed. In other words, the charge has got to be properly and accurately formulated. A looter does not merely "separate", "alienate" or "disconnect"; rather a looter steals, dispossesses and robs. Thus, theories that privilege "connections" and "relationships" with nature and with the environment attempt to sidetrack African aspirations to reclaim their ownership, possession and control of their resources and properties. To own and possess is not merely to have a "connection" or "relationship" with something, rather, it is to exercise rights over one's resources and so this distinction needs to be always clear.

Chapter Outlines

In chapter two, Jairos Kangira and Lazaro Pedro Chissano critically analyse inaugural presidential speeches in a number of southern African countries. Their underlying argument is that, as they vividly presented their speeches, Machel, Mugabe, Nujoma and Mandela aroused imagination that created sights and scenes of freedom, independence and justice in the minds of their audiences; imagination that created images of new egalitarian states in the minds of their audiences; and imagination that presented astute and judicious statecraft of the new leaders, which was the direct opposite of the old, dispossessive, oppressive and fascist regimes. In other words, by unravelling *phantasia* in the four speeches, they reveal the crucial relationship between rhetoric and psyche. They critically argue that while other animals live by impressions and memories, the human beings also live by art and reasoning such as displayed in the speeches. They find sensation, art, experience and reasoning in the aspects of the public epideictic discourses of the new leaders. The authors further argue that all the four speeches gave a strong impression (imagination) of the beginning of the decolonisation of all political and socio-economic systems for the benefit of all the citizens of the four countries.

Artwell Nhemachena; Tapiwa V. Warikandwa and Asteria N. Nauta's chapter three interrogates issues of materiality in relation to the recent Fees Must Fall Movements in some southern African universities. They argue that denied material restitution and restoration of colonially looted resources, Africans have instead had their energies surreptitiously rechannelled [by (neo-)empire] to ideational and ideological matters where minor battles, that do not threaten the material and consequential core of (neo-)empire, are fought on the continent. In other words, their chapter teases out a paradox: the paradox being that while there was much international support for the Fees Must Fall Movements and the "decolonisation" of education in African universities, unfortunately, there is opposition to the decolonisation of African materialities, including the calls to nationalise African mining and other resources, and the restoration of land to Africans. Cited in the chapter is the strident resistance to the early 21st century restoration and reclamation of land in Zimbabwe which attracted sanctions [rather than acclamations] from the (neo-)imperial centres that have hypocritically been supportive of the, imperially less disruptive, Fees Must Fall Movements. Therefore, the authors argue that the opposition to the calls for restoration and reclamation of land and other material resources, including in South Africa and Namibia, underscore the hypocrisy of those who prefer to support only the "decolonisation" of the curricula and the attendant recurriculation. Thus, the authors reveal that the (neo-)imperial frontloading of "decolonisation" of the curricula is meant to mask and elude the more imperially unsettling tasks of decolonising African materialities, including deoccupation of [African] land by settlers and their descendants.

Artwell Nhemachena and Dolphin Mabale's chapter four critically analyses statues as aspects of material culture in South Africa. They argue that while statues constitute national material culture, the African nation states are sadly being destabilised by the global forces that seek to displace and replace the African nation states [as well as replace the African statues and materialities] that are increasingly being portrayed as "failed states", as "exhausted nationalisms" and so on. The authors critically examine the discourses around statues in South Africa in relation to contemporary broader debates around what are called 'new materialities', particularly statues in relation to posthumanism and transhumanism. They conclude that in Africa statues are not necessarily fetished or considered as animated or as agents or actors on the same plane as human beings. In other words, they dismiss theories that presuppose that African ontologies can be understood in terms of post-Cartesianism or Cartesianism. They contend that it is necessary to understand African realities on their own terms.

In chapter five, Munetsi Ruzivo focuses on examining the materialities of civil religion that serve to unify the Zimbabwean nation. It is argued that the paraphernalia and trappings of power show the connections between sacred offices and the material objects that point to their presence. Without these material objects the aura of sacredness is disenchanted. Ruzivo further argues that material objects such as the national flag have been used as a rallying point for national unity. Also, rituals such as the lighting of the Independence flame at Independence Day celebrations point to what is beyond the material. He contends that the flame itself is an embodiment of the aspirations of the Zimbabwean people to remain sovereign and enjoy their independence forever. So, the material objects act as the connecting link between the material world and the spirit world. Ruzivo argues that the Zimbabwean National Heroes' Acre and other smaller shrines dotted throughout the country are rallying points of unity during Independence Day celebrations. For the author, these objects sum up the history of the country from colonisation to independence. In the gatherings, the narratives of the bygone decades are used to reinforce unity. Those who sacrificed their lives in liberating the country from colonialism are praised whilst those who betrayed the liberation struggle are chastised. This is a device meant to unify the nation. The material objects are reinforced by other non-material objects such as the singing of [ideological] liberation war songs to remind the nation where it came from.

Sylvia Juliet Pasi's chapter six incisively analyses the unjustifiable connections between the environment and humans in NoViolet Bulawayo's (2013) *We Need New Names*. The chapter reveals that Bulawayo's narrative addresses social injustices such as land, environmental degradation, and impoverishment. In the novel, the author [erroneously] represents Operation *Murambatsvina* as destroying and endangering the earth's basic life systems in the name of progress. Operation *Murambatsvina* was a government of Zimbabwe execution to demolish urban nonformal settlements and shelters for nonformal business activities. Furthermore, the chapter notes that the disruption of nature is wrongly considered by some thinkers as analogous to the exploitation of humans. In the novel, operation *Murambatsvina* is used wrongly to represent the supposed discontinued "relationship" between humans and nonhuman nature. Using the logics of theorists of animism, the author of the novel adopts a biocentric world-view in which "connections" between humanity, the nonhuman and the environment are deemed to exist. Pasi's chapter posits that as Operation *Murambatsvina* destroyed shacks and other nonformal structures, hardships were visited on the affected citizens. However, she critically argues that putting women, children and nature on the same plane, as some authors do, perpetuates logics of the enslavement and colonial era where [African] women were regarded, by slave-masters and colonialist, as indistinct from beasts/animals of burden. In this sense, portraying women, children and nature as indistinct from each other is not necessarily liberating or decolonising but it replicates colonial portrayals of [African] women as "things", "animals" or "beasts", "chattel".

In chapter seven, Martin Uadiale and Anirejuoritse Awala-Ale examine the gendered effects of ongoing transnational land grabs in Africa. They observe that transnational land grabs have the effect of dispossessing, disinheriting and disempowering African [women] peasants. The authors further argue that the transnational corporations have tried to mask their dispossession and disinheritance of African women by postulation an era of post-feminism. Uadiale and his co-author contend that global capitalism has lured [African] women into the capitalist systems, thereby exposing them to the rapacity of transnational dispossession and exploitation. The authors argue that for its survival, capitalism divides and conquers the world's proletariat as it perpetuates racism, ethnicity, 'tribalism', class differentiations and gender disparities for its own survival. As a socio-economic system, capitalism is committed to racism and sexism. For Uadiale and his co-author, even when men may enjoy freedoms, women will always be regarded as socially inferiors whose tasks are social reproduction as well as production of labour power. The authors hold that the gender, racial, class divisions that capitalism creates only serve to intensify and conceal capitalist exploitations.

Njabulo Chipangura and Pauline Chiripanhura's chapter eight examines Zimbabwe's Mutare Museum's long history of colonially-inspired asportation of ethnographic objects. They argue for the inclusion of African communities in museum activities in a post-colonial milieu. The authors examine how the placing and displaying of traditional drums (ngoma) in one of the museum's galleries was influenced by colonial assumptions that source community interactions with their asported and dislocated objects should go no further than visual observation. More so, Africans were not allowed to perform their rituals which were feared by colonialists who were apprehensive of African prophets that stirred and led rebellions across the continent. Thus Chipangura and Chiripanhura argue that museumising was a tool of capture that did not only serve colonial curiosities but was also a mode of dispossessing and disinheriting Africans of their objects that could potentially influence future anticolonial uprisings. Subsequently, African songs were also banned during the colonial era as they were used together with African drums to stir insurrections, rebellions and resistance to colonial subjugation. Once the drums were asported and placed in museums, they served a dual function in that they became objects of colonial ethnographic investigations and captured 'trophies' meant to block rallying points of African anticolonial insurgencies. Thus, within this discourse, the museum was overwhelmingly used as an institution to propagate the colonial ethnographic gaze, in a context where ethnography and anthropology were used to buttress colonialism, contrary to the socio-cultural histories of the objects which hinged on certain African community values and beliefs. Using the example of ritual drums forcibly seized from the *Jindwi* community in Zimunya, Mutare in the late 1960s the chapter argues that the African sacred ritual and secular uses of the drums were thereafter overshadowed because of the museumising process.

In chapter nine, Paulus Mwetulundila argues that while some scholars assume that the extraction of minerals in Africa started with colonisation, there is evidence that, in Namibia, there was mineral extraction among pre-colonial inhabitants. He further argues that although some scholars presuppose that, in some traditional societies, minerals were regarded as actors, subjects or gods and goddesses, in Namibia, there is evidence that minerals that were/are extracted and sold are/were considered to be objects and not subjects. Mwetulundila argues that when Namibians extract and sell their minerals, they do not consider themselves to be extracting and selling subjects or gods and goddesses. The author further contends that while some scholars argue against Africans' exercising environmental sovereignty, Namibians need to exercise environmental and material sovereignty for them to extract their resources and sell them in order to have material means of survival. For Mwetulundila, the critical question is about how Africans can realise economic sovereignty if they do not exercise environmental and material sovereignty as well, that is, sovereignty over their environments and over the entirety of their materialities? His chapter argues that to deprive Africans of sovereignty over their materialities amounts to legitimising and normalising the dispossession and disinheritance of Africans whose resources are yet to be restituted by colonists and their descendants.

Ruby Magosvongwe's chapter ten analyses post-2000 Zimbabwean White writing and its ecological activism. The chapter concludes that patronising ecological activism that absolves some sections of the society from taking responsibility for ecological damage, which post-2000 Zimbabwe must fight and win, smirks at hypocrisy. Using literary depictions spanning for over a century beginning in 1897 till post-2000 as reference points, the chapter also argues that a-historical approaches that downplay the historical realities that created conditions that nurture and ferment the current ecological challenges will only yield partial solutions that perpetuate the ecological problems. Ecological activism that foregrounds material interests of one section of society whilst downplaying the correction of historical injustices or imbalances and denouncing self-renewal of communities through more equitable redistribution of resources threatens tearing communities apart. Magosvongwe argues that Zimbabwe's solutions to post-2000 ecological challenges lay in holistic solutions to the country's perennial land reclamation question and transparent management of the resources. Her chapter concludes that White commercial farmers' apprehension about land restitution, redistribution and attendant despondency alone does not constitute an ecological crisis of the magnitude that White ecological activism projects portray.

In chapter eleven, Okom Emmanuel Otegwu argues, with a focus on translation, that effective language teaching and learning suggests the application of combined and appropriate strategies or approaches in order to meet the challenges and demands of the present generation of learners with new technologies, and ever evolving learning environments. The bid is to practically find innovative means of making learners be creative and motivated in the learning process. This is where the role of mediating activities is advocated in foreign language learning through the democratic and interactive classroom situation. Otegwu argues that Instructors need to translate knowledge into effective classroom practice, and such knowledge might require further development and investigation. He further contends that, in spite of the value of robotic technologies, it is imperative to note that just as globalisation challenges the sovereignty of some nation states and regions, the use of technology including posthuman robotic technology also challenges the autonomy and sovereignty of human beings in Africa. It is argue that robotic technology challenges the very autonomy and individualised learning that it purports to enhance because the human beings can unwittingly or wittingly become cyborgs or mere appendages of machines or technology.

Colleta Kandemiri and Nelson Mlambo's chapter twelve argues that the natural world is the physical world which is visible to the human eye, and as such it is easy to discuss or make reference to. On the other hand, the metaphysical world, which is invisible but is believed to exist, is understood to be mutually connected to the natural world from an African worldview, especially as presented by Nyathi (2008) through the novel *The Other Presence*. Thus, access to the metaphysical, despite its invisible attribute, was made possible through the qualitative dimension of fiction and its apt ability to represent the un-presentable. Through the fictional work of *The Other Presence* (Nyathi, 2008) the invisible, which is the supernatural is made visible. Kandemiri and Mlambo argue that the text represents typical African social settings including the presence and manifestations of the supernatural. It is also argued that the text revealed occasions on which the supernatural world, through the spirits visiting the natural world therefore manifest in a top-down manner. For Kandemiri and Mlambo, the novel also shows how human beings consult the supernatural world for various reasons. Thus the metaphysical/supernatural is successfully and convincingly represented in a qualitative manner in *The Other Presence* (Nyathi, 2008).

References

Adamo, D T. (2011) Christianity and the African Traditional Religion(s): The Postcolonial Round of Engagement, in *Verbum et Ecclesia* vol 32(1) #285, doi:10,4102/ve.321i 1, 285.

Adams, S. *et al* (eds) (2016) *Under Observation. The Interplay Between eHealth and Surveillance.* Springer.

Akpa, C. O. (2011) The Method of African Science: A Philosophical Evaluation, in *American Journal of Social and Management Sciences.* 2(1) 11-20.

Alberti, B. (2009) Animating Archaeology: Local Theories and Conceptually Open –ended Methodologies. Framingham State University Digital Commons at Framingham State University.

Allen, C. J. (2017) Dwelling in Equivocation, *Journal of Ethnographic Theory,* vol7 no 1.

Amadiume, I. (1997) *Re-inventing Africa: Matriarchy, Religion and Culture.* Zed Books.

Appadurai, A. (2006) The Thing Itself, *Public Culture.* 18: 1: 15-21.

Atkinson, E. (1905) The Negro a Beast, *The North American Review.* Vol 181, no 585: 202-215.

Ballyn, S. (2011) *The British Invasion of Australia, Convicts: Exile and Dislocation.*www.ub.edu/dpfilsa/ballyn.pdf.

Barret, E. (2012) *Carnal Knowledge: Towards a 'New Materialism' through the Arts.* I. B. Tauris.

Bates, R. H. *et al.* (eds) (1993) *Africa and the Disciplines: The Contributions of Research in Africa to the Social Sciences and Humanities.* University of Chicago Press.

BBC News, (29 January 2013) France Returns Smuggled Nok Artefacts to Nigeria. www.bbc.com/news/world-africa-21246767.

Bennett, J. (2010) *Vibrant Matter: A Political Ecology of Things*: Duke University Press.

Bishop, J. M. (2001) Virtual Bodies and Virtual Spaces, in *Kybernetes* vol 30, issue 9/10:1289-1303 https://doi.org/10.1108/EUM000000006553.

Bjerregaard, P. (2006) The Materiality of Museum Politics: Reflections on Objects and Agency in Contemporary Museum Practice. Paper Presented for the Conference Connections, Communities and Collections in Miami Beach F I, USA, July 10-12 2006.

Black, N. J. (1994) The Frontier Mission and Social Transformation in Western Honduras: The Order of our Lady of Mercy: 12-1773, BRILL.

Blatch, S. (2013) Great Achievements in Science and Technology in Ancient Africa, *Journal of Biological Chemistry*. https://www.asbmb.org/asbmbtoday/asbmbtoday-article-aspx?id=32437.

Boaz, D. N. (2014) Witchcraft, Witchdoctors and Empire, the Proscription and Prosecution of African Spiritual Practices in British Atlantic Colonies, 1760-1960s PhD Thesis, University of Miami.

Bower, M. (2017) Husserl on Perception: A Non-Representionalism that Nearly Was. *European Journal of Philosophy*. Doi 10.1111/ejop.12261.

Branch, M. P. and O`Grady, S. (1994) Defining Ecocentrical Theory and Practice Paper for Sixteen Position Papers from the 1994 Western Literature Association Meeting Salt Lake City, Utah-6 October 1994. www.asle.org/wp-content/uploads/ASLE-Primer-DefiningEcocritpddf.

Branch, M. P. and O`Grady, S. (1994) Defining Ecocentrical Theory and Practice Paper for Sixteen Position Papers from the 1994 Western Literature Association Meeting Salt Lake City, Utah-6 October 1994. www.asle.org/wp-content/uploads/ASLE-Primer-DefiningEcocritpddf.

Brown, B. (2001) Things Theory, *Critical Inquiry*. Vol 28 (1): 1-22.

Budge, E. A. W. (1930) *Amulets and Superstition 1930*. Kessinger Publishing.

Butler, J. (1988) Performative Acts and Gender Constitution: An Essay in Phenomenology and Feminist Theory, in *Theatre Journal* vol 40(4):519-531.

Butler, J. *et al.* (2013) *Dispossession. The Performative in the Political.* John Wiley and Sons.

Cadbury, D. (1997) *The Feminization of Nature: Our Future at Risk.* London: Penguin Books.

Chaukura, C. (2015) Africa`s Priceless Heritage. Authorhouse.

Chen, Y. *et al* (2014) Cabons for Wearable Devices, in Science Direct. Vol 121-123.

https://www.sciencedirect.com/science/forrmal/00086.

Ching, K. W. *et al.* (2016) Wearable Technology Devices Security and Privacy Analysis, in *International Journal of Network Security & its Applications* (UNSA) vol 8 (3) :19-30.

Clarke, M. *et al.* (2010) *Lozikeyi Dlodlo: Queen of the Ndebele: "A Very Dangerous and Intriguing Woman"*. African Books Collective.

Cokinos, S. (1994) What is Ecocriticism? Defining Ecocritical theory and Practice: Sixteen Position Papers from the 1994 Western Literature Association Meeting Salt Lake City, Utah 6 October 1994.

Conolly, W. E. (2013) The New Materialism and the Fragility of Things: *Millennium, Journal of International Studies* vol 41 (3): 399-412.

Coole, D. and Frost, S. (2010) *New Materialism, Ontology, Agency and Politics.*

Cornell, P. *et al.* (2009) *Encounters/ Materialities/ Confrontations: Archaeologies of Social Space and Interaction.* Cambridge Scholars Publishing.

Cornu, M. *et al.* (2010) New Developments in the Restitution of Cultural Property: Alternative Means of Dispute Resolution, *International Journal of Cultural Property.* 17:1-31.

Deleuze, G. and Guattari, F. (1987) *A Thousand Plateaus: Capitalism and Schizophrenia.* Minneapolis: University of Minnesota Press.

Diodato, R. *et al.* (2012) *Aesthetics of the Virtual.* Sunny Press.

Dolphijn, R. and Vander Tuin, I. (2012) *New Materialism Interviews and Catographies.* Open Humanities Press.

Douglas, M. (2003) *Purity and Danger: An Analysis of the Concepts of Pollution and Taboo.* Routledge. London.

Dowling, P. J. (1997) A Great Deal of Sickness. Introduced Diseases Among the Aboriginal People of Colonial South East Australia, 1788-1900. A Thesis Submitted for the Degree of Doctor of Philosophy of the Australian National University, Canberra.

Driesen, D. M. (2007) Colonialism`s Climate? *International Studies Review* 9 (3): 484-486.

Dudley, S. (ed.) (2010) *Museum Materialties: Objects, Engagement, Interpretations.* Routledge Lower.

Ebert, T. L. (1986) The Crisis of Representation in Cultural Studies: Reading Postmodern Texts: Critical Angles: European Views of Contemporary American Literature by Marc Chenetier, *American Quarterly* vol 38(5): 894-902.

Edmonds, P. (2010) *Urbanizing Frontiers: Indigenous Peoples and Settlers in 19th Century Pacific Rim Cities,* University of Washington Press.

Elder, G. (2014) Wikis NWO (New World Order): Moving to Collaboration from Domination: Friesen Press.

Fanon, F. (1963) *The Wretched of the Earth.* New York: Grove Press.

Feldhusen, M. (2015) The Social Life of Objects: Interpreting our Material Culture, *Journal of Art Education.* Vol 61 (6): 25-32.

Ferrando, F. (2013) Posthumanism, Transhumanism, Antihumanism, Metahumanism and New Materialisms Differences and Relations, *An International Journal in Philosophy, Religion, Politics and the Arts.* Vol 8 (2):26-32.

Freeland, E. (2014) *Chemtrails, HAARP, and the Full Spectrum Domination of the Planet Earth.* Feral House.

Frost, S. (2011) The Implications of the New Materialisms for Feminist Epistemologies in Grasswick, H. E. (ed.) *Feminist Epistemology and Philosophy of Science, Power in Knowledge.* Doi 10.1007/978-1-4020-6835-5-4.

Gosden, C. *et al.* (1999) The Cultural Biography of Objects. *World Archaeology.* Vol 31 (2): 169-178.

Graeber, D. (2005) Fetishism as Social Creativity: or Fetishes are Gods in the Process of Construction, in *Anthropological Theory.* 5(4), 407 Doi:10.1177/1463499605059230.

Grosfoguel, R. (2011) Decolonizing Post-Colonial Studies and Paradigms of Political Economy: Transmodernity, Decolonial Thinking and Global Coloniality in Transmodernity: *Journal of Peripheral Cultural Production of the Luso-Hispanic World.* 1(1) hhttps:www.escholarship.org.uc/item/21K6t3fg.

Guardida-Rivera, O. (2007) Return of the Fetish: A Plea for a New Materialism, in *Law Critique.* 18:275-307 Doi.10/007/5/10978-9016-4.

Hafner, D. Z. (2015) Ambiguity, Equivocation, Unconscious, in *Language and Psychoanalysis.* 4(1) 75-103.

Hailwood, S. (2015) *Alienation and Nature in Environmental Philosophy.* Cambridge UP.

Harding, S. (1994) Is Science Multicultural? Challenges, Resources, Opportunities, Uncertainties, *Configurations.* 2.2:301-330.

Harman, G. (2011) The Road to Objects, in *Continent.* 1. (3): 171-179.

Hayles, N. K. (1999) *How We Became Posthuman: Virtual Bodies in Cybernetics, Literature and Informatics.* The University of Chicago Press.

Hoffman, B. D. (2016) Biological Invasion and Natural Colonisations: Are They that Different? *Neobiota* 29:1-14 http://neobiota.pensoff.net.

Honwana, A. (2015) `Enough! Will Youth Protest Drive Social Change in Africa`. (7 December 2015.), accessed at African Arguments, https://africanarguments.org/2015/12/07/enough-will-youth-protest-drive-socialchange-in-africa.

Hoving, I. (2013) Earthly Things. Ecocentricism, Globalisation and the Material Turn in *France.* 26(2): 71-85.

Huggan, G. and Tiffin, H. (2009) *Postcolonial Ecocriticism. Literature, Animals, Environment.* Routledge.

Independent, (2 August 2008) Kenya Tells Museums: Give our History Back. www.independent.co.uk/news/world/africa/kenya-tells-museums-give-our-history-back883777 html.

Independent, (26 January 2002) In Demand: The Art Pillaged by Britain www.independent.co.uk/news/uk/thus-britain/in-demand-though-african-art-pillaged-by-britain-9148391.html.

Jing-Hong, Y. *et al.* (2016) The Realization of a Speech-control Unit Used for Intelligent Household Appliances International Conference on Service Science. Technology and Engineering (SSTE2016) ISBN: 978-1-60595-351-9.

Kaunda, C. J. (2016) Towards an African Ecogender Theology: A Decolonial Theological Perspective. *Theological Journal* vol 2 (1): 177-202.

Kruer, M. (2009) Red Albion: Genocide and English Colonialism 1622-1646 M A Thesis, University of Oregon.

Kurzweil, R. (2005) *The Singularity is Near: When Humans Transcend Biology*. London: Penguin Books.

Latham, A. *et al.* (2004) Moving Cities, *Rethinking the Materialities of Urban Geographies*. Vol 28, (6): 701-724.

Latour, B. (2004) *Politics of Nature: How to Bring the Sciences into Democracy*. Cambridge: Harvard University Press.

Latour, B. (2005) *Reassembling the Social. An Introduction to Actor Network Theory*. Oxford: Oxford University Press.

Lebron, C. J. (2017) *The Marking of Black Lives Matter. A Brief History of an Idea*. Oxford UP.

Leong, D. (2016) The Mattering of the Black Lives: Octaria Butters Hyperempathy and the Promise of the New Materialities.

Litau, K. (2016) Translation and the Materialities of Communication in *Translation Studies*. Vol 9 (1): 82-96.

Livingstone, D. (n.d). *Terrorism and the Illuminati: A Three Thousand Year History*. Booksurge llc.

Loayza, M. (2016) Planes of Immanence: Deleuzean Assemblages as a Mode of Thought in the Theatre of Ricardo Monti, *Journal of Dramatic Theory and Criticism,* vol 30(2):79-99.

Lord, B. (2012) *Spinoza Beyond Philosophy*. Edinburgh University Press.

Lovino, S. and Oppermann, S. (2014) *Material Ecocriticism*. Indiana University Press.

MacGaffey, W. (1994) African Objects and the Idea of Fetish, in *RES: Anthropology and Aesthetics*. Vol 25: 123-131.

Magubane, B. M. (2007) *Race and the Construction of the Dispensable Other*. Pretoria: University of South Africa Press.

Mail and Guardian, (14 July 2016) Tatane, Macia, Marikana: South Africa`s Own #BlackLivesMatter Movements is long overdue https://mg.co.za/article-2016-07-14-00-tatane-macia-marikana-south-africas-own-blacklivesmatter-movement-is-long-overdue.

Mail Online, (15 January 2017) Your Boss is Watching You: Companies Fit Staff with Tracking Devices so They Can Follow their Movements Night and Day www.dailymail.co.uk/news/article-4121612/crompanies-fit-thosands-of-staff-wearable-trackers-follow-movements-night-day html.

Mail online, (6 December 2012) How Ancient Africans Were the First nerds: Birth of Technology Traced Back to 70 000 years to the Continents Southern Tip www.dailymail.co.uk/sciencetech/article-2243946/how-ancient-africans-nerds-birth-technology-traced-70000years-continents-southern-tip.html.

Makow, H. (2008) *The Illuminati: The Cult that Hijacked the World.* Silas Green. Winnipeg.

Martin, D. C. *et al.* (2002) Health Conditions Before Columbus: Paleopathology of Native Americans, *Western Journal of Medicine* 176(1):65-68.

Marttin, M. R. (2010) Legal Issues in African Art, Thesis, Dissertations. University of Iowa Research Online.https://ir.uiowa.edu/etal/546 PhD Thesis.

Mawere, M., Chiwaura, H and Thodhlana, T. P. (2005) African Museums in the Making: Reflections on the Politics of Material and Public Culture in Zimbabwe. Bamenda: Langaa.

May, T. (1997) *Reconsidering Difference: Nancy, Derrida, Levinas and Deleuze.* Penn State Press.

Mear, C. (2008) The Origin of the Smallpox Outbreak in Sydney in 1789 in *Journal of the Royal Australian Historical Society.*tretyrepublic.net/node/651.

Merriman, P. *et al.* (2016) Nations, Materialities and Affects, *Progress in Human Geography.* Doi:https://doi.org/10.1177/0309132516649453.

Miller, D. (2007) Materiality: An Introduction www.ucl.ac.uk/anthropology/people/academic-teaching-staff/channel-miller/mil-8.

Mirzoeff, N. (2017) Below the Water: Black Lives Matter and Revolutionary Time in e-flux.www.e-flux.com/journal/79/94164/below-the-water-black-lives-matter-and-revolutionary-time/.

Miura, N. (2013) *John Locke and the Native Americans: Early English Liberalism and its Colonial Reality.* New Castle, Upon Tyne: Cambridge Scholars Publishing.

Morgan, J. L. (1997) Some Could Suckle Over Their Shoulders: Male Travellers; Female Bodies, and the Gendering of Racial Ideology. 1500-1700, in *William and Mary Quarterly* .vol 54, (1): 167-192.

Morgan, J. L. (2011) Labouring Women: Reproduction and Gender, in *New World Slavery*. University of Pennsylvania Press.

Morris, B. (1992) Frontier Colonialism as a Culture of Terror, in *Journal of Australian Studies*, vol 1 (3) 72-87.

Mungazi, D A. (2010) *In the Footsteps of the Master: Desmond M Tutu and Abel T Muzorewa*. Greenwood Publishing Group.

Murphy, P D. (2009) *Ecocritical Explorations in Literary and Cultural Studies. Fences, Boundaries and Fields*. Lexington Books.

Nayar, P. K. (2010) *Contemporary Literary and Cultural Theory: From Structuralism to Ecocriticism*. Delhi: Pearson Education India.

Ndlovu-Gatsheni, S. J. (2015) Decoloniality in Africa: A Continuing Search for a New World Order, *Australasian Review of African Studies*. Vol 36(1): 22-50.

Neyt, F. (2004) *African Fetishes and Ancestral Objects*.5 Continents: Bilingual Edition.

Nhemachena, A and Mawere, M. (2017) Consuming or Being Consumed in the New World Order? GMOs as an Insult to the Dispossessed and Impoverished of the Earth, in Mawere, M. and Nhemachena, A. (eds) *GMOs, Consumerism and the Global Politics of Biotechnology: Rethinking Food, Bodies and Identities in Africa's 21st Century*. Bamenda: Langaa RPCIG.

Nhemachena, A. (2016a) Animism, Coloniality and Humanism: Reversing Empires Framing of Africa in Mawere, M. and Nhemachena, A. (eds) *Theory, Knowledge, Development and Politics. What Role for the Academy in the Sustainability of Africa?* Bamenda: Langaa RPCIG.

Nhemachena, A. (2016b) Double-Trouble: Reflections on the Violence of Absence and the `Culpability` of the Present in Africa, in Mawere, M. *et al* (eds), *Violence ,Politics and Conflict Management in Africa: Envisioning Transformation , Peace and Unity in the Twenty-First Century*. Bamenda: Langaa RPCIG.

Nhemachena, A. (2016c) (Post-)development and the Social Production of Ignorance: Farming Ignorance in 21st Century Africa in Mawere, M . (ed.) *Development Perspectives from the South:*

Troubling the Metrics of [Under-]development in Africa. Bamenda: Langaa Research &Publishing CIG

Nhemachena, A. (2017c) Food, Health and Science in Africa: Locating GMOs Debates in the Shifting Global Epistemological Terrains, in Mawere, M. and Nhemachena, A. (eds) *GMOs, Consumerism and the Global Politics of Biotechnology: Rethinking Food, Bodies and Identities in Africa's 21ˢᵗ Century*. Bamenda: Langaa RPCIG.

Nhemachena, A. (2017b) Hearing the Footfalls of Humanoid Robots: Technoscience, (Un-)employment and the Future of Development in Twenty-First Century Africa, in Mawere, M. (ed) *Underdevelopment, Development and the Future of Africa*. Bamenda: Langaa RPCIG.

Nhemachena, A. (2017a) *Relationality and Resilience in a Not So Relational World? Knowledge, Chivanhu and (De-)Coloniality in 21ˢᵗ Century Conflict-Torn Zimbabwe*. Bamenda: Langaa RPCIG.

Nhemachena, A. and Bankie, F. (2017) Foot Soldiers of the New Empire or Horizontal Saviours? Interrogating Civil Society Organisations and Fundamentalisms in Twenty-First Century Africa, in Nhemachena, A. and Mawere, M. (eds) *Africa at the Crossroads: Theorising Fundamentalisms in the 21ˢᵗ Century*. Bamenda: Langaa RPCIG.

Nhemachena, A. and Dhakwa, E. (2017) When Did The Rains Start to Beat Us? Discursive Dispossession and the Political Economies of Misrecognition about African Mining, in Nhemachena, A. and Warikandwa ,T. V. (eds) *Mining Africa: Law, Environment, Society and Politics in Historical and Multidisciplinary Perspectives*. Bamenda: Langaa Research & Publishing CIG.

Nhemachena, A. and Warikandwa T. V. (2017) On the Challenges of African Mining and Environment in the New World Order: An Introduction, in Nhemachena, A. and Warikandwa T. V. (eds) *Mining Africa: Law, Environment, Society and Politics in Historical and Multidisciplinary Perspectives*. Bamenda: Langaa RPCIG.

Nhemachena, A., Warikandwa, T. V. and Mtapuri, O. (2017) Transnational Corporations' Land Grabs and the On-going Second Mad Scramble for Africa: An Introduction, in Warikandwa, T. V. *et al.* (eds) *Transnational Land Grabs and*

Restitution in an Age of the (De-)Militarised New Scramble for Africa: A Pan African Socio-Legal Perspective. Bamenda: Langaa RPCIG.

Nyamnjoh, F. B. (2015) *"C'est l'homme qui Fait l'homme": Cul-de-sac Ubuntu-ism in Cote D'Ivoire.* Bamenda: Langaa Research and Publishing CIG.

Nyamnjoh, F. B. (2012) Blinded by Sight: Divining the Future of Anthropology in Africa, *Africa Spectrum,* 47 (2-3): 63-92.

Nyamnjoh, F. B. (2012) Potted Plants in Greenhouses: A Critical Reflection on the Resilience of Colonial Education in Africa, *Journal of Asian and African Studies,* 47 (2): 129-154.

O`Sullivan, S. (2010) The Aesthetics of Affect: Thinking Art Beyond Representation, *Journal of the Theoretical Humanities.* Vol 6 (3): 125-135.

Olsen, B. (2013) *Future Esopheric: The Unseen Realisms.* CCC Publishing loot.co.za.

Onyeakar, J. (2012) *Guinea Pigs of the New World Order Blackman the Endangered Breed.* Xlibric Corporation.

Opoku, K. (2015) Germany Must Return Looted Bronzes to Nigeria in Pambazuka News.
https://www.pambazuka.org/governance/germany-must-return-looted-bronzes-nigeria.

Opoku, K. A. (1978) *West African Religion.* Accra FEP International Private Limited.

Opperman, S. (2006) Theorising Ecocriticism: Towards a Postmodern Ecocritical Practice. In *Interdisciplinary Studies in Literature and Environment.* 13.2.

Owomoyela, O. (2002) *Culture and Customs of Zimbabwe.* Greenwood Publishing Group.

Palmer, R. (1977) *Land and Racial Domination in Rhodesia.* Berkeley: University of California Press.

Parekh, B. (1995) Liberalism and Colonialism: A Critique of Locke and Mill, in Pieterse, J. N. and Parekh, B, (eds) *The Decolonisation of Imagination: Culture, Knowledge and Power.* London and New Jersey: Zed books: 81-100.

Parrika, J. (2012) New Materialism as Media Theory: Media and Dirty Matter, in *Communication and Critical / Cultural Studies.* Vol 9(1): 95-100.

Pellizon, A. (2015) The Sentence of Plants: Animals Rights and Rights of Nature. *AAPLJ*:m5-13.

Petrilli, S. (2010) *Sign Crossroads in Global Perspectives: Semiotics and Responsibility.* Transaction Publishers.

Pheko, M. (27 Nov 2013) Liberation without Repossession of Land is Gigantic Colonial Fraud in The Patriotic Vanguard. www.thepatriotic.vanguard.com/liberation-without-repossession-of-land-is-gigantic-colonial-fraud.

Pheko, M. (7 May 2014) How Long Will Africans Celebrate their Land Dispossession? Pambazuka News www.pambazuka.org/land-environment/how-long-will-africans-celebrate-their-land-dispossession.

Pilossof, R. (2012) *The Unbearable Whiteness of Being: Farmers Voices from Zimbabwe.* Harare: Weaver Press.

Prado, F. (2012) The Fringes of Empire: Recent Scholarship on Colonial Frontiers and Borderlands in Latin America, in *History Compass* 10\4:318-333.

Protevi, J. (2008) Deleuze and Cognitive Science. One More Next Step- Paper First International Deleuze Studies Conference, Cardiff University August 13 2008. www.protevi.com/johnDeleuze-cognitive-science-talk-pdf.

Quallen, M. (2016) Making Animals, Making Slaves: Animalization and Slavery in the Antebellum United States Thesis. Georgetown University.

Quarleri, L. (2017) New Forms of Colonialism on the Frontiers of Hispanic America: Assimilationist Projects and Economic Disputes (Rio de La Plata, Late Eighteenth Century) in Tricoire, D. (ed) *Enlightened Colonialism.* Cambridge Imperial and Postcolonial Studies Series. Palgrave Macmillan, Cham.

Sarver, S. (1994) What is Ecocriticism? Defining Ecocritical Theory & Practice: Sixteen Position Papers from the 1994 Western Literature Association Meeting Salt lake City, Utah 6 October 1994.

Schimdt, P. R. (2006) *Historical Archaeology in Africa Representation, Social Memory and Oral.* Oxford: Attamira Press.

Schull, N. D. (2016) Data for Life: Wearable Technology Devices Security and Privacy Vulnerability Analysis, in *International Journal of Network Security and its Applications* (UNSA) vol 8 (3): 19-30.

Shyllon, F. (2009) *Unravelling History: Return of African Cultural Objects Repatriated and Looted in Colonial Times.* Bull Online Books and Journals.

Singh, J. (2017) *Unthinking Mastery: Dehumanism and Decolonial Entanglements.* Duke University Press Books.

Southall, R. *et al.* (2009) A New Scramble for Africa, in Southall, R. *et al* (eds) *A New Scramble for Africa? Imperialism, Investment and Development.* University of KwaZulu Natal Press.

Steblovnik, K. *et al.* (2011) Designing Agent Based Household Appliances, in Pham, D. T. *et al* (eds) *Intelligent Production Machines and Systems-* 2nd 1 PROMS Virtual International Conference 3-14 July Elsevier.

Sullivan, S. (2001) *Living Across and Through Skins: Trannational Bodies, Pragmatism, and Feminism.* Indiana University Press.

Taiwo, O. (2010) How Colonialism Pre-empted Modernity in Africa. Bloomington: Indiana University Press.

Tardiman, R. (2006) *Body and Story. The Ethics and Practice of Theoretical Conflicts.* JHU Press.

The Guardian, (20 June 2015) Classics for the People- Why We Should All Learn from Ancient Greeks https://www.theguardian.com/books/2015/jun/20/classics-for-the-people-ancient-greeks by Edith Hall.

The Guardian, (21 October 2016) Unwillingness to Return Stolen Artefacts is Assault to our Cultural Values, https://guardian.ng/saturday-magazine/unwillingness-to-return-stolen-artefacts-is-assault-to-our-cultural-values.

The Guardian, (28 April 2015) Black Baltimore Residents Aren't Animals, We Punish People for Killing Animals. https://www.theguardian..com/commentisfree/2015/apr/28/black-baltimore-residents-are`nt-animals-we-punish-people-for-killing-animals.

The Herald, (14 August 2015) 2 600 Zimbabweans Artefacts Looted. www.herald.co.zw/2600-zim-artefacts-looted/.

The New York Times, (27 March 2017) Climate Change Denialists in Charge.
https://www.nytimes.com/2017/03/27/us/politics/climate-change-demalists-in-charge.html.

The Patriot, (20 February 2014) Godfrey Huggins. Partnership of Horse and Rider... Zimbabweans Must be Vigilant https://www.the-patriot.co.zw/old-posts/godfrey-huggins-partership-of-horse-and-rider-zimbabweans-must-be-vigilant/.

The Patriot, (16 April 2014) Gwerevende and Rebirth of the Loot Committee.
https://www.thepatriot.co.zw/old_posts/gwerevende-and-rebirth-of-the-loot-committee/.

The Telegraph, (7 April 2010) British Museum under Pressure to Give up Looted Treasures.
www.telegraph.co.uk/news/worldviews/africaandindianocean/egypt/9563963/British-mseum-under-pressure-to-giveup-looted-treasures html.

Thompson, J. (2003) Cultural Property, Restitution and Value, *Journal of Applied Philosophy*. Vol 20, (3): 251-262.

Trindade, I. G. *et al* (2016) Design and Evaluation of Novel Textile Wearable Systems for the Surveillance of Virtual Signals. In *Sensors*. 16,1573; doi:10.3390/516101573.

Tsao, C. L. (2017) The Rise of Wearable and Smart Technology in Labour and Employment Law Presented by the Technology in Practice and Workplace Committee. April 5-7 Washington DC.

Tuck, E. *et al* (2012) Decolonization is not a Metaphor: in *Decolonization Indigeneity, Education and Society* vol 1(1): 1-40.

Turkur, M. M. (2016) *British Colonisation of Modern Nigeria, 1897-1914: A Reinterpretation of Colonial Sources*. Amalion Publishing.

Turner, T. V. (1967) *The Forest of Symbols: Aspects of Ndembu Ritual*. Cornell University Press.

Turner, V. W. (1969) *The Ritual Process: Structure and Antistructure*. Aldine Transaction. New Brunswick & London.

Turner, V. W. (2014) *Betwixt and Between: The Liminal Period in Rites of Passage*. Abe Books.

Utsua, T. P. (2015) The Evaluation of African Indigenous Science and Technology, in *Historical Research Letter* vol 16. www.iiste.org.

Van Gennep, A. (1960) *Rites of Passage.* Psychology Press.

Varner, G. R. (2008) *The History and Use of Amulets, Charms and Talismans.* Lulu.com.

Wallace, D. (2015) Rethinking Religion Magic and Witchcraft in South Africa from Colonial Coherence to Postcolonial Conundrums, in *Journal for the Study of Religion.* Vol 28, (1):23-511.

Warren, C. (2014) Was Sydney`s Smallpox Outbreak of 1789 An Act of Biological Warfare Against Aboriginal Tribes? www.abc.net.au/radionational/programs/ockhamsrazor/was-sydneys-smalpox-outbreak-an-act-of-biolgical-warfare/5395050.

Waterworth, J. A. *et al.* (2014) Distributed Embodiment: Real Presence in Virtual Bodies, in Grimshaw, M. (ed) *Oxford handbook of Virtuality*, edition 1. Oxford: Oxford University Press.

Wolodzko, A. A. (2015) *Materiality of Affect: How Art Can Reveal the More Subtle Realities of An Encounter.* Brill Online.

Wolski, N. (2001) All is Not Quiet on the Western Front – Rethinking Resistance and Frontiers in Aboriginal Historiography, in Russell, L. (ed) *Colonial Frontiers: Resistance and Encounters in Settler Societies.* Manchester University Press.

YaLi, Z. *et al.* (2014) Unobtrusive Sensing and Wearable Devices for Health Informatics, in IEEE Transactions on Biomedic. Vol 61 (5): 1538-1554.

Zondi, S. (2014) The Rhetoric of Ubuntu Diplomacy and Implications for Making the World Safe for Diversity, *African Journal of Rhetoric* vol 6(1): 103-142.

54

Chapter Two

Phantasia and the Rhetoric of Inaugural Speeches: Cases of Samora Machel (1975), Robert Mugabe (1980), Sam Nujoma (1990) and Nelson Mandela (1994)

Jairos Kangira & Lazaro Pedro Chissano

Introduction

Inaugural speeches are epideictic speeches that mark a shift from the old administration to the new one, while at the same time, they signal the beginning of a new administration, and the particular rhetoric is the President (Bennoit, 2009). This chapter critically analyses inaugural speeches of Samora Machel, who delivered his Message of Proclamation of Independence in Mozambique on 25 June 1975; Robert Mugabe, who delivered his Message of Independence in Zimbabwe on 17 March 1980; Sam Nujoma, who delivered his first inaugural speech in Namibia on 21 March 1990; and Nelson Mandela, who delivered his Inaugural Statement in South Africa on 10 May 1994. We argue that, using antithesis in reflecting on the animism practised by the erstwhile white colonial regimes, the rhetors also made use of *phantasia* in imagining the new states they were proclaiming at independence. Longinus in *On the Sublime (15*.1-2) defines *phantasia* as follows:

For the term *phantasia* is applied in general to an idea which enters the mind from any source and engenders (produces) speech, but the word has now come to be used predominantly of passages where, inspired by strong emotion (pathos), you seem to see what you describe and bring it vividly before the eyes of your audience. That *phantasia* means one thing in rhetoric and another in poetry will yourself detect, and so that the object of the poetical form is to enthral, and that of prose form to present things vividly, though both indeed aim at the emotional and the excited.

In simple terms, *phantasia* is imagination.

Our underlying argument is that, as they vividly presented their speeches, Machel, Mugabe, Nujoma and Mandela aroused imagination that created sights and scenes of freedom, independence and justice in the minds of their audiences; imagination that created images of new egalitarian states in the minds of their audiences; and imagination that presented astute and judicious statecraft of the new leaders, which was the direct opposite of the old, oppressive and fascist regimes. In other words, by unravelling *phantasia* in the four speeches, we get to understand the crucial relationship between rhetoric and psyche. According to Aristotle, "… other animals live by impressions and memories, and have but a small share of experiences, but the human race also lives by art and reasoning" (Metaphysics 1a). O'Gorman (2005: 18) illuminates on human *phantasia* by saying that it is different from the *phantasia* of other animals since it "…moves between and among sensation and art, and experience and reason", aspects which we find in the public epideictic discourses of the new leaders. All the four speeches gave a picture of the destruction of the binaries between the coloniser and the colonised, the black and white people, and gave a strong impression (imagination) of the beginning of the decolonisation of all political and socio-ecomic systems for the benefit of all the citizens of the four countries.

We also argue that the totality of the rhetorical situations, exigence and *kairos* of the speeches assisted in buttressing the strong belief in the audiences (both immediate and international) that the new leaders were embarking on nation building processes that were anchored on democratic values which the former colonial governments had failed to do in these countries. We further illustrate the critical role that inauguration plays as "a rite of passage, a ritual of transition in which the newly-elected President is invested in the office of the Presidency" (Campbell & Jamieson, 1989: 395), in each case. In this chapter, we do not investigate the political trajectories of the four countries after the attainment of independence, a task we leave for other commentators interested in judging whether all the new leaders followed the paths to and established the states they imagined in their inaugural addresses, or not.

Rhetorical Situation, Exigence and Kairos

Bitzer (1969:304) states that a rhetorical discourse occurs in response to a rhetorical situation and in a rhetorical situation there is an exigence, "… an imperfection marked by urgency; it is a defect, an obstacle, something waiting to be done, a thing that is other than it should be". Bitzer (1968), in "The Rhetorical Situation", says that "in every rhetorical situation, there will be at least one controlling exigence that functions as the organising principle: it specifies the audience to be addressed and the change to be effected." In all cases, the exigence is the inauguration of the first presidents of the four newly independent African countries, whose audiences were celebrating independence from the shackles of colonialism. In their inauguration speeches, the four presidents were each responding to an exigence: in other words, that which demanded or prompted them to deliver their speeches. What was happening during this time in each of the four countries? Why was this 'thing' important? Who were the major actors at that time? Such questions come to the mind of the readers of the four speeches as a result of what the exigence was. Related to the exigence is the *kairos*, which is also an important part of the rhetorical situation. *Kairos* is "the circumstances that open moments of opportunity" (Kinneavy; Sipiora; Vatz; Bitzer; Hill 217). It is the timeliness or appropriateness for a speech or an event. There is no doubt that the kairos of the four inaugural speeches was appropriate; the speeches were delivered at the right time, that is, at the attainment of independence in each case. The *phantasia* about the new dispensation was roused at the right time when the speakers and the audience were in the euphoria, celebrating the independence of their countries.

In addition to the rhetorical situation, we found that the new leaders employed Aristotle's three rhetorical appeals of ethos, logos and pathos in their speeches to support their claims, and to build imaginations of the new people-oriented nations in the minds of their audiences. What follow are illustrations of some of instances where we found Aristotle's three rhetorical appeals or proofs.

Ethos

The rhetorical appeal ethos, is based on the character, credibility or reliability of the speaker, or other revered personalities. For Lawrie (2006: 21), a character of the speaker means that "the audience's perception of the moral character of the speaker would aid or hinder persuasion". He goes on saying that the audience is more likely to agree with the speaker who displays honesty, balance, reasonability, openness or dependability than the speaker who displays irresponsibleness, secretiveness or instability. In their speeches, the four new leaders were tested revolutionaries who had sacrificed their lives for the liberation of their countries. There is no doubt that the majority of their audiences trusted the ethos of these men who were delivering speeches of the end of colonial rule in their countries. In their speeches, the speakers also used the ethos of other people in the struggle for freedom, independence and social justice.

In his message of the proclamation of independence, Machel established his good character and credibility. The speaker posited himself as a servant of both Mozambican people and FRELIMO Central Committee, a decision-making body of the party responsible for electing the members of the executive committee. The speaker brought balance and established his good image and credibility to the audience in the solemn proclamation of independence of Mozambique. To buttress his cause, he referred to earlier resistance in this country. He recalled the past events of earlier resistance of the people of Mozambique while praising the bravery of Mwenemutapa and Barue. The battle of Barue was one of some of the well-known resistance movements against Portuguese colonial control. The speaker made reference to reputable sources of Mueda and Xinavane uprisings, whereby tens of thousands of people had protested before the Portugal Government demanding independence. He recalled:

> In the course of all the historical process of the wars of conquest, the Mozambican People rose up heroically constantly and everywhere against the colonialist plunder. From the resistance of the Muenemutapa to the insurrection of Barue, Mozambican history prides itself on the glorious deeds of the masses in the struggle for the defense of freedom and independence... popular uprisings as in Mueda and

Xinavane. The blood of the workers ... imprisoned, deported, assassinated and massacred fertilises the national conscience.

The most important part of Machel's ethical appeal is the appeal to Mondlane's *ethos*. Mondlane was the founding father of FRELIMO and the first African from Mozambique to obtain a doctorate:

> It is in this context that on June 25, 1962, Mozambican Patriots, under the direction of Comrade Eduardo Chivambo Mondlane launched the new and victorious phase of national resistance: the creation of FRELIMO, which made possible organised and united struggle of the Mozambican People. The creation of FRELIMO supplies the fundamental and decisive weapon of unity to the combat of the Mozambican People. FRELIMO, rooting itself in the purest traditions of the age-old struggle of the Mozambican working masses, assuming the real interests of the broad strata of exploited, oppressed, and humiliated, is able to define with the clarity he objectives and the methods of the liberating struggle.

By extolling the heroic resistance of the Muenemutapa and Barwe, and the charismatic Mondlane, Machel succeeded in bolstering his ethos in favourable comparison with the ethos of those who had fought Portuguese colonial rule before him and that of his contemporary comrade-in-arms.

Mugabe also established a common ground with the audience at his *exordium*. He praised the people of Zimbabwe, who had participated in the democratic elections, in which he led his party to victory. The choice made by the electorate was essential to legitimise a credible government "they wish to govern them and take policy decisions as to their future". Furthermore, Mugabe acknowledged the support and cooperation of friends, allies and the international community. He re-established his authority as having been also legitimised by the international community. He remarked:

> This, indeed, is the meaning of the mandate my party secured through a free and fair election, conducted in the full glare of the world

spotlight. While my Government welcomes the mandate it has been freely given and is determined to honour it to the letter, it also accepts that the fulfilment of the tasks imposed by the mandate are only possible with the confidence, goodwill and co-operation of all of you, reinforced by the forthcoming support and encouragement of all our friends, allies, and well-wishers in the international community.

Mugabe thanked Her Majesty the Queen for having sent her representative, His Royal Highness, Prince Charles, the Prince of Wales, to officiate the independence ceremony. The presence of the Queen's representative at the ceremony legitimised the speaker's credibility and that of his government, and it created bonds with Britain and other represented countries and organisations. Furthermore, the speaker praised Lord Soames' *ethos*, Britain's last colonial Governor in Rhodesia who presided over its transition to majority rule as Zimbabwe. With the credibility and influential role of such people, Mugabe elevated himself as a credible and reliable person to the audience:

> I wish to thank Her Majesty the Queen for having sent His Royal Highness, Prince Charles, and the Prince of Wales to represent her and officiate at our Independence ceremony, where he will perform the symbolic act of severing our colonial ties with Britain.
> I now wish to pay tribute to Lord Soames, our Governor, for the most important role he has played in successfully guiding this country to elections and independence. He was from the very onset given a difficult and most unenviable task. And yet he performed it with remarkable ability and overwhelming dignity.

Nujoma also established his authority before the audience, appealing to the *ethos* of the Secretary-General of the United Nations and the State President of South Africa. Their presence at the inauguration elevated the status of the speaker as a respected and trustworthy leader with invested mandate to lead the nation. The UN Secretary General and the South African President were part of the UN Resolution 435 which paved the way for elections in 1989. Also, Nujoma thanked the international community and the South African government for the political will and act of statesmanship and realism through President De Klerk, a sign of respect and honesty. He said:

> It is, therefore, profoundly momentous and highly joyous, for the Namibian people and myself, that the highest representatives of the international community - The Secretary-General of the United Nations - together with the State President of South Africa, and the Namibian nation, which I am honoured to lead, are able to announce, here today, to the world that a definitive and final solution to the protracted Namibian problem has, indeed, been unanimously reached by these three parties.
>
> Against this background, Honourable Master of Ceremony, Distinguished Guests and Dear Compatriots I am indebted to the Namibian electorate for giving SWAPO (the South West Africa People's Organisation) an absolute majority, thereby enabling it to form the first government of the Republic of Namibia. In the same vein, I am grateful to members of Namibia's Constitutional Assembly for the confidence they placed in me in electing me as the first President of the Republic of Namibia.

The epitome of Nujoma's *ethos* was realised by displaying his honesty and integrity to uphold the Constitution of the Republic, which is a supreme law of the land to honour the trust bestowed upon him: "I pledge to do my utmost to uphold the Constitution of the Republic, and to honour the trust, which the Namibian people have bestowed upon me to lead this new nation at this critical juncture".

Nujoma displayed his integrity and credibility in his conclusion or *peroratio* by acknowledging that he had been given a mandate by the people of Namibia as the first President of the Republic of Namibia, while paying tribute to those who gave their lives in support for the cause for independence. He positioned himself as a representative of the people of Namibia:

> Master of Ceremony, Sir, In accepting the sacred responsibility which the Namibian people have placed on me, as the first President of the Republic of Namibia, I would like to bow and pay homage to

our fallen heroes and heroines, whose names Namibia's present and future generations will sing songs of praise and whose martyrdom they will intone. In conclusion, I move, in the name of our people, to declare that Namibia is forever free, sovereign and independent.

In his speech delivered on 10 May 1994, Mandela first established his common ground with the audience by sharing the moment with the audience in celebration of a newborn state: "Today, all of us do, by our presence here, and by our celebrations in other parts of our country and the world, confer glory and hope to newborn liberty".

He continued thanking the audience represented in the ceremony for the support and encouragement to produce a new reality in South Africa rooted in justice and confidence in human dignity: "All this we owe both to ourselves and to the peoples of the world who are well represented here". Furthermore, he reinforced his closeness, and he shared the past rooted in the ideologies of racism and racial oppression. "That spiritual and physical oneness we all share with this common homeland explains the depth of the pain we all carried in our hearts as we saw our country tear itself apart in a terrible conflict, and as we saw it spurned, outlawed and isolated by the peoples of the world, precisely because it has become the universal base of the pernicious ideology and practice of racism and racial oppression".

Mandela further expressed his gratitude to the people and leaders of South Africa regardless of their political affiliation, religion, in particular to President De Klerk. De Klerk was instrumental in the negotiations with the ANC, and he was appointed second Deputy President in the first multiracial democratic government for the role he had played in abolishing the apartheid system: "We deeply appreciate the role that the masses of our people and their political mass democratic, religious, women, youth, business, traditional and other leaders have played to bring about this conclusion. Not least among them is my Second Deputy President, the Honourable F.W. de Klerk".

In the exercise of his authority as the first President of South Africa, Mandela appealed to the *ethos* of the interim National Unity Government lead by ANC to address the amnesty of people serving terms of imprisonment as a matter of urgency, while displaying his firm commitment to common justice for all in the country: "As a token of its commitment to the renewal of our country, the new Interim Government of National Unity will, as a matter of urgency, address the issue of amnesty for various categories of our people who are currently serving terms of imprisonment".

It is worth mentioning that all speakers used together-words to show that they shared the same experiences of injustice, oppression, segregation and domination perpetrated by the political regimes in the respective country in one hand, and happiness, joy, exhilaration for the conquest of independence in their countries, on the other.

Pathos

Pathos refers to an attempt to engage the audience's emotions. Lawrie (2006) argues that a speaker can persuade the listeners effectively by appealing to their feelings, values, prejudices or interests. Therefore through the use of pathos, the speaker manages to capture the qualitative facets of life, thus demonstrating that rhetoric manages to provide us with grammars of articulation which can go beyond the limitations of discourses about non-representationalism in life. In essence, emotional appeal was employed in all four inaugural speeches.

In his Message of Proclamation, Machel employed an appeal to pity in order to win the support of the audience by exploiting their feelings. The speaker referred to the audience as people who had been subject to exploitation, barbarism emanating from repression, infamy and humiliation perpetrated by the colonial regime, thus making them inferior. The speaker concluded the argument that the Mozambican people had their ego diminished, negated and enslaved in their own land. He said:

> This watchword found a deep echo in the broad Mozambican masses from the Rovuma to the Maputo, equally subjected to the fierce yoke of the occupier, to the greed of his exploitation, to the barbarism of his repression, to the infamy of his permanent humiliation. The Mozambican saw himself deprived of his national personality, his civilisation and culture denigrated and negated, his manners and

customs ridiculed, saw himself made a foreigner and enslaved in his own country.

The appeal to pity was also used in Mandela Inaugural Statement. The speaker engaged the audience's emotions by referring to the pain sustained as a result of the apartheid regime that had become a practice of apartheid and racial oppression. The speaker engaged the audience as follows: "That spiritual and physical oneness we all share with this common homeland explains the depth of the pain we all carried in our hearts as we saw our country tear itself apart in a terrible conflict, and as we saw it spurned, outlawed and isolated by the peoples of the world, precisely because it has become the universal base of the pernicious ideology and practice of racism and racial oppression".

Nujoma further employed this strategy of appeal to pity to engage the audience. The speaker argued that many Namibians had supported the cause of independence by giving their lives or living in exile in harsh conditions, in an attempt to show how difficult the fight for independence was. The speaker argued: "This is the day for which tens of thousands of Namibian Patriots laid down their lives, shed their precious blood, suffered imprisonment and difficult life in exile. Today, our hearts are filled with great joy and jubilation because our deepest and longest yearning has been realised".

Nujoma continued to apply this strategy and reiterated that the negotiation process was difficult and filled at times with anger and bitterness; however, "It was only perseverance, forbearance and commitment, which helped us to see the process through to its logical conclusion, namely, the birth of the Namibian nation we are here to witness".

Furthermore, Machel adopted *ad populum* fallacy, speaking positive of the leadership of FRELIMO to win popular assent to a conclusion that it defeated the Portuguese colonialism by arousing the feeling and enthusiasm of the audience. The speaker said: "It is under the leadership of FRELIMO, it is integrated in FRELIMO that the Mozambican People redeems the bloodshed for generations, retakes control of its own history, makes useful the sacrifice of its own life, destroys the life forces of the enemy, affirms fully its African and revolutionary personality and imposes defeat on the colonial-fascist regime".

Machel engaged as well the audience's feelings by evoking the basic needs of the audience. He said that his government "will promote the liquidation of elitism and educational discrimination on the basis of wealth". He continued to inspire hope and confidence of the audience that his government "will promote the formation of a new mentality, people's morality, a revolutionary mentality in the heart of the new generations." He said his government would take care of the vulnerable groups in the society: "The People's Republic of Mozambique considers it the duty of honor of all Mozambicans to protect especially the orphans and widows of war, and the wounded and mutilated from the war, the symbol of the sacrifice consented to by millions of Mozambicans in the course of colonial domination and of the armed struggle of national liberation".

Machel appealed similarly to the audience interests and prejudices on the elimination of diseases and extension of health services to the rural areas where the majority of rural populations lived. The speaker assured that: "The elimination of disease, one of the faces of colonialism and underdevelopment, constitutes an essential preoccupation. The People's Republic of Mozambique will extend the network of health services throughout the whole country, especially the rural zones, so as to benefit the working masses".

According to Stiff and Mongeau (2003), emotional appeal is effective when the speaker is trying to influence behaviour, or the speaker wants the audience to take immediate action. In his inaugural speech, Mandela gave hope to the audience for "the construction of a complete, just and lasting peace". The speaker attempted to influence the audience's behaviour by inviting all South Africans to "build the society in which all South Africans, both black and white, will be able to walk tall, without any fear in their hearts, assured of their inalienable right to human dignity".

The appeal to change of behaviour is employed mainly in Mugabe Independence Message. He attempted to influence the behaviour of the audience by calling all Zimbabweans to adapt themselves to the political change, while relating to each other as brother bound to one another. He was persuading the audience to live in harmony and forgiveness. The speaker remarked that:

> Henceforth, you and I must strive to adapt ourselves, intellectually and spiritually to the reality of our political change and relate to each other as brothers bound one to another by a bond of national comradeship. If yesterday I fought as an enemy, today you have become a friend and ally with the same national interest, loyalty, rights and duties as myself. If yesterday you hated me, today you cannot avoid the love that binds you to me and me to you. Is it not folly, therefore, that in these circumstances anybody should seek to revive the wounds and grievances of the past? The wrongs of the past must now stand forgiven and forgotten.

While assuring the audiences that his new government was determined to make changes in the lives of the people by instigating hope for better future, Mugabe engaged the audience's emotions for patience to give time for the newly formed government to develop programs. He further stirred emotions to the audience by acknowledging that people did not own land, a basic commodity for survival, jobs and schools. The speaker assured:

> May I assure you that my Government is determined to bring about meaningful change to the lives of the majority of the people in the country. But I must ask you to be patient and allow my Government time to organise programmes that will effectively yield that change. There are people without land who need land, people without jobs who need jobs, children without schools who need schools and patients without hospitals who need them.

Mugabe continued to appeal to the audience for mutual respect to promote the national unity. The speaker said, "I, therefore, wish to appeal to all of you to respect each other and act in promotion of national unity rather than negation of that unity". Furthermore, he emphasised the need to increase salaries in all sectors, while appealing to the patience of the audience: He commented: "We are also fully aware of the need for increased wages in all sectors of employment.

My Government will certainly do its best to meet the existing needs in these areas. But you have to assist us by being patient and peaceful".

Mugabe appealed, then, to the audience to participate fully in the celebrations of independence and to the basic services employees to continue carrying their duties during the celebrations. The speaker said:

> I now finally wish to appeal to you, wherever you are, to participate fully today and Saturday in the Independence celebrations that have been organised throughout the country. There are, of course, those of you who have the duty to maintain essential services. These services must indeed be maintained so that the celebrations are facilitated. Maintaining such essential services during the celebrations is a significant contribution to their success.

In his message of Proclamation of Independence, Machel talked about the emancipation of women, thus elevating the status of women to achieve total liberation from capitalist oppression. He argued: "The People's Republic of Mozambique, following the line of FRELIMO, will engage itself in the struggle for the emancipation of woman, for total liberation from the diverse forms of traditional and capitalist oppression, so that she may retake her role as citizen with full rights in our society, giving her political, civic and social contribution".

Nujoma evoked joy and jubilation, and instigated hope and confidence while announcing that the country was then in the hands of its people. The speaker engaged as follows: "To the Namibian people, I would like to state, on this solemn occasion, that our nation blazed the trail to freedom. It has arisen to its' feet. As from today, we are masters of this vast land of our ancestors. The destiny of this country is now fully in our own hands. We should, therefore, look forward to the future with confidence and hope"

Weida and Stolley (2013) claim that a good argument will use a combination of all three appeals to make its case. This is the case of Mugabe's argument in his Independence Message. The speaker combined *ethos, pathos* and *logos*. In the argument below, Mugabe started by appealing to the emotions of the audience that independence was never easy. The speaker used loaded language of "countless lives", "death" and "suffering" to stir the emotions (emotional appeal). Secondly, the speaker reasonably argued that death and suffering were reward for independence (cause and effect logical reasoning). Finally, the speaker concluded by showing respect to the audience while raising his credibility that he was an honest man (ethical appeal). The speaker argued as follows: "The march to our national independence has been a long, arduous and hazardous one. On this march, countless lives have been lost and many sacrifices made. Death and suffering have been the prize we have been called upon to pay for the final priceless reward of freedom and national independence. May I thank all of you who have had to suffer and sacrifice for the reward we are now getting".

Logos

The use of *logos* is called a "logical appeal". According to Williams (2015), logos is the use of strategies of logic to persuade an audience. The strategies of logical appeal include the use of deductive and inductive reasoning, analogy, comparison, logical cause, effect strategies and statistics. The four inaugural addresses employed different logical strategies. For example, in his independence Message, Mugabe logically appealed to his audience by saying:

> Tomorrow we shall be celebrating the historical event, which our people have striven for nearly a century to achieve. Our people, young and old, men and women, black and white, living and dead, are, on this occasion, being brought together in a new form of national unity that makes them all Zimbabweans. Independence will bestow on us a new personality, a new sovereignty, a new future and perspective, and indeed a new history and a new past.

Similarly, Nujoma in his Inaugural Speech employed the strategy of logical cause and effect to argue that the achievement of independence was a result of the heroism of those who gave their lives and the conviction for the cause of liberation. The speaker remarked as follows:

For the Namibian people, the realisation of our most cherished goal, namely the independence of our country and the freedom of our people, is a fitting tribute to the heroism and tenacity with which our people fought for this long-awaited day. We have been sustained in our difficult struggle by the powerful force of conviction in the righteousness and justness of our cause. Today history has absolved us; our vision of a democratic state of Namibia has been translated into reality.

The logical cause and effect was also employed in Machel's Message of Proclamation of Independence. Machel was referring to the underlying factors that contributed to the revolution. He put his arguments as follows:

But if colonialism succeeded in its intent of conquest and physical domination, still it never succeeded in dominating the spirits and destroying the will for freedom of the masses. The more blindly repression was asserted, the more hate was evoked against the barbarous aggressors; the greater the oppression and humiliation, the stronger became the desire for freedom; the more brutal became the exploitation and the pillage, the more powerful grew the will for revolution.

Machel repeated the logical strategy to support that the defeat of earlier movements of resistance was "due exclusively to the treason of the feudal ruling classes, to their greed and ambition" that allowed the colonialism to "divide the People and to conquer it". On the other hand, the speaker explained that the unity of liberation movements to form FRELIMO created favourable conditions for the second stage of unity for liberation struggle against colonialism and imperialism. He said: "With the watchword of unity and struggle against Portuguese colonialism and imperialism, in two years FRELIMO creates the appropriate conditions for moving the liberation struggle to the phase of general armed insurrection, thus materialising and making operative the unity of the conquered".

In addition, Machel employed an analogy by comparing the liquidation of Nazism and birth of socialism, including the victory in

China and Indochina as the backbone of national resistance against the colonial oppression: The speaker compared: "The liquidation of Nazism, the creation of the socialist camp, the victory of China, the defeat of the colonial armies in Indochina, the Algerian insurrection, and the emancipation of the Asian and African peoples stimulates the national resistance".

Moreover, Machel gave testimony about the formation of FRELIMO, which is translated as unity in comparison to the earlier movements of resistance with the support of the working masses to uphold the interests of broad strata towards the liberation of the country. The speaker argued that: "The creation of FRELIMO supplied the fundamental and decisive weapon of unity to the combat of the Mozambican People. FRELIMO, rooting itself in the purest traditions of the age-old struggle of the Mozambican working masses, assuming the real interests of the broad strata of exploited, oppressed, and humiliated, is able to define with the clarity he objectives and the methods of the liberating struggle".

Mandela also used the cause and effect strategy while praising the heroes and heroines and the people of the world who sacrificed their lives to liberate the country. The speaker said: "We dedicate this day to all the heroes and heroines in this country and the rest of the world who sacrificed in many ways and surrendered their lives so that we could be free. Their dreams have become reality. Freedom is their reward".

Additionally, in his statement of the inauguration, Mandela employed an analogy while describing the qualities of being attached to the country as compared to that of Jacaranda mimosa trees. The speaker said: "To my compatriots, I have no hesitation in saying that each one of us is as intimately attached to the soil of this beautiful country as are the famous jacaranda trees of Pretoria and the mimosa trees of the bushveld".

In his Inaugural Speech, Nujoma pointed out the qualities of the South African Government to accept the implementation of Resolution 435 to relinquish control over Namibia as an act of statesmanship and realism. The speaker remarked:

As for the government of South Africa, it can be said that the decision to accept the implementation of Resolution 435 was the first demonstration of political will to find a negotiated solution to the problems of our region. Furthermore, President Willem de Klerk proclamation here today that South Africa has reached a final and irreversible decision to relinquish control over Namibia is an act of statesmanship and realism. This, we hope, will continue to unfold in South Africa itself.

Furthermore, Mugabe used syllogism, a logical appeal that applies deductive reasoning to make the audience better understand the point the speaker was making about being born again with the achievement of independence. The speaker commented:

Tomorrow we are being born again; born again not as individuals but collectively as a people, nay, as a viable nation of Zimbabweans. Tomorrow is thus our birthday, the birth of a great Zimbabwe, and the birth of its nation. Tomorrow we shall cease to be men and women of the past and become men and women of the future. It's tomorrow then, not yesterday, which bears our destiny.

Mugabe employed a deductive reasoning strategy over while arguing about the human essence to form the core principles of the political change and national independence. The speaker stated that:

As we become a new people, we are called to be constructive, progressive and forever forward looking, for we cannot afford to be men of yesterday, backward-looking, retrogressive and destructive. Our new nation requires of every one of us to be a new man, with a new mind, a new heart and a new spirit. Our new mind must have a new vision and our new hearts a new love that spurns hate, and a new spirit that must unite and not divide. This to me is the human essence that must form the core of our political change and national independence.

Nujoma used a deductive reasoning strategy too. The speaker set in his argument a general claim that independence imposed a huge responsibility as a starting point. The speaker then drew specific

71

conclusions to defending the liberty, justice and opportunity for all. The speaker reasoned: "Our achievement of Independence imposes upon us a heavy responsibility, not only to defend our hard-won liberty but also to set ourselves higher standards of equality, justice and opportunity for all, without regard to race, creed or colour. These are the standards from which all who seek to emulate us shall draw inspiration".

Mugabe employed another strategy of inductive reasoning. In his argument, the speaker took a specific case of iniquities, such as racism and oppression subjected to the blacks by whites when they had the power, does not have a room in the new political and social system. Because these were inhumane acts perpetrated to those who thought differently, and would remain evil even if perpetrated by the blacks against the whites. In other words, Mugabe was preaching the spirit of reconciliation whose practice assisted in building a united nation. The speaker remarked that:

> If ever we look to the past, let us do so for the lesson the past has taught us, namely that oppression and racism are inequities that must never again find scope in our political and social system. It could never be a correct justification that because whites oppressed us yesterday when they had power, the blacks must oppress them today because they have power. An evil remains an evil whether practiced by white against black or by black against white. Our majority rule could easily turn into inhuman rule if we oppressed, persecuted or harassed those who do not look or think like the majority of us.

Mugabe repeated this technique to explain to the audience that democracy should not be used to harass or intimidate those with different opinions about anything. He emphasised that democracy required compliance to the law and social rules. The speaker reasoned:

> Democracy is never mob-rule. It is and should remain a disciplined rule requiring compliance with the law and social rules. Our independence must thus not be construed as an instrument vesting individuals or groups with the right to harass and intimidate others into

acting against their will. It is not the right to negate the freedom of others to think and act, as they desire…If yesterday I fought as an enemy, today you have become a friend and ally with the same national interest, loyalty, rights and duties as myself. If yesterday you hated me, today you cannot avoid the love that binds you to me and me to you. Is it not folly, therefore, that in these circumstances anybody should seek to revive the wounds and grievances of the past? The wrongs of the past must now stand forgiven and forgotten.

In his Message of Proclamation of Independence, Machel claimed the nature of an independent People's Republic of Mozambique which is "a people's Democratic State". The speaker continued arguing that the new state was going to focus on the "destruction of the results of the colonialism and imperialist dependence for the annihilation of the system of the exploitation of man by man, for the building of the material, ideological, politico-cultural, social and administrative base of the new society." He also used the inductive reasoning strategy. The speaker pointed out representative cases of means used by the colonial regime to dominate the people. The speaker took specific cases of repression, obscurantism, and spread of alcoholism, prostitution, racism and division as supporting facts to represent the larger situation of colonialism. Machel concluded that these were the means used by the colonialists to divide and destroy the people. The speaker said:

The brutality of repression and the terror it sustained, the systematic and deliberate cultural obscurantism which aimed at uprooting the person from his environment, the coldly planned spread of alcoholism and other vices, the prostitution, the implantation of racism and its inherent complexes, the programmed division of the people on the basis of religion, ethnic and regional origin, the systemisation of passivity and submission to colonialism with the active support of the churches, were among many other means used by foreign domination to asphyxiate the spirit of resistance and the creative capacity of the masses and to maintain them divided and impotent.

Phantasia and Imagined States: Nation as an Imagined Community

According to Anderson's (1991) nationalism theory, a nation is an imagined political community. As Anderson (ibid) puts it, a nation "is imagined because the members of even the smallest nation will never know most of their fellow-members, meet them, or even hear of them, yet in the minds of each lives the image of their communion or unity". The most important thing in an imagined community is similar identity and interests of the people – what can be termed as communion. In Table 1 below, we pick some parts of the four leaders' speeches that illustrate the imagined states/communities that the four new leaders said they were going to create together with their respective audiences.

Table 1: The imagined states in the inaugural speeches

Mozambique Samora Machel	Zimbabwe Robert Mugabe	Namibia Sam Nujoma	South Africa Nelson Mandela	Commentary
The Republic which is **born** is the concretisation of the aspirations of all Mozambicans	A new personality, a new sovereignty, a new history, we are being born again, our birthday, the birth of a great Zimbabwe, the birth of a nation	It is therefore **proudly momentous and highly joyous for the Namibian people and myself** -the independence of our country and freedom of our people	Out of the experience of an ordinary human **disaster** that lasted too long **must be born a society which all humanity will be proud of**	**Personification** The birth of the four nations, like birth of a child, gave joy and celebration. The use of antithesis played a role in vividly portraying the imagined nations against the old ones; democratic values versus racial discrimination and oppression by white regimes; jubilation versus disaster
Our People's Republic is **born** from the blood of the people	Confidence, goodwill and co-operation of all of you	The birth of the Namibian nation	Each one of us is as intimately attached to the soil of	Appeal to the pathos of the audience; the birth of the ne nations and the feeling of the

			this beautiful country -each time one of us touches the soil of this land, we feel a sense of personal renewal	renewal at independence were meant to make the audience feel obliged to agree with the speakers; to feel guilty of taking contrary views
Building of the material, ideological, politico-cultural, social and administrative base of the **new** society	Celebrating the historic event (independence)	We formulated and adopted a Constitution acceptable to the broad majority of our people	We are moved by the sense of joy and exhilaration	The audience was made to believe that independence was for them and that was why they were celebrating. The democratic process of constitution making was meant to illustrate that the people were part of the statecraft in the new dispensation
The People's Republic of Mozambiques will **build** an advanced, prosperous and independent economy	Our people, young and old, men and women, black and white, living and dead on this occasion being brought together to form a new form of national unity that makes the all Zimbabweans	I pledge to do my utmost to uphold the Constitution of the Republic of Namibia and to honour the trust which the Namibian people have bestowed upon me to lead this new nation	The spiritual and physical oneness we all share with this common homeland	Emphasis was on unity in building new states. The message was that no one would be left out in the new societies.
People's Democratic Power	**Democratic choice** – free and fair election	We are masters of this vast land of our ancestors We should look forward to the future with	We the people of South Africa feel fulfilled that humanity has taken us back into its bosom -A common victory for	New nations where democratic values would flourish; A new world order in each country which looked

		confidence and hope	justice, for peace, for human dignity	promising for all citizens.
The People's Republic of Mozambique ... will promote the liquidation of elitism ... will promote a **new mentality**, a people's mentality, a revolutionary mentality in the hearts of the new generations	Our nation requires of every one of us to be a new man, with a new mind, a new heart and a new spirit. Our new mind must have a new vision and new hearts, a new we love that spurns the hate, and a new spirit that must unity and not divide	Make great effort to forge national identity and unity -Unity is a precondition of peace and development	The time to build is now -we must act together as a united people for national reconciliation, for national building, for the birth of a new world	Emphasis was again on national unity and oneness; also national reconciliation
The PRM will extend health services throughout the whole country, especially the rural zones, so as to benefit the working masses	Relate to each other as brothers bound one to another by a bond of national comradeship	Set ourselves higher standards of equality, justice and opportunity for all without regard to race, creed or colour	We shall build the society in which all South Africans, both black and white will be able to walk tall, without fear in their hearts -a rainbow nation at peace with itself and the world	National reconciliation
Establishment of a **new and just social order**	Our majority rule could easily turn inhuman rule if we oppressed, persecuted or harassed those who do not look or think like the majority of us		The people of South Africa have bestowed on me as the first President of a united, democratic, non-racial and non-sexist government	National reconciliation
The PRM – establishment of real **peace and social justice**	Let us enjoin the whole of our nation to march to			Peace and unity

	perfect unison; we have			
This is the **first State in which Power belongs to us,** this is our free and independent country born from the sacrifice of the blood and from ruins	There are people without land, people without jobs who need jobs, children without schools need schools and patients without hospitals who need them			First state, Most important here, the land question was a contentious issue in all the new states at the time of their independence. Obviously the audience would support a leader who talked about giving them the land that had been stolen from their ancestors by the colonisers.

The overarching theme in the speeches was the freedom the people in the four countries were going to enjoy in the new states. To unpack freedom, and consolidate the visions the new leaders had for their countries, we found the words of Eleanor Roosevelt, America's former First Lady, fitting in this discussion. Addressing the UN General Assembly on 9 December 1948, she said:

> We must not be confused about what freedom is. Basic human rights are simple and easily understood: freedom of speech and free press; freedom of religion and worship; freedom of assembly and right of petition; the right of men [and women] to be secure in their homes and free from unreasonable search and seizure and arbitrary arrest and punishment ... Democracy, freedom [and] human rights have come to have a definite meaning to the people off the world which we must not allow any nation to change that they are made synonymous with suppression and dictatorship (Williams, 2013:42-43).

In their speeches, Machel, Mugabe, Nujoma and Mandela accentuated freedom, democracy, the rule of law and the observation of human rights in the new states they were creating.

Statement of Facts (Narratio)

According to Lawrie (2006: 23), statement of facts is "The narrative or an overview of the facts of the case (*narratio*): It is this part that the speaker summarises the events that led up to the speech or relevant "facts or cases. This background information is usually given in the form of a story, so the name narrative."

Machel's *narratio* comprised nine paragraphs in which the speaker provided a narrative of background information that led up the speech. The first paragraph set a chronology of events dating back to the launch of armed struggle on September 25, 1964, the date on which "the Central Committee of FRELIMO launched the historic watchword of the unleashing of the general armed insurrection of the Mozambican People against Portuguese colonialism and imperialism". The second and third paragraphs of the *narratio* are startling facts providing some dramatic facts that Mozambican people were subject to "exploitation, to the barbarism of his repression, to the infamy of his permanent humiliation" as well as a description of "other means used by foreign domination to asphyxiate the spirit of resistance and the creative capacity of the masses, and to maintain them divided and impotent". The fourth and fifth paragraphs provide a transition with an adversative conjunction "but" and they present information on the early resistance of Mwenemutapa and Barue against the Portuguese that were defeated due to "the treason of the feudal ruling classes, to their greed and ambition, which allowed the enemy to divide the People and to conquer it". The sixth and seventh paragraphs provide information on the uprisings that started in urban areas and the transformation of colonialism into colonial-fascism that never "succeed in shaking the determination of the people". The eighth paragraph narrates the birth of socialism, "the victory of China, the defeat of the colonial armies in Indochina, the Algerian insurrection, the emancipation of the Asian and African peoples that was key to "stimulate the national resistance". The last paragraph of *narratio*, provides information about the popular uprisings of Mueda and Xinavane where thousands of Mozambican people were "assassinated and massacred".

Mugabe's *narratio* consisted of three paragraphs. The first paragraph refers to the holding of democratic, free and fair elections, in which Zimbabweans "made a democratic choice of those who, as their legitimate government, wish to govern them and take policy decisions as to their future". The second paragraph reaffirmed the mandate conferred by the people and appealed to "the confidence, goodwill and co-operation of all of you, reinforced by the forthcoming support and encouragement of all our friends, allies, and well-wishers in the international community". The last paragraph provided startling facts that independence was long, arduous and hazardous where "countless lives have been lost, and many sacrifices made."

Similarly, Nujoma's *narratio* comprised three paragraphs. In the first paragraph, the speaker set a chronology of time "for the past 43 years or so, this land of our forbearers was a bone of contention between the Namibian people and the international community, on one hand, and South Africa, on the other". The second paragraph referred to negotiations made where "The United Nations and other international bodies produced huge volumes of resolutions, in an attempt to resolve this intractable problem". The third paragraph praised the achievement of independence that "is a fitting tribute to the heroism and tenacity with which our people fought for this long-awaited day. We have been sustained in our difficult struggle by the powerful force of conviction in the righteousness and justness of our cause."

The first paragraph of Mandela's *narratio* reveals the experience of apartheid that purported a birth of a "society of which all humanity will be proud". The second paragraph provides background that the victory was due to the support of "the people of the world who are well represented here today". The last paragraph of *narratio*, provides more information about the effects and impacts of the apartheid regime that tore the country apart and was "isolated by the peoples of the world, precisely because it has become the universal base of the pernicious ideology and practice of racism and racial oppression".

In his *peroratio*, Mandela ended with most appealing metaphor and ended on a positive note by saying "the sun shall never set". In the real world, when the sun sets, darkness follows and darkness is associated with evil deeds. In other words, all bad things happen in darkness. In contrast, when the sun rises, it signifies joys, and all good things are supposed to happen during day time. The metaphorical expression "sun shall never set" meant that the apartheid (a period resembling darkness) had been abolished and everlasting freedom had been achieved for the people of South Africa.

Mugabe also used metaphors in his Independence Message. The speaker used the word "march to our national independence" and did not mean the exact walk steadily, but meant a struggle for independence, whereby people died, and sacrifices were made to achieve independence. Moreover, Mugabe used another metaphorical expression "we are being born again", a Christian metaphor which means to undergo spiritual rebirth or regeneration from human spirit to Holy Spirit while attempting to appeal to the audience for reconciliation among Zimbabweans.

Nujoma also used a metaphor in his *exordium*. The speaker was attempting to engage the audience by saying that "The Namibian problem was at the centre of a bitter international dispute over a decade". By using the expression "bitter international dispute", the speaker did not mean the taste or smell but a dispute that lasted longer to resolve at the international level, which included the UN, the Government of South Africa and the Namibian people.

Machel also used a metaphor in his Message of Proclamation of Independence, when arguing about the acts of colonialism that were essentially meant to exploit and oppress the people of Mozambique that were "made foreigner and enslaved in his own country. The speaker compared the native people of Mozambique as those coming from a different country to demonstrate how colonialism regime acted against the people of Mozambique. Furthermore, the speaker used "youth sap of the nation" comparing the youth as the tree fluid that transports water and other nutrients. The speaker did not mean exactly that the youth will be transporting water or nutrients, rather youth as the backbone of the country.

Another trope found in the inaugurals is irony. According to Crick (2014), Irony is the use of a word or phrase in such way that it conveys the opposite meaning. This trope was found in Mugabe's Message of Independence. The speaker was emphasising the fact that the walk to independence was achieved through death as "the price we have been called upon to pay for the final priceless reward of freedom and national independence". The speaker was provoking the audience into thinking that freedom was a human right for everyone that required no price, but instead a struggle was the way to get through. The trope is also found in Mandela speech while praising the fallen heroes and heroines on which "freedom was their reward". The speaker was saying the opposite that South Africans had to die for the country to get its freedom.

Mugabe also employed personification in his message of independence. According to Crick (2014), personification is a description of the abstract or nonhuman object as if they possess human qualities. The speaker used the expression "sons and daughters of Zimbabwe" to bring a deeper meaning of all people born in Zimbabwe and thus giving a voice to the country. The expression "sons and daughters [of the soil]" signified black Zimbabweans' quest for reclamations of ownership of the [colonially disinherited] land for which they fought during the liberation wars. In Zimbabwe the Shona term *mwana wevhu* (literally 'child of the soil') became synonymous with a freedom fighter [for the restoration and reclamation of land to Black Zimbabweans] during the liberation struggle. In contrast, the coloniser was not *mwana wevhu* since he/she did not rightly, justly and legally **own** this *vhu* (the land of Zimbabwe).

Furthermore, Mandela used another trope called metonymy, which refers to "a description of something personal and abstract in terms of a concrete object associated with it" (Crick, 2014: 39). Related to this, the speaker used the term "South Africans" in the place of the citizens of South Africa as a whole. The speaker attempted to break up the awkwardness of repeating the people of South Africa over and over making the sentence more interesting and more inclusive.

Conclusion

What we have not done in this chapter is to judge Machel, Mugabe, Nujoma and Mandela as either villains or saints, but we found that the rhetorical situation in each case presented them as heroes who were delivering masses of people from the colonial bondage of colossal magnitude. The analysis of their rhetorical situations revealed that the inaugural speeches responded to an apparent problem that triggered the speakers to respond with a rhetorical act concerning the independence in Mozambique, Zimbabwe, Namibia and South Africa. The rhetorical situations also revealed that the speakers delivered the inaugural speeches primarily to an intended audience, with whom they shared common values and experiences of colonisation and the struggle for liberation. It is evident from the speeches that the leaders used *phantasia* in imagining the states that they were creating, states that would uphold democratic practices for the good of all the citizens regardless of the "tribes", races, creed or colour. We also conclude that the speakers took advantage of the exigence and kairos of the moment of independence celebrations to sell to the audiences the directions of their statecraft after the fall of colonial powers. We also argued that their inaugural speeches were appealing to the liberated masses who also imagined new dispensations which promised to uphold their freedom and human dignity. In these new dispensations, the black majority saw themselves as free people who were going to live side by side, all **as human beings**, with the white people who had perpetrated injustices of great magnitude on them and their ancestors. The new states were inclusive and their inclusiveness were expressed in the four speakers' together-words such as "our People's Republic", "our people", "let us build", "our state", "our national independence", "as we become", "we are called", "we cannot", "if we ever look", "our majority rule", "our most cherished goal", "our achievement", "all of us do", "our daily deeds", "we are moved", and "we deeply appreciate". The use of these words was aimed at inviting the audience to be part of celebration of independence in their countries. At the same time, by using these words, the speakers evoked the shared experiences of pain, oppression, segregation and brutality endured in the long walk to independence. Furthermore, the speakers recognised that their countries had achieved a cherished goal of independence that required everyone to play a role in uniting, building and consolidating the countries that had been torn apart by the evil colonial machinery. Contrary, the new states were built on the principles of democracy and equality. There was not going to be a divide between 'us' and 'them' in the new states, but only 'us'. Othering and animism were things of the past colonial times, never to be practised again – the sun would never set again in the four countries.

References

Abell, P. (1987) *The Syntax of Social Life: The Theory and Method of Comparative Narratives*, New York: Oxford University Press.

Anderson, B. (1991) *Imagined Communities: Reflections on the Origins and Spread of Nationalism*. Verso.

Aristotle, (2001) *Rhetoric* Translated by W. Rhys, London: Oxford University Press.

Aristotle, (2007) Rhetoric: *A Theory of Civic Discourse*, 2nd edition, Translated by G. Kennedy, New York: Oxford.

Aristotle's Metaphysics 1a:
https://www.loebclassics.com/view/aristotle-metaphysics/1933/pb_LCL271.3.xml?rskey=asA1ZM&result=3

Benoit, W. (2009) 'Nature and Context of Inaugural Addresses' in J. A. Kypers (ed.), *Rhetorical Criticism: Perspective in Action*, pp. 84-87, Lanham, MD: British Library Catalogue.

Bitzer, L. F., and Black, E. (1971) *The Prospect of Rhetoric*, Eaglewood Cliffs: Prentice Hall.

Bitzer, L. F. (1968), *The Rhetorical Situation: The Power of Rhetoric*, New York: Macmillan Publishing Company.

Bogdan, R., and Biklen, S. K. (2007) *Qualitative Research for Education: An Introduction to Theories and Methods*, London: Pearson A & B.

Bucher, N. R. (2005) 'A Rhetorical Analysis of the Joint Sitting on the Final Report of the Truth and Reconciliation Commission Held at Parliament on 15 April 2003' Master's Thesis, University of Cape Town, South Africa.

Burke, K. (1969) *Rhetoric of Motives*, Berkeley: University of California Press.

Burton, G. O. (2011) Deliberative Rhetoric in *Silva Rhetoricae,* viewed March 2016, from http://rhetoric.byu.edu/Branches%20of20oratory/Deliberative .htm

Campbell, K. H., Huxman, S. S., and Burkholder, T. R. (2014) *The Rhetorical Act: Thinking, Speaking and Writing Critically* 5th edition. Stamford: Cengage Learning.

Campbell, K. K., and Jamieson, K. H. (1989) Inaugurating the Presidency. *Presidential Studies Quarterly* 15(2): 394-411.

Comrade, (n.d) in *Oxford Dictionary,* viewed 27 November 2015, from http://www.oxforddictionaries.com/definition/english/comra de

Condit, C. M. (1985) 'The Functions of Epideictic: The Boston Massacre Oration as Exemplar', *Communication Quarterly* 33(4): 284-299.

Covino, W. and Jolliffe, D. (1985) *Rhetoric: Concepts, Definitions, Boundaries.* Massachusetts: Allyn and Bacon.

Crick, N. (2014) *Rhetorical Public Speaking* 2nd edition, New York: Routledge.

Crowley, S., and Hahwee, D. (1999) *Ancient Rhetorics for Contemporary Students* 2nd edition, Needham Height: Allyn and Beacon.

Crowley, S., and Hawhee, D. (2004) *Ancient Rhetorics for Contemporary Students* 4th edition, New York: Pearson Education.

Darch, C., and Hedges, D. (2013) *Political Rhetoric in the Transition to Mozambican Independence: Samora Machel in Beira, June 1975,* viewed March 2016, from http://www.scielo.org.za/pdf/kronos/v39n1/04.pdf.

Denscombe, M. (2010) *The Good Research Guide for Small-scale Social Projects* 2nd edition, Philadelphia: Open University Press.

Duke, R. K. (1990) *The Persuasive Appeal of the Chronicle: A Rhetorical Analysis,* Sheffield: Almond Press.

Fikameni, S. (2015) 'A Discourse Analysis of Metropolitan and Sanlam Namibia's English Print Advertisements in the Namibian Newspaper: A Comparative Study' Master's Thesis, University of Namibia, Namibia.

Foss, S. K. (1996) *Rhetorical Criticism: Exploration and Practice* 2nd edition, Prospect Heights: Waveland.

Funada-Classen, S. (2012) *The Origins of War in Mozambique: A History of Unity and Division* Translated by Masako, Somerset West South Africa: African Minds.

Glenn, C., and Goldthwaite, M. A. (2008) *The St. Martin's Guide to Teaching Writing* 7th edition, Boston: Bedford/St. Martin's.

Haart, R. P. (2000) *Modern Rhetorical Criticism*, Boston: Allyn and Bacon.

Hase, D. R. (1989) 'Modelling Event Structures', *Journal of Mathematical Sociology* 14(1): 139-169).

Henning, R. (2001) 'Reading and the 'Written Style' in Aristotle Rhetoric', *Rhetoric Society Quarterly* 2(1), 25-109.

Horn, R. (2009) *Researching and Writing Dissertations: A Complete Guide for Business and Management Students* 2nd edition, London: Chartered Institute of Personnel and Development.

Isocrates (1980) *Isocrates with an English Translation in Three Volumes*, Translated by George Norlin, London: William Heinemann Ltd.

Jang, R. (1980) 'General Purpose of Research Designs', *American Journal of Health- System Pharmacy* 37(3), 398-403.

Kangira, J., and Mungenga, J. N. (2012) 'Praiseworthy Values in President Hifikepunye Pohamba's Epideictic Speech Marking Namibia's 20th Anniversary', *Journal of Studies in Humanities and Social Sciences* 3(1), 109-116.

Kasula, B. (2012) *Prominent African Leaders Since Independence*, Dar es Salaam: New Africa Press.

Kennedy, G. A. (1999) *Classical Rhetoric and Its Christian and Secular Tradition from Ancient to Modern Times*, Chapel Hill: University of North Carolina Press.

Kinneavy; Sipiora; Vatz; Bitzer; Hill 217 https://sites.google.com/site/rhetoricanddiscourseclass/home

Kuypers, J. A., and King, S. (2009) *Rhetorical Criticism: Perspective in Action*, Lanham, MD: British Library Catalogue.

Lawrie, D. G. (2006) *Speaking to Good Effect: An Introduction to the Theory and Practice of Rhetoric* 1st edition, Stellenbosch South Africa: Sun Press.

Leedy, P. D., and Ormrod, J. E. (2001) *Practical Research: Planning and Design* 10th edition, Upper Saddle River: Merrill Prentice Hall.

Lindlof, T. R. and Taylor, B. C. (2010) *Qualitative Communication Research Methods* 3rd edition, London: Sage.

Longinus in *On the Sublime (15*.1-2) Translated by W. Rhys Roberts (2013).
https://docs.google.com/viewer?a=v&pid=sites&srcid=ZGV mYXVsdGRvbWFpbnxkYXZrYW5wdXJ8Z3g6N2YxMTBlZj UyNzdjNGVl

Lott, D. N. (1969) *The Presidents Speak: The Inaugural Addresses of the American Presidents from Washington to Kennedy,* New York: Holt, Rinehart and Winston.

Machel, S. (1975) *Message for Proclamation of Independence for Mozambique at His Inauguration as the President of the Republic of Mozambique,* Machava Stadium: Maputo.

Magyar, A. (2010) *Psychology of Persuasion,* New York: Nova Science Publishers.

Mandela, N. R. (1994) Statement of the President of the African National Congress, at his inauguration as the President of the Democratic Republic of South Africa. Unions Building: Pretoria.

Mathe, A. I. (2006) 'Canons of Classical Rhetoric in Sam Nujoma's State of Nation Addresses (11)', Mini Dissertation, University of Free State, South Africa.

Mathe, A. I. (2009) 'Persuasion as a Social Heuristic: A Rhetorical Analysis of the Making of the Constitution of Namibia', Doctoral Dissertation, University of Cape Town, South Africa.

Mbenzi, O. E. (2014) 'The Political Rhetoric of Bishop Kleopas Dumeni in the Pre Independence Era in Namibia', Doctoral Thesis, University of Namibia, Namibia.

Mensah, O. E. (2014) The Rhetoric of Kwame Nkrumah: An Analysis of His Political Speeches', Doctoral Dissertation, University of Cape Town, South Africa.

Meyer, D. (2005) 'The Media and Northern Ireland: Censorship, Information Management and the Broadcasting Ban' in Greg Philo (ed) *Glasgow, Media Group Reader,* London: Routledge.

Mugabe, R. G. (1980) Message of Independence by His Excellency Robert Mugabe at His Inauguration as the Prime Minister of the Republic of Zimbabwe, Rufaro Stadium: Harare.

Nayeni, N. N. (2014) DR. 'Sam Nujoma's Rhetoric: An Analysis of Selected Epideictic Speeches during His Tenure of Office as President of the Republic of Namibia', Master's Thesis, University of Namibia.

Ngesi, S. E. (2001) 'A Rhetorical Study of the Open Democracy Bill: A Parelmanian Approach', Master's Thesis, University of Cape Town.

Ngesi, S. E. (2014) 'Treading a Tightrope: A Rhetorical Study of the Tension between the Executive Leadership of the African National Congress (ANC): From Nelson Mandela to Thabo Mbeki', Doctoral Thesis, University of Cape Town.

Nujoma, S. (1990) The Inaugural Address of His Excellency Sam Nujoma at His Inauguration as President of the Republic of Namibia, Windhoek Athletic Stadium: Windhoek.

O'Gorman, N. (2005). 'Aristotle's Phantasia in Rhetoric: Lexis, Appearance, and the Epideictic Function of Discourse', *Philosophy and Rhetoric*, 38(1), 16-40.

Osborn, M. and Osborn, S. (1994) *Public Speaking*, Harcourt: Houghton Miffin.

Quaye, C. O. (1991) *Liberation Struggles in International Law, Philadelphia*: Temple University Press.

Rhetoric (n.d) In *Ask Define,* viewed 20 November 2015, from http://rhetorical.askdefinebeta.com.

Robert Mugabe (n.d) In Wikipedia, viewed on 17 September 2015, from http://en.wikipedia.org/wiki/Robert_Mugabe.

Still, J. B. and Mongeau, P. A. (2003) *Persuasive Communication* 2nd edition, New York: Guilford Press.

Valenzano, J. M., and Braden, S. W. (2012) *The Speaker: The Tradition and Practice of Public Speaking* 2nd edition, South Lake: Fountainhead Press.

Vendome, M. (1980) *The Art of Versification Translated* by A. E. Galyon, Ames: Iowa State University Press.

Vickers, B. (1989) *In Defence of Rhetoric*, Oxford: Clarendon Press.

Weida, S., and Stolley, K. (2013) 'Using Research and Evidence' in *Prude Writing Online,* viewed on 19 September 2015, from http://owl.english.purdue.edu/owl/resources/588/02/

Welma, C., Kruger, F., and Mitchell, B. (2005) *Research Methodology*, Cape Town: Oxford University Press Sothern Africa.

Williams, G. H. (2015) Ethos, Pathos, Logos: The 2 Rhetorical Appeals, viewed 23 August 2015, from http://georgewilliams.pbworks.com/w/page/14266873/Ethos-Pathos-Logos-The-3-Rhetorical-Appeals

Williams, H. (2013) *Great Speeches of our Time*, London: Quercus.

Windt Jr., T. O. (1986) 'Presidential Rhetoric: Definition of a Field Study', *Presidential Quarterly* 16(1), 102-116.

WynSculley, C. (2004) 'Rhetorical Analysis of Budget Speeches: 1985, 1993, 1994, 2002', Mini Dissertation, University of Cape Town, South Africa.

Yin, R. K. (2003) *Case Study Research: Design and Methods* 2nd edition, London: Sage.

Yoos, G. E. (1984) 'The Teacher and the Author', *Teaching Philosophy* 7(2), 96-172.

Chapter Three

Materialities and Human Rights in Contemporary African Higher Education: the Case of the "Fees Must Fall Movements" in Southern African Universities

Artwell Nhemachena; Tapiwa V. Warikandwa &
Asteria N. Nauta

> *Yet we wonder whether another settler move to innocence is to focus on decolonizing the mind, or the cultivation of critical consciousness, as if it were the sole activity of decolonization; to allow conscientization to stand in for the more uncomfortable task of relinquishing stolen land. We agree that curricula, literature, and pedagogy can be crafted to aid people in learning to see settler colonialism, to articulate critiques of settler epistemology, and set aside settler histories and values in search of ethics that reject domination and exploitation…However the front-loading of critical consciousness building can waylay decolonization…Until stolen land is relinquished, critical consciousness does not translate into action that disrupts settler colonialism (Tuck et al, 2012: 19).*

Introduction

Denied material restitution and restoration of colonially looted resources in the supposedly postcolonial [global] world order, Africans have instead had their energies surreptitiously rechannelled [by (neo-)empire] to ideational and ideological matters where sideshow battles that do not threaten the material and consequential core of (neo-)empire are fought on the continent. In other words, this chapter teases out a paradox: the paradox being that while there was much support for the Fees Must Fall movements and the "decolonisation" of education in African universities, unfortunately, there is opposition to the decolonisation of African materialities. There is "international" opposition to calls to nationalise African mining and other resources, and the restoration of land to Africans (Al Jazeera, 1 May 2016; Hall *et al*, 2017; du Plessis, 2013; Nhemachena, 2016). In this regard, we need to note paradoxical Euro-American opposition to calls for the humanisation of African who are currently demanding compensation for enslavement and colonisation (Nhemachena, 2016). The massive resistance to the restoration and reclamation of land in Zimbabwe [which attracted sanctions rather than acclamations from the (neo-)imperial centres] underscores the hypocrisy of those that support the "decolonisation" of education only while paradoxically opposing the decolonisation of African materialities.

While it is true that Western knowledge has been used for epistemicide or the killing of other [African] knowledge systems (Hall *et al*, 2017), it is imperative to also note that Western material dispossession of Africans has also impoverished Africans many of who are dying of impoverishment related causes. Similarly, while it is true that there have been no changes in epistemologies since apartheid as the curricula remain colonial, apartheid, western oriented, Eurocentric and continues to reinforce white and western dominance (Heleta, 2016); it is equally imperative to note that the same applies to materialities which remain colonised by Westerners and by descendants of colonists who still "own" and control much of African materialities. Thus, while it is noted that Africa needs to tackle and dismantle epistemic violence and hegemony of Eurocentrism completely (Heleta, 2016), it is also necessary to note that the same applies to the need to decolonise African materialities where (neo-)imperial hegemony still prevails.

Thus, while (neo-)empire and its [supportive] networks of institutions, organisations and individuals have celebrated the recent Fees Must Fall Movements and the calls for the "decolonisation" of education in Africa (Nhemachena *et al*, 2017), (neo-)empire paradoxically continues to deny Africans decolonisation in the material senses of getting back their [material] resources which have been looted and robbed since the colonial era. In other words, while material restitution and restoration of what was and is being stolen by (neo-)colonists from Africa can help resolved the challenges of material impoverishment on the continent, the (neo-)imperial world order chooses to hoodwink Africans into believing that ideational and ideological battles are all that is needed to free Africa. In this regard, the fact which (neo-)empire hides is that materialities are the foundations of life in Africa, much as they are the foundations of life everywhere else in the world. In this sense, to claim and have access to human rights, one requires material means of subsistence and existence; for one to claim and have access to education, one needs to first of all have ownership and control over materialities that define one's life trajectories. Similarly, for one to claim and realise human rights to dignity, freedom of conscience, freedom of opinion, freedom of movement and so on, it is imperative to have ownership and control of material resources and other affordances which are foundational to life (Warikandwa and Nhemachena, 2017). In other words, the problem with (neo-)imperial provisions of human rights including rights to life is that they remain in the logics of virtualities that do not materialise in Africa. In a context where colonially dispossessed Africans are denied material restorative relief by the resilient global matrices of power, human rights are understandably elusive in Africa, precisely because African materialities and those that looted them are still at large. In this sense, denial of restitution, compensation and restoration of material resources and property amounts to denying human status to Africans.

Apparent from the foregoing is the fact that the elusiveness of [higher] education in Africa is a function of the elusiveness of restoration of African materialities, at large. The elusiveness of higher education is not merely because African states, governments and parents have failed to provide for [free] education but it is *a fortiori* because African states, governments and parents have not yet recovered their material resources from colonists and from descendants of the colonists. In this vein, civil society organizations or Non-Governmental Organizations and some apartheid era Professors who sponsored the Fees Must Fall Movement in South Africa would have been better off if they spent their energies persuading the colonists and their descendants, including in metropolitan centres, to restitute and restore resources stolen from Africans (Nhemachena *et al*, 2017). The fact that African education systems themselves depend on restoration and compensation in the form of material resources is often conveniently ignored by those that are anxious to circumvent restitution and restoration of African materialities. We argue in this chapter that in an African context where African resources are still at large and where transnational corporations which are often erroneously defined as "investors", still evade paying taxes to [liberally demonised] African governments (Nhemachena *et al*, 2017); the battles by African students could have been broadened and fought on the core and more consequential (neo-)imperial fronts and not just on the sites of African universities. In other words, the argument here is that the Fees Must Fall Movements should have been properly directed at the resilient transnational (neo-)imperial capital that continues to claim, "own" and control African material resources. Put another way, the Fees Must Fall Movements should have been properly conceived in terms of what we shall call **(Neo-)empire Must Fall Movements**.

Tracing the Fees Must Fall Movement at the University of Namibia, this chapter provides a critique of the movements and argues that fees cannot meaningfully fall in Africa if the structuring (neo-)imperial context subsists, as it does; we argue also that even if fees were to meaningfully fall in Africa, the (neo-)imperial world order is not receptive of the mass educated Africans being churned out by the African academies. In this sense, while the right to education is provided for in some African jurisdictions and in some international conventions, there are sadly no meaningful provisions for rights to ownership of resources: there is no right to employment by Africans. The presumption here is that African investments in education are not treated as at par with other transnational corporation investments. In other words, in spite of massive investments in education, postcolonial African states, governments and parents are sadly not internationally and even nationally regarded as investors. In Africa, governments and individuals who invest in education are unfortunately not generally and conventionally treated as investors even when they migrate to invest their knowledge in other countries. Thus, investors who are deemed to be worth sacrifices, are sadly only those who come from outside the continent, including from the global north. However the investors manifesting in the form of transnational corporations are in essence merely recycling colonially looted resources and replicating global colonial structures of apartheid, dispossession and exploitation of Africans.

While "poverty", which is deemed by some thinkers to be an explanatory variable in lack of access to education, is often defined as the condition where people have insufficient basic needs in terms of food, shelter and clothing; we argue here that Africa is not necessarily poor but it is rather materially and epistemically impoverished via resilient (neo-)colonial dispossession and exploitation. So, the World Bank's (1999) identification of information and knowledge [ignoring as it does the restoration of African materialities] as vital resources in overcoming "poverty" and other forms of deprivation is flawed. Equally flawed are contentions that knowledge has become as important as the other factors of production such as land, capital, and labour. These conceptualisations of "poverty" neglect the global (neo-)imperial processes of impoverishment including dispossession and exploitation of Africans who have not been restituted for the (neo-)colonial and (neo-)enslavement dispossession and exploitation. Similarly flawed are the understandings of "poverty" by the Namibian National Poverty Reduction Action Programme (2001-2005) which defines it as the inability to afford the minimum basic necessities of life and as the lack of capabilities necessary to perform optimally in society. These understandings of "poverty" ignore the global (neo-)imperial networks that haunt Africa with impoverishment and with what Harvey (2004) calls new imperialism's "accumulation by dispossession".

Part of the impoverishment of Africa has been the (neo-)imperial creation of mirages of decolonisation when in fact (neo-)empire repositions itself in order to intensify dispossession and exploitation of contemporary Africa. In other words, one of the key points of decolonisation should be the demystification of ideologies that paint transnational corporations as indispensable "investors" when in fact they come to the continent to exploit African labour and resources (Nhemachena et al, 2017). In fact, as Nhemachena (2016) argues, universities and other academies in Africa are guilty of the social production of ignorance about (post-)developmental issues wherein they uncritically portray Africans and their traditions and cultures as the antithesis of development. They ignore the stark reality that [paradoxically celebrated] transnational corporations are the very antithesis of development on the continent. In this sense, while Africans are sadly advised by Westerners that human rights necessarily entail getting rid of [African] traditional institutions, the same Westerners have retained their queens and kings who continue to exist in Europe, including Britain (Nhemachena, 2016). Though Africans are advised that their traditional chiefs, kings and queens, and often even their elected political leaders are an excruciating financial exaction for their countries; Westerners take the liberty to pay their queens, nobility and kings out of transnational corporations' proceeds from dispossession and exploitation of Africans. In other words, Africans are being surreptitiously and indirectly taxed by transnational corporations [which often evade paying taxes to African states and governments] whose proceeds are used to pay for the sustenance of traditional institutions of European kings and queens, even as the Africans are advised to hack down their own [traditional] institutions (Nhemachena, 2016).

Much as in the arguments above, if transnational corporations are evading taxes due to Africans and their governments yet in their home governments they pay taxes that sustain Western traditional institutions, including queens and kings, the upshot is that financial challenges which African institutions are facing are partly explicable in terms of transnational corporations' tax evasions (Nhemachena and Dhakwa, 2017). The upshot of the above is also that while Africans are encouraged to hack down their own universities and academies, Westerners retain their own universities and academies which are paradoxically sustained directly or indirectly via transnational corporations' dispossession and exploitation of Africans. Thus, even as Africans are busy hacking down not only their traditional institutions including chiefdoms and queendoms, their universities and academies; Westerners retain their own. While the International Monetary Fund and the World Bank neoliberal reforms brought about problems in African universities [and other institutions] by introducing "cost recovery measures", devaluation of African currencies, deregulation of African wages and so on (Mamdani, 1997); some Africans continue to narrowly view their problems as emanating from within national boundaries. In this respect, it is necessary to note that the internationalisation of economies, polities, academies including universities mean that some of the problems of these institutions emanate from the international realm and not, narrowly, from the national realms. For this reason, we argue that narrow perceptions of problems in Africa are a manifestation of epistemic impoverishment of Africans (see Nhemachena *et al*, 2016).

Namibia is threatened by impoverishment. Although some have defined "poverty" in term of life below the "poverty" line, we argue here that impoverishment of Africans entails living within the ambit of resilient (neo-)colonial dispossession and exploitation. In other words, the line that marks "poverty" in Africa is not necessarily narrowly a financial monetary one but it is a broad material one in the sense of including (neo-)colonial dispossession and exploitation. It is not narrowly and simplistically lack of [Western] education, unemployment, lack of money that defines impoverishment in Africa - impoverishment is *a fortiori* (neo-)colonial dispossession and exploitation. Lack of access to education, presence of unemployment and lack of money are mere symptoms of (neo-)colonial impoverishment, including dispossession and exploitation. While some would argue that a very thin population in countries like Namibia is enjoying considerable wealth, we argue that an even thinner band of [invisible and haunting] global elites is enjoying the African wealth, resources and proceeds from exploiting Africans (see Nhemachena, 2016). Thus, while some sources like Schmidt, (2009) and the Republic of Namibia National Planning Commission, (2015) narrowly understand "poverty" by regions in Namibia, we argue that there is need to understand impoverishment of Africa in terms of global networks of material, ideological, cultural and epistemic plunder.

The critical question in the Fees Must Fall Movement is whether African students should struggle for "inclusion" in a global [education] world that has sadly normalised and legitimised the (neo-)colonial plunder, dispossession and exploitation of Africans? In other words, the question is about whether African students should struggle, including to the extent of destroying universities in Africa, simply in order to be included in the global world that is premised on logics of plunder, dispossession and exploitation of Africans? Similarly, the question is whether African students should struggle for "inclusion" of their knowledge systems in a global world that is marked by plunder, dispossession and exploitation of African tangible and intangible property? The point here is that Africans and their indigenous knowledge systems have not necessarily been historically excluded from the global (neo-)imperial world: Africans and their knowledge systems have always been included in the global (neo-)imperial world but they have been included as underdogs to be used, exploited and dispossessed (Nhemachena, 2016). In this vein, the game changer on the continent does not lie in Africans simplistically struggling for "inclusion", rather it lies in Africans struggling for restitution and restoration of their material and nonmaterial resources. The theft of African indigenous knowledge which some Western institutions, companies and individuals have for long been patenting, the theft of African land, mineral resources, water, medicines and the theft and enslavement of African human beings are all instances of historical inclusion in the (neo-)imperial global world but it is inclusion as underdogs and as sacrificial victims in this vampirish, vagarish and thuggish global (neo-)imperial world. In short, the term inclusion is an instantiation of neo-colonial equivocations: in a global context where Africans and their resources have been "included" by fiat and by looting, the term inclusion does not sound enticing for contemporary critical Africans. Looters and robbers can equally and simply claim that they have not committed any crime but rather that they have simply "included" the looted and robbed to whom the robbers extend "aid" from plunder. Thus, to uncritically struggle for "inclusion" is to miss the imperatives and essence of African historical struggles for restitution, restoration and autonomy and sovereignty.

In spite of the above critique, Western academies and epistemologies have since the era of African independence emphasised phantoms of "inclusion" and of having access and availability, equity and so on. They have neglected the more fundamental issues and imperatives about restoration of African ownership and control: Africans need not merely have access, inclusion, equity and availability - rather they should own and control their material resources as well as epistemic [spaces] resources. This notwithstanding, in 2016, Namibian students from the University of Namibia and the Namibian University of Science and Technology engaged in protests for tuition fees to be reduced in the interest of broadening **access** to higher education. Thus, Simataa (2010) raised the point that higher education, specifically **access** thereto, has a fundamental bearing on the extent to which Namibia as a nation can realise its objectives as set out in the nation's Vision 2030. It was argued further that **access** to higher education is the conduit through which many Namibians currently excluded from the mainstream economy, can be "included". The Namibian students' Fees Must Fall protests were in fact a copy of the South African Fees Must Fall Movements which were launched in mid-October 2015.

Some scholars portray African students who cannot **access** education as underprivileged, less privileged, disadvantaged and marginalised (Malele, 2011). However, we argue in this chapter that the root problem for Africa is not merely access but (neo-)colonial dispossession and exploitation. To merely and simplistically describe Africans as marginalised, disadvantaged, less or underprivileged is to effectively seek to sidestep the historical (neo-)colonial dispossession and exploitation. It is to leap frog the colonial thuggery and robbery of African material and nonmaterial assets. (Neo-)colonialism does not merely disadvantage, under-privilege or marginalise Africans - it *a fortiori* dispossesses and exploits them, and this point needs to be stressed in contemporary discourses about African materialities. We argue that policies [whether donor driven or African governments driven] that are premised on simplistic, erroneous and superficial descriptions of African materialities are doomed to failure right from the onset.

The upshot of the above is that freedoms, including broader human rights and democracy depend on ownership and control of materialities and not necessarily vice versa. If freedom, human rights and democracy were not dependent on the ownership and control of materialities, (neo-)colonists and their descendants would have long given back, to Africans, the looted materialities. To excel in democracy, one needs to own, possess and control one's property

97

and resources. In fact Euro-American states that claim to champion democracy own and control not only their own resources – they also "own" and control resources that they have looted from other people. Without ownership, possession and control over their resources, Africans cannot engage in democracy – they only engage in puppetry which is sadly misrecognised as democracy. In this regard, the protests in Africa need not be understood in isolation from questions of [restitution and restoration] African materialities.

Democracy and freedom in African universities will remain elusive if questions of African materialities are not addressed: in fact Westerners will continue to dictate to African academies [governments and states] on the premise that they are funding the African universities and academies (Nyamnjoh, 2004). In this sense, academic freedom and human rights (Nyamnjoh, 2015) depend on whether impoverished African academies [states and governments] continue to receive "aid" including research funding from Westerners who then call the tune for the African politicians and academic pipers they have paid (Nyamnjoh, 2004). Thus, the issues in the Fees Must Fall Movements should not be construed simplistically as pertaining to supposed bad governance of African states or the governance of African universities. The issues are not simplistically about the existence of hierarchies and supposed domination within African universities. The key issue is about [restitution and restoration] African materialities of which absence affects the governance of African institutions from universities to African polities and families. In this respect, human rights and freedoms must include, as a core issue, the African rights to restitution and restoration of (neo-)colonial materialities and nonmaterialities. In fact these need to be included and buttressed in the Universal Declaration of Human Rights and in the work of international courts some of which have sadly focused only on prosecuting African leaders as if they are the only international criminals in the world (Bankie and Nhemachena, 2017).

Voices of the Students

A research was done, in 2016, at the University of Namibia to determine students' views about the Fees Must Fall Movement in Namibia. The students interviewed at the University of Namibia suggested that the university management needs to critically reconsider its services: they noted that it charges students on services that still need improvement or are unavailable. While some students celebrated the Fees Must Fall Movement, it is necessary to consider the broader issues about African materialities as discussed above. The students also pointed out that it was mainly those from low income households that engaged in the "Fees Must Fall Movement". While the fees were reduced following the Fees Must Fall protests, it is also important to note that there was a risk in that the reduction in fees would compromise on the operations of the institution and that this would also likely have negative impacts on the students as stakeholders. Students indicated that they benefited from the protests in that, following the protests, the tuition fees were not increased and that the government noticed that students were suffering from high tuition fees. Indicated also was the fact that many students were subsequently granted loans, and some even said that they were promised that their loans would be turned into grants. Thus, it was reported by the students that the fees were not increased, the registration fees were reduced, new loan contract systems were designed and there was the granting of the loans to some students who had never had access to the loans.

As indicated above, the world operates as networks including global networks of plunder, networks of dispossession and exploitation of Africans. In this sense, there is a problem in that protests that are often supported by some Western backed "civil" society organisations, Western institutions and governments are those that are narrowly directed against African governments, states and institutions and not at the broader networks of [global] plunder. In other words, the problem is that the protests are not directed at the entire global networks of plunder, dispossession and exploitation. In this regard, transnational corporations evade paying taxes to African states and governments (Nhemachena *et al*, 2017) and

Western institutions such as the World Bank and the International Monetary Fund have been responsible for the atrocious neoliberal marketisation of African [higher] education, yet the Fees Must Fall protests were not also directed at them. In fact the transnational institutions and corporations retained the privilege to fund "civil" society organisation to support the protests, which were narrowed down to protesting only against African governments and institutions. In this sense, it is necessary to note that pushing African governments to provide free [higher] education or to reduce fees would not only benefit African students - it would also help Western institutions that benefit when dispossessed African states and governments are forced into debt traps as they struggle to sustain their [African] academies.

The protests that (neo-)empire supports are only those that can be described as postmodern protests which do not challenge the material core of the (neo-)empire but which are redirected against Africans' own institutions and polities. In fact, the map for the transformation of African universities into postmodern universities, which will not necessarily be controlled by Africans and their governments/states, is theoretically available in the postmodern theorisations of future universities in which students will be taught by humanoid robots-deemed to be cheaper (Nhemachena, 2017; Nhemachena *et al*, forthcoming). In this way, protesting African students are directly and indirectly, wittingly and unwittingly furthering the global (neo-)imperialist and postmodernist university of the future. Although the protests may be understood to further human rights and freedoms, the postmodernist, posthumanist robotic future of the university threatens to be in fact antihumanist, posthumanist and [African] postanthropocentric and thus without human rights to protect human [African] beings. In the postmodernist and poststructuralist theories, Africans are animistically portrayed to be on the same plane of immanence as the humanoid robots and animals. In fact there are some Western theories that are already circulating in academies, wherein humans [Africans] are portrayed as in processes of becoming, including "becoming animals" (Nhemachena, 2017). In this sense, in so far as contemporary "African" postmodern protests support postmodern dedifferentiation between the human and nonhuman, they effectively prop up the posthumanist, antihumanist and transhumanist agendas of the New World Order in which [African] human beings will be regarded as not distinct from animals and the rest of nature (Nhemachena, 2016; Nhemachena, Warikandwa and Mtapuri, 2017). In short, it is necessary to note that while postmodern protests are celebrated by some as indicating democracy, postmodernism is at its core about dedifferentiating the human and the nonhuman and hence it is about something else other than human rights and humanistic democracy – it is about dehumanising [African] others to a point where they "become" animals and at par with nonhumans. Dispossession, disinheritance and exploitation are instances of dehumanisation and hence of coercing [African] others to become animals for carrying (neo-)imperial burdens. Burdens do not necessarily have to be carried by thinkers and hence the contemporary emphasis in the postmodernist and poststructuralist theories is on "actors" and "agency" rather than on thinking or cogitation. We therefore argue that for Africa to be genuinely decolonised there is need not necessarily for emphasis on "action" or "agency" alone but on thinking and cogitation as well, and such cogitation necessarily has to include thinking about the historical, (neo-)colonial foundations of African impoverishment. Unfortunately, postmodernist protests enjoin "actors" or "agents" to act [much like animals] without reflecting on the deeper, historical, foundational and (neo-)colonial causes of [African] impoverishment and suffering.

Fees Must Fall Movement: The Case of a Misdirected Battle?

The Fees Must Fall Movement cultivates intellectual engagement of the highest order on higher education from an African perspective. This is attributed to the fact that the "liberation" of Africa, on the face of it, has not translated to a holistic socio-economic emancipation of the impoverished African majority. It is without doubt that Africans have been denied their material restitution and restoration of colonially looted resources, a development which has been perpetuated by the post-colonial education system which promotes hegemonic Euro-American theories of education. The adoption of educational systems that are devoid of African philosophy (Higgs, 2003: 5; Higgs, 1999) has undermined the development of African oriented educational systems thus advancing the hegemony of Western forms of questionably "universal" knowledge. The useful philosophical framework for the construction of empowering knowledge (Letseka, 2000; Lumumba-Kasongo, 2002) that will enable Southern African countries to participate in the development of foundationally emancipatory education systems has thus been relegated to an afterthought by Western educated as well as by captured African leaders and academics.

African universities thus have resisted the compelling need to decolonise African education along with African materialities. It is accepted that education is a tool to emancipation (Ahmad *et al*, 2014) and thus must be affordable. In fact, education is a human right that should be afforded to all. However, African institutions of higher learning must be alert to the dangers of championing the cause of (neo-)colonial powers through making toxic education affordable without paying attention to the need to detoxify such dangerous forms of education (Nyamnjoh, 2012a; 2012b). The argument here is that beyond the mere clamouring for the plausible notion of affordable higher education, the quality of the education should be of benefit to African communities in which the graduates will work (Hoppers, 2000). Placing emphasis on the factory model of education in which there is a mass production of ignorance (see Nhemachena, 2016) at affordable rates, at the expense of noble initiatives to decolonise African education and African materialities will be a fatal mistake for the already impoverished Africans. As such, the Fees Must Fall Movement should be subsumed in the overarching and more important concept of the Rhodes Must Fall Movement (see Nyamnjoh, 2016) and by extension the envisaged (Neo-)Empire Must Fall Movement".

The Rhodes Must Fall Movement is generally accepted as a legitimate and plausible attempt by South African university students to realise the rewriting of African history much as to eradicate institutional racism and more importantly decolonise education and African materialities that were looted by (neo-)imperialism of which

Cecil Rhodes was the architect (Chaudhuri, 2016). Chaudhuri argues that beyond the mere act of problematising the existence of Rhodes' statute at the University of Cape Town in South Africa, and indeed anywhere else in Africa, emphasis must be placed on an "ethos that gives space and even pre-eminence to such a figure and hesitates to interrogate Rhodes' [colonial] legacy (*Ibid*). Rhodes' legacy does not simply represent his financial bequests to institutions of higher learning and their educational offshoots such as the Rhodes scholarships, amongst others, but the vision embodied in his will (*Ibid*). In his testamentary will, Rhodes pointedly provided for:

> ...the establishment, promotion and development of a Secret Society, the true aim and object whereof shall be for the extension of British rule throughout the world, the perfecting of a system of emigration from the United Kingdom, and of colonisation by British subjects of all lands where the means of livelihood are attainable by energy, labour, and enterprise, and especially the occupation by the British settlers of the entire Continent of Africa, the Holy land, the Valley of Euphrates, the Islands of Cyprus and Candia, the whole of South America, the Islands of the Pacific not heretofore possessed by Great Britain, the whole of the Malay Archipelago, the seaboard of China and Japan ... (*Ibid*; Rhodes, 1902).

The Rhodes Must Fall Movement sought to challenge and address the unequal vision being engendered by the New World Order proponents (Allen & Jobson, 2016). Such inequalities have significantly manifested themselves in African universities where the "education" aspirations of impoverished Africans are being arguably "realised". It is improper to contend that the education aspirations of Africans are arguably being "realised" in universities because imperialism has a toxic effect to "education" on the continent. It must not be forgotten that colonial projects have never pursued the best interests of Africans but to exploit them in pursuit of the coloniser's interests. As such, to unyoke Africa from the slavery that presents itself like a chronic disease on the continent, African education must be decolonised. This debate is not about necessity but of a long overdue and imperative policy and legislative objective.

Decolonisation of the African education systems must be construed to imply the proactive eradication from Africa's educational system of any knowledge systems that perpetuate the reprehensible wrongdoings, moments, and ambitions of the (neo-)colonialists. Such an approach will help Africa disabuse itself from practices of viewing Western education systems and values as progressive modern forms of science and civilisation whilst relegating non-western forms of education to being outdated and uncivilised knowledge and value systems. It is therefore evident that the Fees Must Fall Movement is a side-dish whose main meal should be the Rhodes Must Fall Movement. This view leads to the analysis of the human right to education and what it ought to imply in the African context.

The Human Right to Education and the Fees Must Fall Movement

Education is frequently discussed in the language of economics. African governments, like other governments in the world, often simply equate an investment in education with an investment in the national economy. As such, educational services in Africa, especially at the tertiary level, are habitually considered tradable goods which are far removed from a wider human rights context. It is important for Africans to start thinking about the development of their societies rather than mere Western driven economic agendas. Africans must move towards understanding that sound education [as it was offered in pre-colonial Africa] begets sound knowledge and appropriate abilities. Whilst it is generally accepted that most Africans hope to gain economic benefits from education and literacy in order to overcome the prejudices of their (neo-)colonial past, it is a different matter entirely to think that these benefits are education's sole aim.

The Fees Must Fall Movement has been advanced on the understanding that education is a fundamental human right. Education is imperative to the promotion of human rights; it is both a human right in itself and an indispensable means of realising other human rights. It is the precondition for the enjoyment of many economic, social and cultural rights; for instance, the right to receive higher education on the basis of ability, the right to enjoy the benefits of scientific progress and the right to choose work can only be exercised in a meaningful way after a minimum level of education is reached. Similarly, in the ambit of civil and political rights, the freedom of information, the right to vote and the right to equal access to public service depends on a minimum level of education, that is, literacy. As a vehicle for empowerment, education can give marginalised adults and children the means to escape from impoverishment and participate meaningfully in their societies. Education is vital to empowering women, to safeguarding children from exploitation and hazardous labour, to the promotion of human rights and democracy and to the protection of the environment.

Two major dimensions may be distinguished in the right to education: the social dimension and the freedom dimension (Haugaard, 2016). The social dimension requires states to make various forms of education available and easily accessible to all and to introduce progressively several forms of free education. The freedom dimension applies to the right to academic freedom and institutional autonomy and it implies the personal freedom of individuals or their parents or guardians to choose the educational institutions meeting their educational standards, or their religious or moral convictions. This freedom implies, in addition, the freedom of individuals and bodies to establish and direct their own educational institutions.

The right to education has been included in several international instruments. The Universal Declaration on Human Rights (UDHR) proclaims that, "education shall be directed to the full development of the human personality and to the strengthening of respect for human rights and fundamental freedoms" (Article 26). Articles 13 and 14 of the International Covenant on Economic, Social and Cultural Rights (ICESCR), Articles 28 and 29 of the Convention on the Rights to the Child (CRC), Articles 10 and 14 of the Convention on the Elimination of All Forms of Discrimination against Women (CEDAW), Article 5 of the International Convention on the Elimination of All Forms of Racial Discrimination (ICERD), and Article 24 of the Convention on the Rights of Persons with Disabilities (CRPD) contain detailed provisions on education. In addition, the Convention Relating to the Status of Refugees provides for the right to education in Article 22. The United Nations Educational, Scientific and Cultural Organisation (UNESCO) Convention against Discrimination in Education seeks not only to ban discrimination, but also to promote equal opportunities and equal treatment in education for the individual.

At the regional level, Articles 13 and 16 of the Protocol of San Salvador contain detailed provisions on education. In particular, Article 13 lays down the normative content of the right: respect for human rights and fundamental freedoms, friendship amongst all, pluralism, tolerance and the maintenance of peace. The aim of education is human dignity and the full development of the human personality. In Europe, Article 2 of the First Protocol to the European Convention on Human Rights (ECHR) is phrased in negative terms: "No person shall be denied the right to education"; and focuses on the liberty of parents to ensure education in conformity with their own religious and philosophical convictions. In the context of Africa, Article 17 of the African Charter on Human and People's Rights (ACHPR) only contains provisions regarding the duty of the state to promote and protect 'morals and traditional values recognised by the community'. Provisions of the Cairo Declaration on Human Rights in Islam from 1990 stress the right of every human being to 'receive both religious and worldly education' (Article 9). **The rights to education are separated into three levels:**

- **Primary (Elemental or Fundamental) Education**. This shall be compulsory and free for any child regardless of their nationality, gender, place of birth, or any other discrimination. Upon ratifying the ICESCR, States must provide free primary education within two years.
- **Secondary** (or Elementary, Technical and Professional in the UDHR) Education must be generally available and accessible.
- **Higher Education** (at the University Level) should be provided according to capacity. That is, anyone who meets the necessary education standards should be able to go to university.

Both secondary and higher education shall be made accessible "by every appropriate means, and in particular by the progressive introduction of free education". The realisation of the right to education on a national level may be achieved through compulsory education. The fulfilment of the right to education can be assessed using the 4 As framework, which asserts that for education to be a meaningful right it must be available, accessible, acceptable and adaptable. The 4 As framework was developed by the former United Nations Special Rapporteur on the Right to Education, Katarina Tomasevski, but is not necessarily the standard used in every international human rights instrument and hence not a generic guide to how the right to education is treated under national law. The 4 As framework proposes that governments, as the prime duty-bearers, have to respect, protect and fulfil the right to education by making education available, accessible, acceptable and adaptable. The framework also places duties on other stakeholders in the education process: the child, which as the privileged subject of the right to education has the duty to comply with compulsory education requirements, the parents as the 'first educators', and professional educators, namely teachers.

The 4 As have been further elaborated as follows:

- **Availability** - funded by governments, education is universal, free and compulsory. There should be proper infrastructure and facilities in place with adequate books and materials for students. Buildings should meet both safety and sanitation standards, such as having clean drinking water. Active recruitment, proper training and appropriate retention methods should ensure that enough qualified staff is available at each school.

- **Accessibility** - all children should have equal access to school services, regardless of gender, race, religion, ethnicity or socio-economic status. Efforts should be made to ensure the inclusion of marginalised groups including children of refugees, the homeless or those with disabilities in short there should be universal access to education i.e. access to all. There should be no forms of segregation or denial of access to any students. This includes ensuring that proper laws are in place against any child labour or exploitation to prevent children from obtaining primary or secondary education. Schools must be within a reasonable distance for children within the community, otherwise transportation should be provided to students, particularly those that might live in rural areas, to ensure ways to school are safe and convenient. Education should be affordable to all, with textbooks, supplies and uniforms provided to students at no additional costs.

- **Acceptability** - the quality of education provided should be free of discrimination, relevant and culturally appropriate for all students. Students should not be expected to conform to any specific religious or ideological views. Methods of teaching should be objective and unbiased and material available should reflect a wide array of ideas and beliefs. Health and safety should be emphasised within schools including the elimination of any forms of corporal punishment. Professionalism of staff and teachers should be maintained.

- **Adaptability** - educational programs should be flexible and able to adjust according to societal changes and the needs of the community. Observance of religious or cultural holidays should be respected by schools in order to accommodate students, along with providing adequate care to those students with disabilities.

A number of international NGOs and charities work to realise the right to education using a rights-based approach to development.

The Fees Must Fall Movement: A Battle for Free Education Which is Void of Knowledge Indeed

The Fees Must Fall Movement has placed significant emphasis on realising affordable education. However, little regard has been placed on the need to ensure that the affordable education sought must be contextually relevant and pursue an African agenda. In the contemporary African society, discourses relating to the Africanisation of the African education system have been frowned upon with preference being given to Western education systems. The Western education systems are greatly informed by the Prussian system of education which specialises in the mass production of ignorance. Watters (2015) has branded the Prussian system as a factory model of education which produces docile products suitable for use and not independence. Toffler (1970) decried the Prussian system of education or "Industrial Era School" when he posited that:

Mass education was the ingenious machine constructed by industrialisation to produce the kind of adults that it needed. The problem was inordinately complex. How to pre-adapt children for a new world – a world of repetitive indoor toil, smoke, noise, machines, crowded living conditions, collective discipline, a world in which time was to be regulated not by the cycle of the sun and moon, but by the factory whistle clock. The solution was an educational system that, in its very structure, stimulated this new world. This system did not emerge instantly. Even today it retains throw-back elements from pre-industrial society. Yet the whole idea of assembling masses of students (raw material) to be processed by teachers (workers) in a centrally located school (factory) was a stroke of industrial genius. The whole administrative hierarchy of education, as it grew, followed the model of industrial bureaucracy. The very organisation of knowledge into permanent disciplines was grounded on industrial assumptions … The inner life of the school thus became an anticipatory mirror, a perfect introduction to industrial society. The most criticised features of education today – the regimentation, lack of individualisation, the rigid systems of seating, grouping, grading and marking, the authoritarian role of the teacher – are precisely those that made mass public education so effective an instrument of adaptation for its place and time.

At its inception, the Prussian System of Education was aimed at training soldiers to be subject to the control of their superiors in order to defeat Napoleon Bonaparte, the historically renowned French military leader. The soldiers (students) were trained to listen to teacher (superior) when they are instructed to charge into the battlefield even though their instincts, intellect and emotions required them to escape with their lives from the cannons firing at the battlefield. Similarly, the African educational system has embraced the Prussian system of education laced with Western oriented dominant theories of education which have led to the loss of African materialities. Even though "some" Africans realise the need to decolonise to arrest the continual loss of African materialities to the Western countries and Asia, they still continue to subject themselves to the toxic education system which impoverishes African indigenes.

It is thus evident that the thrust of the Prussian system of education imported into the African education system is to train docile and **unreasonably obedient citizens** who will do what the Western sponsored media and captured African governments tell them to do at the expense of their materialities. University students in Africa are placed into Western biased institutions of higher education for a minimum period of three (3) years and told to embrace Western ideological views and think and behave and talk like the supposedly "superior" Western people. The media in the capitalist oriented African society tells university students what to buy, who to vote for and a million other things pertaining to mainstream contemporary lifestyle.

The approach to training a docile and non-critical crop of university students has worked exceptionally well for colonial powers. Today, most African societies laced by the Prussian system of education have a homogenous and well controlled/submissive citizenry that is eager to promote profits of foreign investors and the ruling class. The same citizenry is willing to die for the interest of the foreign investors and ruling class and care less about decolonising the African education system and the loss of African materialities. Such systems of education which induce docility, puppetry, zombification and/or parrotology have been made compulsory in African universities across all disciplines. Anyone who is not equipped with such a "toxic waste" type of education is condemned to abject impoverishment. Inglis (1918) aptly pointed out that compulsory schooling was intended, "... to be just what it had been for Prussia in the 1820s: a fifth column into the burgeoning democratic movement that threatened to give the peasants and the proletarians a voice at the bargaining table." The point here is that, as was the case in the industrial era, the modern compulsory education in African has been tailor-made to make a sort of surgical incision into prospective unity of the lower classes in society which seek to decolonise their education systems and materialities. Thus, Inglis (1918) correctly concludes that the Prussian system of education sought to, "Divide children by subject, by age-grading, by constant rankings on tests, and by many other more subtle means, and it was unlikely that the ignorant mass of mankind, separated in childhood, would ever reintegrate into a dangerous whole" (*Ibid*). Such a divide and rule type of education explains why Africans are divided in so far as the need to decolonise African education and materialities is concerned. Inglis (1918) then proceeded to break down the purpose [actual purpose] of modern schooling into six basic functions. The six basic functions of modern education are:

1) **The adjustive or adaptive function**: Schools (including universities) are to establish habits of reaction to authority. This approach totally precludes critical judgement completely. It destroys the idea that useful or interesting material should be taught because you cannot test for reflexive obedience until you know whether you can make learners learn and do <u>foolish and boring things</u>.

2) **The integration function**: This can also be termed the "conformity function" because its intention is to make learners as similar as possible. People who conform are predictable. This is of significance to colonial masters and the captured ruling class who seek to harness and manipulate a large labour force.

3) **The diagnostic and directive function**: Education is meant to determine each learner's proper social role. This is done by logging evidence mathematically and anecdotally on cumulative records. This approach is conducive for social engineering.

4) **The differentiating function**: Once learners' social roles have been "diagnosed" they are to be sorted by role and trained only so far as their destination in the social machine merits - and not one step further.

5) **Selective function**: The selective function focuses on Darwin's theory of natural selection as applied to what he called "favoured races". Emphasis in this regard is not on human choice but rather to help things along by consciously attempting to improve the breeding stock. Institutions of higher learning are meant to tag the "unfit" – with poor grades, remedial replacement, and other punishments – clearly enough that their peers will accept them as inferior and effectively bar them from the reproductive sweepstakes.

That is what all those little humiliations from first grade onward were intended to do: wash the dirt down the drain (This approach is inconsistent with the Ubuntu spirit which focuses on the greater good of every individual in the collective and focuses on realising the best for every individual based on their capabilities).

6) **The propaedeutic function**: The societal system implied by these rules will require an elite group of caretakers. To that end, a small fraction of the learners will quietly be taught how to manage this continuing project, how to <u>watch over and control a population deliberately dumbed down and declawed in order that government might proceed unchallenged and corporations might never want for obedient labour</u> (*Ibid*; Gatto, 2008).

It is therefore clear that, in Africa's higher education institutions, emphasis is not placed on the conception of a grand warfare between classes so as to realise decolonisation and the protection of African materialities (Le Grange, 2016). Rather, emphasis is placed on a system of education that serves the best interests of complex management, economic or political superiors through the production of docile learners and graduates. Such learners and graduates are often demoralised, divided and powerless such that they can be discarded if they do not conform to the directives of the superior authority. Vast fortunes are thus made by corporations at the expense of indigenous Africans in an economy based on mass production and organised in favour of the same businesses (Nyamunda, 2016). The net implication of this model of education is that today's Africa suffers from a dearth in intellectual maturity informing all aspects of Africans' lives (Watkins, 2013; Kahuni, 2017). Divorce laws have removed the need to work hard on relationships, New World Order entertainment initiatives in the media and social networks have removed the need for Africans to learn to entertain themselves, template answers to complex problems have removed the need to ask critical questions, and easy credit has removed the need for fiscal self-control. Africa has reduced itself to a continent of a docile citizenry which is happy to surrender its judgments and wills to Western and Asian captured political exhortations and capitalist commercial blandishments that under normal circumstances would insult adults of sound minds. There is no desire amongst many Africans to critically engage with historical and foundational injustices, distorted literature, philosophies, economic environment and theological issues informing the contemporary African society. The brilliant graduates from [African] universities who have excelled in Western education systems and have been resultantly branded geniuses are simply dirt to the African society. They do not espouse the decolonisation of African education and promote the theft of African materialities through employing the capitalist oriented Prussian system of education. In their cheap minds, to do so is a hallmark of brilliance. God forbid! It must be clearly understood that to the extent that the Fees Must Fall Movement focuses on free education, it is misguided if it does not place emphasis on decolonising the toxic free education currently offered in [African] universities. African materialities will continue to be lost in the pursuit of a flawed right to education whose education is not context relevant. There must be radical shift from the Fees Must Fall Movement to Rhodes Must Fall Movement. Such radical shift must be informed by informed calls for place-based Afro-centric learning rights and educational values.

Conclusion

The Fees Must Fall Movement, as discussed in this chapter has placed significant emphasis on the right to education and the negative effect of reducing fees on service delivery in institutions of higher education in Southern Africa. Emphasis has also been placed on the globalised nature of education with any radical student activism aimed at disrupting education activities in universities being regarded as being anti-globalist and counterproductive. However, little regard was placed on how much the academy in African institutions of higher education is productive of ignorance, overwhelmingly white, Eurocentric space and suffocating experience for black students (Everatt, 2016). Such is the nature of the African universities and the Prussian system of education employed therein those university graduates of all races, creed, and/or colour obtain education that leads to ultimately a capitalist state that has no interest in the impoverished emerging from capture; overlapping with Black people in a society dominated by Whiteness; creating an unreconstructed racial capitalism that needs to be toppled (*Ibid*). As such, this chapter has argued that whilst there must be concerted efforts by African States to realise affordable if not free higher education for all students, there is also a significant and competing interest of ensuring that the education offered is decolonised so that African materialities are not continually lost to Western and Asian countries. The Fees Must Fall Movement has plainly placed emphasis on free education which ensures that students in African universities will receive a quality colonised education rather than quality Africanised and context relevant education. Emphasis thus should be placed on ensuring the decolonisation of African education to arrest the loss of African materialities to the West.

References

Ahmad, A.T. *et al* (2014) "Reconsidering the Philosophy of Education for Self-Reliance (ESR) from an Experimental Learning Perspective in Contemporary Education in Tanzania," *Educational Research for Social Change,* vol 30(1), 3-19.

Al Jazeera (1 May 2016) Julius Malema Vows to Seize White-Owned Land, www.aljazeera.com/news/2016/04/south-africa-malema-eff-draws-huge-crowds-polls-160430203336402.html.

Allen, J.S. and Jobson, R.C. (2016) "The Decolonising Generation: (Race and) Theory in Anthropology since the Eighties," *Current Anthropology*, vol 57(2), 129-148.

Chaudhuri, A. (2016) The Real Meaning of Rhodes Must Fall, The Guardian United Kingdom, 16 March 2016.

Council of Europe, European Convention for the Protection of Human Rights and Fundamental Freedoms, as Amended by Protocols Nos. 11 and 14, 4 November 1950, ETS 5.

Du Plessis, S. (2013) Nationalizing South African Mines: An Economic Assessment, in *Journal of the Southern African Institute of Mining and Metallurgy* vol 113 (1): 31-38.

Everatt, D. (2016) "What Must Fall: Fees or the South African State?" available at https://www.wits.ac.za/news/latest-news/in-their-own-words/2016/2016-10/what-must-fall-fees-or-the-south-african-state.html (accessed 27 August 2017).

Fanon, F. (1963) *The Wretched of the Earth*. London: Grove Press, Inc.

Gatto, J.T. (2008) "How Public Education Cripples our Kids, and Why" available at http://www.naturalchild.org/guest/john_gatto2.html (accessed 27 August 2017).

Hall, B. L. *et al*. (2017) Decolonisation of Knowledge, Epistemicide, Participatory Research and Higher Education, in *Research for All*, vol 1 (1): 6-19.

Hangula, F. S. M. (2008). *A Report of a Review of Poverty and Inequality in Namibia*. Namibia: Central Bureau of Statistics, National Commission Planning.

Haugaard, M. (2016) "Two Types of Freedom and Four Dimensions of Power," *Revue Internationale De Philosophie*, vol 275(1), 37-65.

Havery, D. (2004) The 'New Imperialism": Accumulation by Dispossession, in *Actuel Marx*, vol 35 (1): 71-90.

Heleta, S. (2016) Decolonisation of Higher Education: Dismantling Epistemic Violence and Eurocentrism in South Africa, in *Transformation in Higher Education* vol 1 (1), a9 http://dx.doi.org/10.4102/the.v1i1.9.

Higgs, P. (1999) "A Reconstruction of South African Philosophy of Education," *Interchange*, 30(2): 121-142.

Higgs, P. (2003) "African Philosophy and the Transformation of Educational Discourse in South Africa," *Journal of Education*, vol 30: 5-22.

Hoppers, C.A. (2000) African Voices in Education: Retrieving the Past, Engaging the Present and Shaping the Future. In Higgs, P., Vocalise, N.A.G., MDA, T.V., and Assis-Lumumba, N.T. (eds). *African Voices in Education*. Cape Town: Juta.

Inglis, A. (1918) *Principles of Secondary Education* Boston: Houghton Mifflin Harcourt.

Kahiurika, N. (2016). *The Namibian Newspaper. Must Fees Fall?* Windhoek

Kahunai, P. (2017) "Africa Suffers from Lack of 'Intellectual Hygiene'," The Herald Zimbabwe, 5 July 2017, available at http://www.herald.co.zw/africa-suffers-from-lack-of-intellectual-hygiene/ (accessed 27 August 2017).

Le Grange, L. (2016) "Decolonisng the University Curriculum," available at http://jsaa.ac.za/index.php/sajhe/article/viewFile/709/204 (accessed 27 August 2017).

Letseka, M. (2000) "African Philosophy and Educational Discourse" in Higgs, P., Vocalise, N.A.G., MDA, T.V., and Assis-Lumumba, N.T. (eds). *African Voices in Education*, Cape Town: Juta.

Lumumba-Kasongo, T. (2002) "Reflections on the African Renaissance and its Paradigmatic Implications for Deconstructing the Past and Reconstructing Africa" *Black Renaissance/Renaissance Noir*, vol 5(1), 1-6.

Melucci, A. (1989) *Nomads of the Present: Social Movements and Individual Needs in Contemporary Society*. Philadelphia: Temple University Press.

Namibia (2004). National Planning Commission. Namibia Vision 2030. Windhoek: Government of Namibia. Retrieved from www.npc.gv. nalv.is.OIJ2.Q3.Q pdf.

Namibian National Poverty Reduction Action Programme (2001-2005). NPC. Windhoek

Ndlovu-Gatsheni, S. J., (2013) *Coloniality of Power in Postcolonial Africa: Myths of Decolonisation*. Dakar: CODESRIA.

Nhemachena, A. (2016) (Post-) development and the Social Production of Ignorance: Farming Ignorance in 21st Century Africa, in Mawere, M. (ed) *Underdevelopment, Development and the Future of Africa*. Langaa RPCIG: Bamenda.

Nhemachena, A. (2016) Hearing the Footfalls of Humanoid Robots: Technoscience, (Un-)employment and the Future of "Development" in Twenty-First Century Africa, in Mawere, M., (ed) *Underdevelopment, Development and the Future of Africa*. Bamenda: Langaa RPCIG.

Nhemachena, A. and Bankie, B. F. (2017) Foot Soldiers of the New Empire or Horizontal Saviours? Interrogating Civil Society Organisations and Fundamentalisms in Twenty First Century

Africa, in Nhemachena, A. and Mawere, M. (eds) *Africa at the Crossroads: Theorising Fundamentalism in the 21st Century*. Bamenda: Langaa RPCIG.

Nhemachena, A., Warikandwa, T. V. and Mtapuri, O. (2017) Transnational Corporations' Land Grabs and the On-going Second Mad Scramble for Africa: An Introduction, in Warikandwa T. V. et al (eds) *Transnational Land Grabs and Restitution in an Age of the (De-)Militarised New Scramble for Africa: A Pan African Socio-Legal Perspective*. Bamenda: Langaa RPCIG.

Nhemachena, A. (2017) *Relationality and Resilience in a Not So relational World: Knowledge, Chivanhu and (De-)Coloniality in 21st Century Conflict-Torn Zimbabwe*. Bamenda: Langaa RPCIG.

Nhemachena, A. (2016) Animism, Coloniality and Humanism: Reversing the Empire's Framing of Africa, in Mawere, M. and Nhemachena, A. (eds) *Theory, Knowledge, Development and Politics: What Role for the Academy in the Sustainability of Africa?* Bamenda: Langaa RPCIG

Nhemachena, A. and Dhakwa, E. (2017) When Did the Rain Start to Beat Us? Discursive Dispossession and the Political Economies of Misrecognition about African Mining, in Nhemachena, A. and Warikandwa, T. V. (eds) *Mining Africa: Law, Environment, Society and Politics in Historical and Multidisciplinary Perspectives*. Bamenda: Langaa RPCIG.

Nhemachena, A. and Mudimu, R., (2017) Fighting Fellow Comrades in the Trenches of Poverty in Africa? Interrogating the Fees Must Fall Movement at the University of Namibia, in Mawere, M. (ed) *Poverty, Vulnerability and Disaster Risk Management: Building Bridges of Resilience and Development in Africa's 21st Century*. Bamenda: Langaa RPCIG.

Nhemachena, A. Mlambo, N. and Kaundjua, M. (2016) The Notion of the "Field" and the Practices of Researching and Writing Africa: Towards Decolonial Praxis, *Africology: The Journal of Pan African Studies*, vol.9, no.7: 15-36.

Nyamnjoh, B. F. (2015). *Students and Scholar Protests in Africa: PAX ACADEMICA African Journal of Academic Freedom Revenue*. Nos. 1&2

117

Nyamnjoh, F. B. (2004) From Publish or Perish to Publish and Perish: What 'Africa's 100 Best Books Tell Us about Publishing in Africa". *Journal of Asian and African Studies* Vol 39 (4).

Nyamnjoh, F. B. (2012a) Blinded by Sight: Divining the Future of Anthropology in Africa. *Africa Spectrum*, 47, 2-3, 62-92.

Nyamnjoh, F. B. (2012b) Potted Plants in Greenhouses: A Critical Reflection on the Resilience of Colonial Education in Africa, *Journal of Asian and African Studies*, 47, 2, 129-154.

Nyamnjoh, F. B. (2016) *#RhodesMustFall: Nibbling at Resilient Colonialism in South Africa.* Bamenda: Langaa RPCIG.

Nyamnjoh F B. (2016) *Rhodes Must Fall: Nibbling at Resilient Colonialism in South Africa.* Bamenda: Langaa RPCIG.

Nyamunda, T. (2016) "The State and Black Business Development: Small Enterprises Development Corporation and the Politics of Indigenisation and Economic Empowerment in Zimbabwe," *Historia*, vol 16(1), 41-65.

Organization of African Unity (OAU), African Charter on Human and Peoples' Rights ("Banjul Charter"), 27 June 1981, CAB/LEG/67/3 rev. 5, 21 I.L.M. 58 (1982).

Organization of American States (OAS), Additional Protocol to the American Convention on Human Rights in the Area of Economic, Social and Cultural Rights ("Protocol of San Salvador"), 16 November 1999, A-52.

Organization of the Islamic Conference (OIC), Cairo Declaration on Human Rights in Islam, 5 August 1990.

Republic of Namibia National Planning Commission (2015). *Poverty and Deprivation in Namibia.* NPC. Windhoek.

Rhodes, C. J. (1902) *The Last Will and Testament of Cecil John Rhodes,* available at https://www.amazon.com/last-will-testament-Cecil-Rhodes/dp/1240024924#reader_1240024924 (accessed 27 August 2017).

Schmidt, M. (2009). *Poverty and Inequality in Namibia.* Windhoek: Institute of Policy Research.

Simataa, M. S. (2010). *In Pursuit of Access to with Education System in Namibia,* Windhoek.

Tofller, A. (1970) *Future Shock* New York: Random House.

Tsholofelo. (2015). *Fees Must Fall: Part of Increase at South Africa Universities*. Retrieved from en.m.wikipedia.org.

Tuck, E. *et al.* (2012) Decolonization is Not a Metaphor, in Decolonisation, *Indigeneity, Education and Society* vol 1 (1): 1-40.

United Nations Educational, Scientific and Cultural Organisation (UNESCO), *Convention Against Discrimination in Education*, 14 December 1960.

United Nations General Assembly, Convention on the Rights of Persons with Disabilities: resolution / adopted by the General Assembly, 24 January 2007, A/RES/61/106.

United Nations General Assembly, Convention on the Rights of the Child, 20 November 1989, United Nations, Treaty Series, vol. 1577, p. 3.

United Nations General Assembly, Convention Relating to the Status of Refugees, 28 July 1951, United Nations, Treaty Series, vol. 189, p. 137.

United Nations General Assembly, International Convention on the Elimination of All Forms of Racial Discrimination, 21 December 1965, United Nations, Treaty Series, vol. 660, p. 195.

United Nations General Assembly, International Covenant on Economic, Social and Cultural Rights, 16 December 1966, United Nations, Treaty Series, vol. 993, p. 3.

United Nations General Assembly, Universal Declaration of Human Rights, 10 December 1948, 217 A (III).

University of Namibia (2014). Student Fees Prospectus 2015.

Watkins, K. (2013) "Too little Access, Not Enough Learning: Africa's Twin Deficit in Education," available at https://www.brookings.edu/opinions/too-little-access-not-enough-learning-africas-twin-deficit-in-education/ (accessed 27 August 2017).

Watters, A. (2016) The invented History: 'The Factory Model of Education', available at http://hackeducation.com/2015/04/25/factory-model (accessed 25 August 2017).

World Bank. (1999) World Bank Development Report 1998! 99. Knowledge for Development. Oxford University Press.

Chapter Four

Conjugating Materialities and Symbols in Contemporary Africa? The Case of the Statue of King Nghunghunyani, South Africa

Artwell Nhemachena & Dolphin Mabale

Introduction

When the University of Cape Town (UCT) Student Maxwele Chumani poured human waste on the Rhodes statue at the UCT, the subsequent Rhodes Must Fall Movement was interpreted in various ways. Some interpreted it as a symbol of lack of meaningful transformation [of higher education] at the University of Cape Town, others interpreted it as a sequel of the legacy of the ["past"] apartheid that explains the impoverishment of Blacks in South Africa. Still others interpreted it as Blacks' lack of appreciation of the fact that Cecil John Rhodes was a "generous" man who donated the land on which the University of Cape Town was built. While some celebrated the hybridity [impurity] of culture including the hybridity of statue cultures in the rainbow nation of South Africa, there was a paradox in that some could not countenance the hybridisation with impurities that were pelted at the statue [of Rhodes]. Thus, while some consider pelting impurities including excrement at statues as protests, other scholars paradoxically urge the celebration of "hybridity", in Africa, and the associated impurities. This chapter interrogates the conjugation of materialities – material impurities [including human excrements and paints] that are pelted at statues, the materialities of statues in relation to the materialisation of impoverishment in Africa and the materiality of statues in relation to the materialisation of [African] freedom and nation states on the continent. While situated in the discourses on statues, the chapter interrogates the broader discourses on new materialities in relation to various forms of [statue] materialisations in Africa. By dwelling on the statue of King

Nghunghunyani [who fought for decolonisation] the chapter argues for a form of decolonisation of materialities that materially and consequentially unsettles the (neo-)imperialism that has settled in Africa for centuries. It argues that to merely privilege symbolisms, multiple meanings of things [including statues], multiculturalism, decolonisation of ideologies and epistemologies rather than materially unsettling (neo-)imperialism is to engage in mere skirmishes with (neo-)imperialism.

While the Rhodes Must Fall Movement can be understood as a symbolic struggle against the symbols of (neo-)empire in South Africa, the challenge with symbolic struggles is that they exhaust energy that would be better directed to real material struggles that are more consequential in unsettling (neo-)empire. Fighting against symbols does not translate to fighting against the real materialities and materialisations of (neo-)empire – thus, the African liberation heroes did not merely fight imperial symbols and statues. In other words, while Rhodes and other (neo-)imperialists have dispossessed and disinherited Africans not merely of symbols but of real and consequential materialities including land (Mbembe, 2016), Africans are often decoyed into fighting symbols [skirmishes] of empire. Thus, in the sham concessions, (neo-)empire frontloads its symbols, semiotics and its shadows against which Africans and other indigenous people are supposed to battle before symbolic inconsequential truces are made. In other words, symbolic struggles about semiotics of (neo-)empire, struggles merely around multiplicities of meanings of things and so on merely facilitate rituals of rebellion which anthropologists note (Gibson, 1955; Gluckman, 1954) serve to reaffirm support for [empire] kingship. The question then is whether the recent South African songs of hate and rejection of (neo-)imperial statues were not merely serving to produce a cathartic effect, to reaffirm support for (neo-)empire and to renew the unity of the (neo-)imperial system. The defacing of statues of Rhodes, of Paul Kruger, General Louis Botha, King George VI and others that constitute symbols of (neo-)empire in South Africa (Maune, 2015; Mbembe, 2016; Kubeka, 2015; Laband, 2015; The Guardian, 10 April 2015; Nyamnjoh, 2016) may have been necessary symbolic struggle against (neo-)empire but it was not a sufficient one.

Real material and more unsettling struggles that get to the core of (neo-)empire are necessary so that Africans do not just keep on [inconsequentially] fighting statues [shadows], which statues [shadows] are for (neo-)imperial convenience currently being portrayed as animate and as actors or agents.

If statues are construed as symbols of (neo-)empire or as shadows of (neo-)empire, it becomes possible to understand Africans who fight (neo-)imperial statues as in fact engaged in battles against the shadows rather than the real and more consequential materialities of (neo-)empire. While it is humiliating to be asked to bow in deference before the statues of (neo-)empire, that is, the statues of those that did not consider Africans to be human (Mbembe, 2016), it is necessary to remember that statues are mere symbols or shadows of empire against which Africans are often permitted to engage in ritualised skirmishes. An example that indicates how Africans often fight shadows of (neo-)empire is the recent Afrophobia in South Africa. In this regard, some South Africans have engage in Afrophobia that directly attacks the [human] Africans while on the other hand in their (neo-)imperial struggles they only engage in battles against symbols and statues or shadows of empire. In other words, instead of fighting the real, material and consequential core of (neo-)empire, there is preoccupation with fighting shadows and ideologies of (neo-)empire but when it comes to Afrophobia, the South Africans did not hesitate to attack the real [African] humans. The Afrophobic South Africans killed, maimed and destroyed the physical material properties of fellow Africans who have sadly been similarly dispossessed and disinherited by (neo-)empire whose shadows are the subject of battles in South Africa. Such paradoxes in the Afrophobic violence in South Africa imply that fellow Africans subjected to violence are equated with statues or shadows of (neo-)empire. The Afrophobic violence sadly assumes that fellow Africans are equivalent to the (neo-)imperial nonhuman statues that are similarly attacked. Furthermore, the underlying assumptions in the Afrophobic violence are that African immigrants to South Africa have been turned into statues – that they have become statues materially and developmentally immobilised by impoverishment even as they seek to move into the South African polity populated by

123

shadows and other statues of (neo-)empire. However, unlike (neo-)imperial statues, fellow Africans are not merely defaced or rendered alternative housing in museums – they are rather deported, brutalised, killed, and they are made to suffer privations.

Figure 1 below shows the defaced statue of a late British Queen

Statue of Queen Victoria (1903) in front of the library in Port Elizabeth was splattered with black paint in 2010 (Photo by Gallo Images/foto24wener Hills).

Although some politicians in South Africa have defended the (neo-)imperial statues as part of the "rich" symbolic history [heritage] of South Africa (Kubheka, 2015), it is imperative to note that impoverishment of Africans is also a "heritage" or history from (neo-)imperialism. In this regard, while the politicians defend the (neo-)imperial statues as part of the history or heritage of [South] Africa, the challenge is that in the Afrophobic violence [where human beings rather than statues are attacked], it is hardly acknowledged by the politicians and citizens that it is part of [Ubuntu] African heritage to care for one another. Besides, it is hardly acknowledged that the South African economy is a heritage from (neo-)colonial exploitation

124

of fellow Africans from the north who are paradoxically currently being subjected to Afrophobia. Thus, it is seldom recognised that the South African economy is a heritage of colonial forced labour migration [from other African countries] to South African mines (Nyamnjoh, 2006). It is hardly recognised that the transnational corporations that have recently taken [capital] flight from other African countries are indebted to the citizens of the African countries who now follow the absconding transnational corporations that have exploited them (see Makochekanwa, 2007; Mario, 2009; Asongu, 2014; Kwaramba et al, 2016; NewsDay, 30 October 2013. There is therefore need not only to consider the fact that transnational corporations currently transfer profits across borders of nations which they exploit but also necessary to cognise is the fact that historically colonialist drove cattle and other livestock ,which they looted from various group of Africans, across different national borders (Palmer, 1977). In this regard, transnational corporations shift African heritages across different borders such that what are often narrowly deemed to be national heritages are in fact heritages of the generalities of the dispossessed, disinherited and exploited [African] people.

In the light of the foregoing, we argue that (neo-)imperial impoverishment, dispossession, disinheritance and exploitation of Africans has turned them into "statues" that cannot exercise their mobility in physical senses of being able to successfully migrate and settle in different countries. Conceived as statues by host citizens, the impoverished and materially demobilised Africans are expected to remain locked up within the borders of their nations. Similarly, conceived as nonhuman statues that are supposed to be immobile they are denied access to human rights – they are treated less as humans than as nonhuman statues. In this sense, while other scholars conceive statues as constituting immortalisation of the deceased we argue that, from the African historical point of view, to be turned into a statue is in fact to be mortified to be demobilised as in the case of the majority of Africans who have not only suffered colonial dispossession and disinhertance but also the (neo-)colonial forms of disablement. While, as will be explained below, other scholars argue that in a post-Cartesian world there is no radical distinction between the dead (statues) and living [African] human beings it is necessary to contextualise these arguments in the (neo-)colonial history of deprivation, dispossession and exploitation of Africans in ways that eroded the distinctions between the humans and animals, the human and the nonhuman. In short Africans were (neo-)colonially **mortified into statues** rather than **immortalised as statues**.

Thus, mortification can be construed in a number of ways and some of the forms of mortification are the destruction of Ubuntu, the destruction of Africanness, the destruction of Pan-Africanism and Afrocentricity all of which mortifications explain the contemporary demobilisation of Africa. While some commentators have interpreted the Rhodes Must Fall Movement in terms of struggles to decolonise, transform or to Africanise the governance of universities, Africanise the curricula and to fit the universities to African realities (Laban, 2015: 15), Afrophobia indicates otherwise. Afrophobia indicate detestation of Africanisation, it underscores hankering for (neo-)colonisation, that is, for what is colonial and unAfrican. In fact the paradox of defending the Rhodes statues in South Africa as part of South African heritages while rejecting fellow Africans as liabilities underscored the detestation of Africanisation of South Africa. When descendants of architects of colonialism and apartheid collectively defend their embattled [statue] heritage in South Africa, while South Africans brutalise and kill their fellow Africans, the implication is that Africans remain captured in the stasis [and statuehood] of apartheid divide and rule. It is such stasis that has rendered Africans into human statues without human progress. Thus, noting ways in which Whites in South Africa defend their apartheid [statue] heritage, The Guardian (10 April 2015) states:

> The drive has sparked protests from white minority parties and the Afrikaans singer Steve Hofmeyr and Sunette Bridges, who sang the former apartheid anthem Die Stem in front of Kruger's statue, watched by an audience of white people, some dressed in quasi-military uniforms. Bridges chained herself to the monument... AfriForum, a white civil rights group, warned that string emotions around the debate meant that communities were becoming dangerously polarised...The Afrikaner is from a historical perspective, increasingly being portrayed

as criminals and land thieves. But apartheid freedom fighters are certainly not the untainted heroes government is making them out to be.

In a context where apartheid and colonial era descendants are animating their statues and singing apartheid era national anthems so as to protect their statues, literature is proliferating around animism as well as about new materialities wherein statues are portrayed as subjects and not mere objects. Thus, statues and other materialities are being portrayed by some scholars as spiritualised, as subjects, as agents, as actors, as endowed with feelings, emotions and so on (Eipper, 2007; Meskell, 2005; Croucher, 2012a; Croucher, 2012b; Bynum, 2012; Marie-Aude *et al*, 2015; Fontein, 2009). Thus, plastered skulls are regarded as recreation of fleshed and lifelike appearances and these plastered skulls are deemed to be affective, to influence and evoke emotions; they are presented as demonstrating a close link between the dead and the living in ways that are argued to blur the distinctions between a person and object (Croucher, 2012a). The plastered skulls are presented as the materiality of "ancestors", as images of "ancestors" including anthropomorphic pillars and pastered statues which are represented as veneration of "ancestors" (Croucher, 2012b). In this sense, animism and fetishism are presented as ways in which to think about humans' interactions with religious statues (Whitehead, 2015; Fontein, 2009). So, some scholars argue that bones are regarded as both emotive and affective "persons" and "objects" in politics of heritage in Zimbabwe where the bones are portrayed as extension of the consciousness of the dead, as spirit "subjects" or "persons" which are deemed to make demands on the living (Fontein, 2009).

In the context of the foregoing, Africans are presented as having had cultic devotion to statues which they are portrayed to have "provided with food and clean clothes each day in addition to drink offerings" (Meskell, 2005). Meskell (2005) argues that a statue is a temple which was believed to be the body of a divinity and a spirit medium that likewise provided the divinity with a temporary body. Thus, Meskell (2005) argues that in Egypt, statues were not simply vehicles but materialisations of gods themselves, in this sense; it is argued that the materialisation of the gods was central in Egypt, with obsession in preserving the living body and beyond the zone of death. In this regard, it is noted that Egyptians sought to abjure or defeat death through artificiality: specificality, via elaborate bodily rituals and preparations to evade the unbearable moment when flesh became nothing. In this regard, it is argued that magical spells were required to explicitly bring those functions back to the corpse, to make the dead body akin to its living counterpart. Citing Armstrong, (1981: 43), Meskell (2005: 61) further notes that mummies are powerful ambiguous entities, for Meskell, they are things and beyond things, subjects and objects, physical and cognitive categories, perceptible and apperceptible. In this respect, it is noted that bodies and body parts could be apprehended as prostheses replacing the frailty of the body and thought of as supplementing the body and coextensive with it, thereby extending the self through material means.

For purposes of this chapter, we note that if statues were provided with food and clean clothes each day then the implication is that Africans in this sense the Egyptians must have been excellent farmers with the abilities to produce sufficiently not only for human consumption but for the statues also. In other words, the scholars who portray Africans as feeding and clothing statues imply that there were great farmers in Africa and so we argue here that there is need to ensure that Africans get back their land which (neo-)colonialist are still holding onto on the pretext that Africans are not good farmers. As argued above, the problem in Africa is that (neo-)colonialist mortified Africans into statues by dispossessing, exploiting and disinheriting them. Now, just like the statues described above, African human beings are being forced to rely on food donations from the centres of (neo-)empire and unfortunately the genetically modified food that is being donated has been proven to cause sterility and impotence in ways that deny Africans the possibility of becoming ancestors (see Nhemachena and Mawere, 2017).

Apart from noting that (neo-)empire has always used technology and other mediums as its extensions, we argue herein that the contemporary celebrations of animism and the new materiality of statues should be understood in the light of the emergent humanoid robots that are being set to usher in a New World Order that threatens to be in fact a PostAfrican World (Nhemachena *et al*, 2017). In a context where (neo-)empire seeks to multiply its imperial extensions including by producing and selling humanoid robots for purposes of replacing human beings in employment and marriage [sex robots] (Nhemachena, 2017), it should not be surprising that there is proliferation of literature on animism, extensions to human bodies and new materialities. While some scholars argue that new materialities are essentially about immanent embodied agency, paradoxically, Africans who have been disinherited, dispossessed and impoverished do not have the privilege to embody food. In this regard, harpings about embodiment and immanence can be understood as irrelevant particularly because they also do not address the absence of embodiment of food and drink by the dispossessed, disinherited and exploited Africans who have, for centuries since the beginning of colonialism, been forced to fast incessantly.

In fact there are resilient arguments against [African] preservationism of heritages, statues and monuments which are increasingly being taken over by "international" heritage bodies including "civil society" stakeholders who contest African national control of heritages (Marie-Aude *et al*, 2015). In this sense, the rise of "civil society" engagements and the contestations around the commemoration of [African] liberation heroes, heritage and memory have generated sites of struggle, ethically and emotionally charged (Marie-Aude *et al*, 2015: 542). Thus, organisations like UNESCO designate African heritages as "World Heritages Sites" thus speaking to debates about universalism and particularism, nation-ness and border crossing, "soft power" and "cultural policies" Dominguez (2017: 120).

Even though the Afrophobic Africans think that South Africa is a particularistic and distinct nation state, we note that the presence of the (neo-)imperial statues in South Africa presupposes that South Africa does not exist as a nation. If South Africans can welcome and preserve (neo-)imperial statues, the question is how come they are not prepared to welcome and preserve the lives of fellow human Africans? If South Africans are ready to turn their cities into battlefields brutalising, killing and demanding that their fellow

Africans be deported, on allegations of taking their jobs (Tshishonga, 2015; Masenya, 2017; Jacobs, 2016), how is it the case that South Africans are prepared to preserve both (neo-)imperialist statues which by extension celebrate imperial mockery of Ubuntu? The question is whether, for South Africans, jobs are more important than demanding restoration of their material resources that were looted by colonialist and their descendants whose statues are being portrayed as animate, as imbued with agency and affect? The question we raise here is, if [as argued by some scholars cited above] the (neo-)imperial statues have agency, affect, emotions, vitality, intimacy, feelings and so on, why are they not addressing their imperial and apartheid wrongs, including restoration of the land, mines and other material resources to Black South Africans?

The contemporary discourses that seek to foreground unemployment issues, political domination, alienation or separation rather than dispossession and disinheritance of Africans are aimed at generating amnesia about the dispossession and theft of African resources. Apart from the then visible statue of Cecil John Rhodes, Africans need to notice the invisible presence of the gigantic statues of transnational corporations that are feasting on Africans. The same transnational corporations fund or sponsor education systems that foreground discourses about political oppression, political domination, problematise hierarchies, political power, political corruption in Africa and discourses about 'separation" or "alienation". These discourses foreshadow the more relevant and significant discourses and battles over (neo-)imperial restoration of African material resources. Instead of fighting together to recover their stolen resources, some Africans fight one another in competition for employment that is provided by those that have dispossessed them or stolen their material resources. For this reason, we argue that the (neo-)imperial statues and pillars of dispossession and impoverishment require visibilisation so that Africans do not fight sideshow battles against supposed political domination, hierarchies, oppression, "separation" and "alienation": they need to fight for restoration or recovery of materialities that were stolen so that they regain ownership and possession of their materialities. The struggles need not be merely for "connections" or "relationships" with nature or with the environment – the struggle should be for repossession, for restoration or for recovery of their possession and ownership of their material resources. For such struggles, Africa requires heroes and heroines like those [including King Nghunghunyani] who resisted colonialism

The Materiality of the Statue of King Nghunghunyani

Although colonial and (neo-)imperil forces would want to deny Africans their history including about the past and the present African heroes and heroines, King Nghunghunyani has been acknowledged as warrior King-hero of the Nguni. Thus, while (neo-)colonial and (neo-)imperial media vilify African heroines and heroes African states have made efforts to honour those that fought against (neo-)imperialism and (neo-)colonialism. In this sense, colonial and contemporary neo-colonial antipathy to African hierarchies is an exemplification of (neo-)imperial presumptions that there are no exceptional people or individuals in Africa. However, we note exceptionalism in the legacy of 19th century Nguni Warrior King, Nghunghunyani whose statue is currently in the midst of a public debate in the Limpopo Province of South Africa. Nghunghunyani is part of the current national narrative as he is regarded as one of the Warrior Kings who fought off colonialism in southern Africa. Whereas King Nghunghunyani's legacy represents the current celebrated heroes of South African cultural heritage who fought against colonialism and apartheid, the challenge with contemporary South African society is that there are some who would want to distinguish themselves by Afrophobic violence – and therefore create and sustain a new culture of violence against fellow Africans rather than sustain the historic culture of struggles against (neo-)colonialism. Put another way, some contemporary Africans sadly want to distinguish themselves by fighting their own mothers, fathers, brothers and sisters.

Since national narratives are given structure by collective memory, it is necessary for South Africa to [in addition to recovering ownership of material resources] Africanise its education system so that collective national memory will not be eroded by irrelevant

131

Eurocentric education institutions. According to Marshall (2008), collective memory is a product of memories of the past that serve as a foundation for the new political order, thereby creating a new national narrative (Leibowitz, 2008). While new national narratives may be necessary, it is essential to ensure that African history and heritages including about resistance to (neo-)colonialism and apartheid are preserved. This is particularly so because Eurocentrism has tended to summarily consider everything Africa to belong to the ignoble past and to the dustbins of history. While Hodgkin & Radstone (2003) argue that selected stories for collective memories are connected to a specific landscapes, the unfortunate thing is that African heroes and heroines have been demonised since the colonial era while paradoxically (neo-)imperial heroes and heroines were celebrated not only in the imperial centres but also in the (neo-)colonies and postcolonies. When (neo-)imperial powers chose to ignore African heroes and heroines, they played amnesia (Johnson, 2002: 295) for those sections they choose to omit. In Nhemachena's (2016) terms, the (neo-)imperialists have for long been producing ignorance about African materialities, heroes and heroines. Although scholars like Baines (2003) attribute the selection to the fact that older versions of the past no longer fit into the picture, as they are either redundant or unacceptable, it is necessary to note that such scholars rely on (neo-)imperial notions of linear time premised on Darwinist evolutionism.

If Euro-American states selectively honour their heroes (Marschall, 2008) [including architects of apartheid and colonialism] of the past, the question is why the honouring of African [living and deceased] heroines and heroes is contested by Euro-Americans including via the so-called civil society organisations? The question is why African states are coerced into honouring the statues of Cecil John Rhodes rather than recognise and commemorate African [liberation war] heroes and heroines? The challenge here is that African nations are populated by statues not so much of the liberation war but by (neo-)imperial statues which in spite of current Euro-American discourses about animism, affect, agency and so on cannot exercise the agency to restore (neo-)imperially plundered resources. Thus, instead of African states being premised on foundation myths revolving around selected African precolonial and postcolonial heroes and heroines, sadly African states that house (neo-)imperial statues appear to be based on heroes and heroines of the empire. We argue herein that the fact that even in Euro-America, they have their heroes such as George Washington, Thomas Jefferson, Winston Churchill and others signals the necessity of recognising African heroes and heroines as compasses that guide and shape the identities of postcolonial Africa. Without men and women of distinction who constitute the heroes and heroines, Africa will remain flattened and without erections [in metaphorical and literal senses] to oppose (neo-)imperial machinations (Chingozha and Nhemachena, 2017). In this sense, heroes and heroines are the ones that spur erections – it is not mere political elections that are needed to propel Africa forward – Africa also needs erections to ward off (neo-)imperial disinheritance and exploitation. Of course (neo-)empire would want [statues] of its own heroes to monopolise erections on the continent while it forces Africans to merely engage in vacuous political elections, in prostration (Nhemachena and Bankie, 2017). In this regard, using various guises, Africans are often incited against their own heroes, against their own grandfathers and grandmothers, against their fathers and mothers, against their brothers and sisters who happen to erect or compete for erections with (neo-)imperial heroes that are presented as universal heroes whose erections know no boundaries.

In post-apartheid South Africa, city-texts and history have been rewritten in order to replace the public art that corresponded with the collective memory of the Great Trek. The mythology of the Great Trek and Afrikanerdom that has been canonised in the Voortrekker Monument has been replaced by the "Struggle" (Marschall, 2003), thus, revitalising African history. Resuscitating the history of South Africa has been more about redress (Rassool, 2000) considering that, during apartheid, inequality was evident even when it came to the declaration of monuments by the National Monuments Council (hereafter NMC) (Baines, 2003). The NMC was the statutory body of the apartheid government that was responsible for the declaration of national monuments. Memories of the colonial past and of apartheid now form the basis of the new national narrative, including

133

dispossession, disinheritance, oppression, massacre, and resistance. Hlongwane (2008) notes that the Soweto student uprising of 16 June 1976 has been commemorated since 1977, but now officially commemorated at the Hector Peterson Memorial in Orlando West, Soweto. Rasool (2000) has, however noted that of all the memories that served to form the basis of the new national narrative, the Nelson Mandela narrative was central to the new South African history, as he is regarded as the 'founding father' of the new political regime (Marschall, 2006).

Thus, as with all new political orders, monuments and memorials of the memories are erected. Foote *et al* (2000) are correct in stating that the erection of monuments inscribing a national identity in the landscape is affected by political and wartime upheaval. According to Marschall (2008: 3): "Virtually all new monuments and cultural heritage sites built in post-apartheid South Africa, are in one way or another linked to the notion of struggle or resistance". Such memorials include the Walter Sisulu Memorial in Kliptown, Steve Biko statue in King Williams Town, Constitution Hill in Braamfontein and Hector Peterson Memorial in Soweto. The people who died in Sharpeville during protests against the apartheid era Pass Laws on 21 March 1960 are memorialised in a monument (Saunders, 2007).

While it is still necessary to struggle for an African new economic order, it is understood that the national narrative is incomplete without the people who made possible the new political order. Some African heroes and heroines fought off colonial rule, and are significant and regarded as heroes of the past, who had been marginalised by the apartheid regime (Rassool, 2000). The latter can be illustrated by the statues of King Makhado in the town of Makhado, formerly known as Louis Trichardt in the Limpopo Province (Thotse, 2010). All these heroes are also canonised by statues.

Nghunghunyani the Warrior King

The new South African regional narratives of the Limpopo Province eulogise the warrior leaders who fought resistance battles against the Boers who were bent on dispossessing indigenous people of their land. These narratives are the heart of the doctoral thesis of scholar and researcher, Tlou Setumu (2010). His work highlights the common elements amongst the leaders of the former Northern Transvaal. The element that, among others, stood out was that they resisted colonial invasion and dispossession of indigenous people. The warrior leaders were chiefs such as Makhado, Malebogo, Mokopane, and Sekhukhune whose statues now feature in public spaces. The provincial Department of Sports, Arts and Culture used Setumu's work to form the basis of the erection of statues all over the Limpopo Province (Setumu Pers. Com. 10 November 2011).

Fig. 1 The statue of King Nghunghunyani at the Tourist Information Centre in Giyani (Photographed by researcher)

In the *Mapungubwe News Heritage Month Souvenir Edition* 2009, former Member of Executive Committee (MEC) of Sports, Arts and Culture Mrs. Happy Joyce Mashamba, announced that during the previous five years, the department had been involved in rolling out a programme to honour warrior kings. At the time of her speech, the statue of King Makgoba was yet to be erected and unveiled, and she remarked that the programme was not complete until that task was carried through. She then added that the department would "...launch Warrior Kings' Day to commemorate their fearless and ferocious resilience in the crucible of resistance to savage imperialist conquest, dispossession and settler colonial domination" (*Mapungubwe News Heritage Month Souvenir Edition,* 2009). She then thanked Tlou Setumu for allowing the department to utilise his historical records. The same publication pays tribute to the following kings:

- King Malebogo of the Bahananwa people, whose statue was unveiled on Heritage Day, 24th September 2006;
- King Mokopane of the Matabele of Kekakana;
- King Sekhukhune of the Bapedi;
- Rain Queen Modjadji of the Balobedu;
- King Makgoba of the Batlhalerwa;
- And finally King Nghunghunyani of the Tsonga

Nghunghunyani (Figure 1) resisted Portuguese imperialism in the early 1800s and fought battles against them. The statue of Nghunghunyani was unveiled in December 2006 by Mashamba in the town of Giyani, the capital town of the former homeland of Gazankulu.

The Legacy of the Gaza Nguni

It is rather impossible to discuss King Nghunghunyani and the Gaza Nguni without discussing their history and heritage. The narrative is traced back to the *difecane*, a period of turmoil and disturbances during the 1920's (Harries in Vail, 1989) in Zululand after King Shaka succeeded his father to the Zulu royal throne. The *difecane* was marked with numerous migrations of off-shoots of the Zulu warriors and groups, some fleeing from Shaka, while some were subjects that had been entrusted with fighting other clans in an attempt to expand the Zulu Kingdom. Nghunghunyane was the grandson of the Zulu warrior Manukosi, or Soshangana who fled from Shaka in 1819 after the latter defeated Zwide and incorporated his people into the Zulu Kingdom.

The Gaza Nguni, together with their leaders, were despots who killed other clans, burned their villages, and took their women and children, and practised slavery (Setumo: 2005). They also participated in the East coast slave trade whereby slaves were taken as prisoners of war. Clans that assumed the Nguni culture were acculturated and incorporated into the Gaza Nguni, and their girls supplied the much needed wives that would perpetuate and maintain the purity of the Nguni. This was a deliberate act that served to exclude non-Nguni from social and economic benefits. There are, however, people who resisted incorporation into the Nguni. According to Harries (1981), these people were easily recognisable as they stuck to their material culture and language. These people were regarded by the Gaza Nguni as "*amatonga*" and were subjected to exploitation. Amatonga was a pejorative term meaning slave or dog with no human rights whatsoever. The Nguni regarded them and the Chopi as subhuman and as such, a justifiable source of slaves (Harries, 1981).

Tsonga Speaking Communities of the Limpopo Province

The north eastern region of the Limpopo Province is inhabited by Tsonga speaking communities in areas that used to form part of the former homeland of Gazankulu, whose capital, as mentioned above, was Giyani. The homeland of Gazankulu was originally formed in 1962, and then named Matshangana Territorial Authority (Harries in Vail, 1989). That Authority brought together disparate groups of Tsonga speakers from four regions of the Transvaal: Spelonken and Giyani, Malamulele, the areas around Letaba, and the Shangana in Bushbuckridge. The groups from the four regions, save for those from the Bushbuckridge, had immigrated into the Transvaal from southern Mozambique, fleeing from Nguni rule. These people were not in any way culturally homogenous, but "...a conglomeration of people from various coastal chiefdoms" according to Harries (*ibid*: 84). The refugees were no powerful clans and had no rulers or leaders of their own (Van Warmelo, 1935) and this, according to Van Warmelo (*ibid*) and later Harries (in Vail, 1989) prompted them to settle virtually under any chief to whom they could offer services and pay tribute to. Their only quest was finding a place to live. They had come from various cultural traditions and their roots could not be linked to any single clan or chief. The Tsonga speaking people of the Bushbuckridge area are the descendants of the Gaza Nguni and were the last group to arrive in South Africa, after the arrest and subsequent exile of Nghunghunyani.

The two groups, comprising of refugees fleeing Nguni rule and the descendants of the same Nguni, forged a unity based on similarities in language, material culture, and historical affiliation, to form the homeland of Gazankulu. The unity is even evident in the founding phrases of the former homeland, namely, *"vatukulu va Gwambe na Dzavana"* and *"swihluke swa Nghunghunyani"* respectively (Rikhotso, 1984). The first phrase is about mythical ancestors of the Tsonga speaking people of the Northern Transvaal, while the second simply states that the Bushbuckridge people are offshoots of Nghunghunyani.

The Statue of Nghunghunyani and the Public Debate

The erection of the statue of Nghunghunyani is controversial. There are various sectors of the Tsonga speaking community, amongst whom the statue has been erected, who regard the statue as insulting. These various groups argue that the statue should not be located in Giyani as the Nguni leader it represents never led the chiefs of the region. Four scholars created a blog that was initially aimed at contesting the Tsonga-Shangana kingship, but also mention how the statue of Nghunghunyani is misleading as regards the history of the region (http://tsonga-history.blogspot.com/).

Several articles were written about the dissatisfaction of people about the statue. An article in the *Daily Sun* (6 December 2005) titled *"The statue of the king is wrong"* reported that both Shangaan and Vatsonga leaders indicated that it was wrong for the government to erect a statue in Giyani in honour of Nghunghunyani. In response to the protestations, the then spokesperson for the Department of Sports, Arts and Culture Mmbangiseni Masia announced, "King Nghunghunyani is undoubtedly a hero who fought colonialism. Our government is honouring such leaders and will continue to build monuments to (sic) the wars of resistance".

The Social Narratives of the Tsonga Speaking Communities of the Limpopo Province

Guided by the history of the Tsonga speaking communities in the Limpopo Province of South Africa, it is not surprising that their individual social narratives are void of the great figure represented by Nghunghunyani. This can be illustrated by the fact that the social narrative of the Valoyi, the Van'wanati (Maluleke), the Vankuna, and the Vahlengwe include totems and praise poems that are void of the Gaza Nguni, and more specifically and notably Nghunghunyani. Each of these groups has its own distinct foundation myth and heroes which do not include Nghunghunyani.

For instance, the Vankuna celebrate their Chief *Shilubana* as their founding hero. When asked where they originated from the Nkuna stated that:

> ...We came from *ka-Zulu*. From there some went to Mozambique. Along the way battles were fought with other groups, more especially the Gaza Nguni. This prompted for us to leave Mozambique in different directions. Some of our people went to Rhodesia. Some settled with Joao Albasini. Some of us settled in Bushbuckridge. Some went and came back via Modjadji and Politsi. We left and settled at *Monareng* with the *Mmamatola*. That's where *Shiluvani* died. We then settled at *Bokgakga* under *Hosi Maake* and established a very good relationship with us. We were given a place to settle there. Later after then Shiluvani's son *Muhlava* became chief.
>
> We had good relations with the people of *Maake*. On leaving Mozambique, our *n'anga* had informed us that we would encounter the land of a female chief who will take care of us, and that we should not pass there, but settle.
>
> We also had good relationship at first with the *Banareng*, but things later changed. *Shiluvani* had requested that *Banareng* look after his son. He did. The relationship changed only much later (Interview with a Nkuna Representative, 2013).

The Vankuna have two praise poems dedicated to their heroes, Hosi Muhlava I and Hosi Muhlava II. They also have a praise for all the clan, which is shorter than the other two, and will thus be presented here. We note that this is a shortened version of the Hosi Muhlava I praise poem;

"Nkhwashu wa pindza mahalambeni,
Gegetsu ra nhlonge xi lwa na dzana,
Khume ri lwa ni matoya ni mayeka.
N'wapala ra ndlopfu ro tsandza ni timhisi ku kutsa.
Muhosi a va potsi ku potsa vankulunge wa tsune.

Makombela mati a nga ri na torha,
A kombelele ku fundza a halata.
Nkunankulu, Nkuna lonene,
Ku nga ri hi ku khonza,
kambe hi xinkavana eka Nkuna" (Courtesy of Rhunali N'wa-Hulana Muhlava Shiluvana)

Translation of the Totem:
Here's to you Nkhwashu
The one who fights with hundreds,
Ten men fight with cowards and the useless.
You are an elephant pole that not even hyenas can sink their teeth into.

Here's to you, the great Nkuna, the kind Nkuna,
Not that we are paying tribute, but that Nkuna is indeed your birthright.
You the one, who asks for water even when not thirsty,
You simply ask just for the fun of it, and then spill.

The Van'wanati people have a hero in *Malenga* who is also their founding father. The N'wanati praise has four totems in it, namely, the meerkat, the elephant, the lion and the mamba. The lion totem seems to be old as the family traces it back to the Great Lakes, while the other three seem to be recent as they are traced to southern Africa. When the praise is explained in detail, it reveals some interesting information, like the fact that one of the N'wanati leaders was Maxakadzi, an ivory trader whose trading post was at *Nyembani* (Inhambane, Mozambique):

...The Van'wanati are Vatsonga. We trace existence back to 1200 when we left the Great Lakes. We belong to the beja-thonga group of the great lakes. Van'wanati "i vaka betsa ra matsalatsala". That is how we pride ourselves. The totem from the great lakes was a lion, standing for kings. In southern Africa we are called Van'wanati, Nkala. We also have another southern African totem, the elephant. The kingdom we belonged to of the Monomutapa Empire, we were under Utheve. After the collapse of the empire, the Van'wanati became prominent, and defeated a number of people including the Vacopi. Van'wanati clans are numerous; including the Makwakwa people, the Mkhwananzi, Masangu, Vambhani, Makhubele, and Maluleke. The Maluleke group is the only one that retained the Vunwanati, due to migrations, assimilations and other problems. It is also possible to find a Maluleke in Swaziland. The area from what is today Kruger National Park up to the Zambezi was Tsonga territory. Vatsonga are traders.

Malenga left N'wanati and started a kingdom in Pfhukwe, around 1550s. He was succeeded by his third son Maxakadzi who established his head kraal at Nyandwini, at Shingwedzi in the area that is now the Kruger National Park in 1640. Maxakadzi was succeeded by Ximambani. His kraal established at Phafuri where Thulamela is today. Nkuri took over after Ximambani. His kraal was at Dzundzwini, on a hill, in the area that is now the Kruger National Park.

...the sons of Ximambani include Mavuva, Nkomisi, Hohlwani, Tsuvuka, Matsilele At Valdezia, Xigalo, Nkuri, Mulamula, Mhinga, Xikole (also known as Vambani), Xihahele, Makuleke, Malavi, Xikhumba at Phafuri, Matsilele in southern Mozambique. We had land and our own kingdom... (Interview with a N'wanati Representative, 2013).

The Valoyi mention *Changamere* and *Mbhekwana* as their founding figures. Their narrative as indicated below is part of their history:

...The Valoyi belong to the kingdom of the Munomutapa. When Changameri died in Zimbabwe the Valoyi moved to Vutsonga. In around the year 1818 the Mfecane upheavals started, and Soshangana moved to Mozambique. He wanted to incorporate clans. In 1825 the Valoyi then moved to the Transvaal refusing to be incorporated into the kingdom that Soshangana was building up starting at the confluence of the Levubu and Limpopo Rivers. Under the leadership of Mbhekwana, the Valoyi had the following six regiments; N'wakhada, N'wamitwa, N'waxihuku, N'wavucema, Mavokweni, and Mirurhu. These regiments represent the sons of Mbhekwana… (Interview with a family representative, 2013).

Of note is the fact that some the social narratives of these individual groups mention encounters with the Gaza Nguni, Nghunghunyani's predecessors. A case in point is the Vankuna who migrated to the north coast into Tsonga speaking territories (see also Harries in Vail, 1989; Jacque, 1984). While some scholars present precolonial Africans as without notions and practices of ownership and possession of resources and property, the narrative in this chapter shows that Africans resisted colonial dispossession because they knew that the land that was being looted belonged to them and their progeny. The reason why Africans commemorate their heroes is that the heroes and heroines fought to resist colonial dispossession and disinheritance of Africans. So, while (neo-)imperial discourses would present Africans and their societies as flat and without hierarchies and as without heroines and heroes, this chapter shows that African societies had hierarchies and order wherein heroes and heroines were celebrated and commemorated and villains were mocked. Whereas contemporary discourses around posthumanism and transhumanism seek to efface [African] societies, there is evidence that precolonial Africans had social organisations including kings, chiefs, and queens who constituted the leadership within the social organisations (Nhemachena, 2016). So, while Eurocentric theorists would want to apply Hobbesian postulation of orderless, anarchic existence in precolonial Africa, there is evidence that there was social order which colonialists disrupted before claiming the presence of disorder in Africa (Nhemachena, 2017). Whereas some scholars presuppose that African states originated from Westphalianism, this chapter has shown that states existed in precolonial Africa – that Africans had their own states prior to colonisation and therefore the presence of [African] states should not be simplistically interpreted as a function of Westphalianism.

Leaders, like King Makhado and King Nghunghunyani, within the African states who fought against colonial dispossession constitute the new heroes in postindependence South Africa which has erected statues to commemorate them.

Conclusion

While some scholars argue for new materialities wherein they posit that statues are animated embodiments of "ancestors" and therefore that the statues have feelings, emotions, agency, affect and so on, in South Africa as indeed in Africa more broadly indications are that statues are symbols rather than embodiments of ancestors. For this reason statues are not considered to be animated, they are not deemed to have feelings or emotions or affect and they are not provided with food and clean clothes each day as argued by some scholars. The narratives in this chapter were made by human beings rather than by statues themselves because in Africa statues are not regarded as endowed with speech and they are not embodiments [rather symbols] of ancestors. In this sense, the chapter underscores the need to carefully and critically engage with Eurocentric theories particularly on animism, ecocriticism, earth jurisprudence as well as Eurocentric philosophies on affect, immanence, embodiment, becomings, agency and action. In fact it is erroneous to presume, as the Eurocentric theories do, that all objects are embodiments, with agency, affect, emotions, feelings and action. In a continent where the majority of Africans cannot afford to [ingest] and embody food and drink because of transnational corporations and (neo-)imperial dispossession and disinheritance, to emphasise embodiment is to err. Instead of overdramatising [assumed] spiritual embodiments, there is need to critically consider whether the majority of people on the continent can afford to ingest [embody] materialities such as food and drink. To postulate theories of animism, vitality and vibrancy of matter without considering the more fundamental questions about the possession, recovery and ownership of materialities by the African people is to be guilty of attempting to sidetrack African struggles for restoration of their material resources. In other words, animistic theories that privilege [spiritual] embodiment are not relevant on a continent where the majority of Africans cannot afford to embody materialities like food and drink.

Acknowledgements

1. The Office of the DVC Academic, University of Venda is heartily thanked for the provision of the Capacity Development Fund that funded the mobility of the researcher [second author] during her MA studies.
2. Geoffrey Tshibvumo drove the researcher to research sites and helped manage interview appointments. He also assisted in data collection at the Giyani Archives and National Archives, Pretoria.
3. Phindani Mulaudzi assisted in data collection at the Giyani Archives and National Archives, Pretoria.
4. A special thanks to Rhulani N'wa-Hungana Muhlava Shiluvana for making the Vankuna praise poems available for research.

References

Asangu, S. A. (2014) Fighting Capital Flight: Empirics on Bench-Marking Policy Harmonisation in *The European Journal of Comparative Economics* vol 11(1):93-122.

Baines, G. (2003) *The Politics of Public History in Post-Apartheid South Africa*. Grahamstown: Rhodes University.

Biney, A. (23 March 2017) Cry My Beloved South Africa: the Cancer of Afrophobia, in Pambazuka News https://www.pambazuka.org/human-security-cry-my-beloved-south-africacancer-afrophobia.

Bynmun, C. W. (2012) The Sacrality of Things: An Inquiry into Divine Materiality in the Christian Middle Ages: In *Irish Theological Quarterly* 78(1):3-18.

Carastathis, A. (2016) *Intersectionality: Origins, Contestations, Horizons.* University of Nebraska Press.

Croucher, K. (2012) *Death and Dying in the Neolithic Near East*. Oxford: Oxford University Press

Croucher, K. (2012) *The Materiality of 'Ancestors': Plastered Skills, Statues, and Stone Gods.* Oxford: Oxford University Press.

Daily Sun (6 December 2005) *"The statue of the king is wrong"* Page 11.

Dominguez, V. R. (2017) World Anthropologies: Special Section on Cultural Heritage/Management, in *American Anthropology* vol 119(1):120-121.

Eipper, C. (2007) Moving Statues and Moving Images: Religious Artefacts and the Spiritualisation of Materiality, the *Australian Journal of Anthropology*, vol 18(3):253-664.

Else, C. A. (2014) In the Aftermaths of Xenophobia: A Critical Analysis DPhil Linguistics. University of Free State.

Esselen, R. (2007) Living with the Past. Unpublished Master of Architecture [Professional] thesis. University of the Witwatersrand: Johannesburg.

Fentress, J. (1992). *Social Memory.* Oxford: Blackwell.

Fontein, J. (2009) The Politics of the Dead: Living Heritage, Bones and Commemoration in Zimbabwe in *Association of Social Anthropologists of the UK and Commonwealth Online* no 01/2:1-27.

Foote, K. E. T.; Attila Árvay A. (2000) Hungary after 1989: Inscribing a New Past on Place. *Geographical Review*, 90 (3), 301-334.

Geismar, H. (2015) Anthropology and Heritage Regimes, in *Annual Review of Anthropology* vol 44:71-85.

Gibson, G. D. (1955) Rituals of Rebellion in South-East Africa. Max Gluckman (The Frazer Lecture, 1952). Manchester: Manchester University Press, 1954. 36pp 3/6d.

Gluckman, M. (1954) *Rituals of rebellion in South-East Africa.* Manchester: Manchester University Press.

Graham, B., Gregory, G. & Ashworth, J. (2004) The Users and Abusers of Heritage in Corsane, G. (ed), *Heritage, Museums and Galleries: an Introductory Reader.* London: Routledge.

Harries, P. (1981) Slavery, Social Incorporation and Surplus Extraction: The Nature of Free and Unfree Labour in South-East Africa. *The Journal of African History.* 22 (3), 309-330.

Harries, P. (1989) Exclusion, Classification and Internal Colonialism: The Emergence of Ethnicity among Tsonga-Speakers of South Africa. In Vail, L. (ed.) *The Creation of Tribalism in Southern Africa.* Cape Town: David Phillip.

Hesse-Biber, S. N. & Leavy, P. (2006) *The Practice of Qualitative Research. Thousand Oaks*: SAGE.

Hlongwane, A.K. (ed.) (2008) Footprints of the "Class of 76": Commemoration, Memory Mapping and Heritage. Hector Pieterson Memorial and Museum. Johannesburg.

Hodgkin, K. & Radstone, S. (2003) *Contested Pasts: the Politics of Memory*. London & New York: Routledge. http://tsonga-history.blogspot.com/.

Jacobs, J. U. (2016) The Trauma of Home and (non)belonging in Zimbabwe and its Diaspora: Conversion Disorder in Shadows by Novuyo Rosa Tsuma. *Journal of Literary Criticism, Comparative Linguistics and Literary Studies* 37(1) a1237.

Jaques, A.A. (1984) *Swivongo swa Machangana. Morija Printing Works.* Lesotho: Morija.

Johnson, N. C. (2002) Mapping Monuments: the Shaping of Public Space and Cultural Identities. *Visual Communication*, 1 (3): 293-298.

Kockel, U. & Nic Craith, M. (eds.) (2007) *Cultural Heritages as Reflexive Traditions*. New York: Palgrave Macmillan.

Kubheka, T. (7 April 2015). Removal of Apartheid Statues is an Insult to SA`s Rich History ewn.co.za/2015/04/07/Removal–of-apartheid-statues-is-an-insult-SA`s-rich-history.

Kwaramba, M. *et al.* (2016) Capital Flight and Trade Misinvoicing in Zimbabwe, in *African Development Review* vol 28, issue (510:50-64.

Laband, J. (2015) Toppling Statues, Burning Books and the Humanities in South African Universities. The Journal of the Helen Suzman Foundation issue 76:15-21.

Liebowitz, V. (2008) Making Memory Space: Recollection and Reconciliation in Post-Apartheid South Africa. Unpublished Master of Architecture Thesis. RMIT University.

Makochekanwa, A. (2007). An Empirical Investigation of Capital Flight from Zimbabwe, University of Pretoria Space Institutional Repository https://repository.up.ac.za/handle/2263/4400.

Mapungubwe News. Heritage Month Souvenir Edition. (2009) The Official Newsletter of the Department of Sports Arts & Culture. Polokwane.

Maree, K. (ed.) (2012) *First Steps in Research*. Pretoria: Van Schaik Publishers.

Marie-Aude, F. *et al.* (2015) Heritage and Memory in East Africa today: A Review of Recent Development in Cultural Heritage Research and Memory Studies, Azania: *Archaeological Research in Africa*, vol 50(4):542-558.

Mario, P. (2009) *Zimbabwe's Cry for Hope*. Lulu.com.

Marschall, S. (2003) Canonizing New Heroes: The Proposed Heroes Monument in Durban. *South African Journal of Art History*. Vol. 18, 80-93.

Marschall, S. (2006) Commemorating 'Struggle Heroes': Constructing a Genealogy for The New South Africa. *International Journal of Heritage Studies*. Vol. 2, 176-193.

Marschall, S. (2008) Reordering the Past: Monuments and Architectural Heritage in Post-Apartheid South Africa. *Collections électroniques de l'INHA*.

Masenya, M. J. (2017) Afrophobia in South Africa: A General Perspective of Xenophobia, in *Bangladesh e-Journal of Sociology* vol 4(1): 81-88.

Maune, B. (2015) These Africans Statues Could Still Fall. https://www.timeslive.co.za/new/south-africa/2015-04-10-these-south-african-could-still-fall/.

Mbembe, A J. (2016) Decolonising the University: New Directions in Arts & Humanities in *Higher Education* vol 15(1):29-45.

Merriam, S. B. (2009) *Qualitative Research: A Guide to Design and Implementation*. San Franscisco: Jossey-Bass.

Meskeli, L. (2005) 'Objects in the Mirror Appear Closer than They Are', in Miller, D. (ed) *Materiality*. Duke University Press.

Neocosmos, M. (2006) *`Foreign Natives` to `Native Foreigners`. Explaining Xenophobia in Post-Apartheid South Africa: Citizenship and Nationalism, Identity and Polities*. CODESRIA Monograph Series, Dakar.

News Day. (30 October 2013) Curbing Capital Flight: Optimising Tax from Non-Renewable Resources https://www.newsday.co.zw/2013/10/30/curbing-capital-flight-optimising-tax-on-non-renewsble-resources/.

Nhemachena, A. (2017) *Relationality and Resilience in a Not So Relational World: Knowledge, Chivanhu and (De-)Coloniality in 21st Century Conflict-Torn Zimbabwe*. Bamenda: Langaa RPCIG.

Nhemachena, A; Warikandwa, T. V. and Mtapuri, O. (2017) Transnational Corporations' Land Grabs and the On-going Second Mad Scramble for Africa: An Introduction, in Warikandwa T V; Nhemachena, A. and Mtapuri, O. (eds.) *Transnational Land Grabs and Restitution in an Age of the (De-)Militarised New Scramble for Africa: A Pan African Socio-Legal Perspective*. Bamenda: Langaa Publishers.

Nhemachena, A and Mawere, M. (2017) Consuming or Being consumed in the New World Order? GMOs as an Insult to the Dispossessed and Impoverished of the Earth, in Mawere, M and Nhemachena, A (eds) *GMOs, Consumerism and the Global Politics of Biotechnology: Rethinking Food, Bodies and Identities in Africa's 21st Century*. Bamenda: Langaa RPCIG.

Chingozha M. P. and Nhemachena, A. (2017) Africa without Genetically Modified Organisms: On the need for National Food Sovereignty, in Mawere, M and Nhemachena, A (eds) *GMOs, Consumerism and the Global Politics of Biotechnology: Rethinking Food, Bodies and Identities in Africa's 21st Century*. Bamenda: Langaa RPCIG.

Nhemachena, A. (2017) Food, Health and Science in Africa: Locating GMOs Debates in the Shifting Global Epistemological Terrains, in Mawere, M and Nhemachena, A (eds) *GMOs, Consumerism and the Global Politics of Biotechnology: Rethinking Food, Bodies and Identities in Africa's 21st Century*. Bamenda: Langaa RPCIG.

Nhemachena, A. (2016) (Post-)development and the Social Production of Ignorance: Farming Ignorance in 21st Century Africa in Mawere, M. (2016) *Development Perspectives from the South; Troubling the Metrics of [Under-]development in Africa*. Bamenda: Langaa Research &Publishing.

Nhemachena, A. and Bankie, F. (2017) Foot Soldiers of the New Empire or Horizontal Saviours? Interrogating Civil Society Organisations and Fundamentalisms in Twenty-First Century Africa, in Nhemachena, A. and Mawere, M. (eds) *Africa at the*

Crossroads: Theorising Fundamentalisms in the 21ˢᵗ Century. Bamenda: Langaa RPCIG.

Nhemachena, A. (2017) Hearing the Footfalls of Humanoid Robots: Technoscience, (Un-)employment and the Future of Development in Twenty-First Century Africa, in Mawere, M (ed) *Underdevelopment, Development and the Future of Africa.* Bamenda: Langaa RPCIG.

Niewenhuis, J. (2012) Introducing Qualitative Research, in: Maree, K. (ed.) *First Steps in Research.* Pretoria: Van Schaik Publishers.

Nyamnjoh, F. B. (2006) *Insiders and Outsiders: Citizenship and Xenophobia in Contemporary Southern Africa.* London: CODESRIA – Zed Books.

Nyamnjoh, F. B. (2016) *#RhodesMustFall: Nibbling at Resilient Colonialism in South Africa.* Bamenda: Langaa RPCIG.

O`Meara, D. (1991) The Collapse of Mozambican Socialism, in *Transformation.* 14: 82-103.

Palmer, R. (1977) *Land and Racial Domination in Rhodesia.* Berkeley: University of California Press.

Qurjano, A. (2000) Coloniality of Power, Eurocentricism and Latin America in *Nepantla: Views from South* 1(3): 533-580.

Rassool, C. (2000) The Rise of Heritage and the Reconstitution of History in South Africa. *Kronos.* No. 26, 1-21.

Rikhotso, F. (1984) *Matimu ya mfumo wa Gazankulu (History of the Gazankulu Government).* Emmanule Press.

Saunders, C. (2007) The Transformation of Heritage in the New South Africa, in Stolten, H. E. (ed.) *History Making and Present Day Politics: The Meaning of Collective Memory in South Africa.* Nordiska Afrikaintitutet. Uppsala, Sweden.

Savransky, M. (2017) A Decolonial Imagination: Sociology, Anthropology and the Politics of Reality in *Sociology* vol 51(1): 11-26.

Setumo, T. (2005) *Hosi Ngungunhane of the Tsonga.* Polokwane: J.P Publishers.

Sowetan Live, (30 November 2010) Xenophobia is in Fact Afrophobia in Disguise www.sowetanlive.com.za/columnist/2010/11/30/xenophobia-is-in-fact-afrophobia-in-disguise.

Stolten, H. E. (ed.). (2007) *History Making and Present Day Politics: The Meaning of Collective Memory in South Africa.* Uppsala: Nordiska Afrikaintitutet. Uppsala.

The Guardian. (10 April 2015) Vandalism of Apartheid Era Statues Sparks Fevered Debate in South Africa. 10 April 2015. https://www.theguardian.com/world/2015/apr/10/vandalism-of-apartheid-statues-sparks-fevered-debate-in-south-africa.

Thotse, M. (2010) Contesting Names and Statues: Battles over the Louis Trichardt /Makhado 'City-text' in Limpopo, South Africa. *Kronos.* 36 (1), 173-183.

Till, K. (1999) 'Staging the Past: Landscape Designs, Cultural Identity and Erinnerungspolitik at Berlin's Neue Wache', *Ecumene* 6: 251–83.

Tshishonga, N. (2015) The Impact of Xenophobia- Afrophobia on the Informal Economy in Durban CBD, South Africa, 11(41): 163-179.

Vail, L. (ed.) (1989) *The Creation of Tribalism in Southern Africa.* Cape Town: David Phillip.

Van Warmelo, N. J. (1935) A Preliminary Survey of the Bantu Clans of South Africa. Ethnological Publications, Vol. V. The Government Printers. Pretoria.

Whitehead, A. (2015) *Religious Statues and Personhood: Testing the Role of Materiality.* Bloomsbury Academic.

Chapter Five

Materialities and Symbols of Zimbabwe's Civil Religion

Munetsi Ruzivo

Introduction

After attaining its independence in 1980, Zimbabwe embarked on a process of unifying the nascent state. The country was divided and fragile at independence because of the 16 years of war. Since colonisation, in 1890, Zimbabweans had not accepted the colonial yoke. Four factors provoked the war and these were: theft of African land by the British South African Company (BSAC) agents, forced labour exacted on the Africans and the brutality of the BSAC police and crop and cattle scourges as well as plagues of locusts and the rinderpest that robbed Africans of their possessions, heritages and sources of livelihood (Murdoch, 2015:22). In the 1896-1897 war, both the Ndebele and the Shona people waged a war that ended with their defeat. Between 1898 and 1930 Africans made use of associations such as the Rhodesian Native Association, the Industrial and Commercial Workers Union, Matabeleland Home Society and the Southern Rhodesian Bantu Voters Association to express their concerns about colonial dispossession, disinheritance and exploitation (West, 2002:122; Hallencreutz, 1998: 219).

When mild forms of persuasion and militant forms of protest failed more militant parties were formed such as National Democratic Party (NDP). When it was banned Zimbabwe African People's Union (ZAPU) succeeded it in 1961 and the following year it was banned. The leadership went into exile (Hallencreutz, 1998: 365). ZAPU was the earliest party to send people outside the country for military training (Sadomba, 2011:10). Due to banning of the National Democratic Party in 1961 and ZAPU in 1961, the nationalist movement split in 1963 when Joshua Nkomo expelled a group of rebels in Highfields. The split generated animosity between supporters of the two parties. In 1971, ZAPU members, namely James Chikerema, George Nyandoro and some Zimbabwe African National Union (ZANU) members such as Nathan Shamhuyarira and others who had split from ZANU formed a Front for the Liberation of Zimbabwe (FLORIZ). Jason Moyo and Hebert Chitepo formed a joint operations command between their forces. The Zimbabwe African National Union (ZANU) and the Zimbabwe African Peoples Union (ZAPU) through their military wings namely, Zimbabwe African National Liberation Army (ZANLA) and Zimbabwe African People's Revolutionary Army (ZIPRA) waged an armed struggle against the colonial system. Back home the liberation movement had fractured along ethnic lines. The Ian Smith Government wielded immense influence on farm workers, civil servants and domestic workers as well as on clergymen such as Bishop Abel Muzorewa and Ndabaningi Sithole and some African chiefs such as Ndiweni and Jeremiah Chirau had made a pact with the Rhodesian Government (The Patriot, 2017 November, 27). This, alone, shows how fragile the New Zimbabwe was. The type of religion that could unify the state was civil religion. Civil religion would not be objectionable to both Christians and African Traditional religion practitioners. The African people were divided between those who supported the Rhodesian Front Government and those who supported the nationalist parties and their armed wings.

One way of unifying the nascent state was by inventing a national religion of some sort. This religion we shall call it civil religion meaning a kind of religious nationalism. In this religion, some elements of African Traditional Religion blended with Zimbabwean Patriotism. The religion also embodies elements of Christian religion. It resembles African traditional religion in that it is a public affair for those who share the same ideals with its practitioners. Its national saints or heroes are similar to those in African Traditional Religion. It is no longer practised in the crude traditional way where traditional beer is served. The old has been absorbed into the new religion. Civil religion was not only a cult of the state in the precolonial Africa but was practised at the family level, regional and National levels. The Zimbabwe precolonial society practised civil religion. Colonisation and the introduction of Christianity led to the abrogation of African rule and its civil religion as its linchpin. Many of the nationalists were educated in mission schools like many of their fellow countrymen. Upon attaining independence in 1980, aspects of African traditional religion and Christian religion were blended with patriotism to serve the interests of the nascent state.

Definition of Materiality

This chapter, first and foremost, shall make a study of the material culture of civil religion as it was used and deployed by the postcolonial state. Civil religion here shall be understood as a national cult of the state. In the second place, the chapter will highlight materialities that constitute this cult of the state. Materialities being understood here as aspects of civil religion that pertain to state actors, objects, places and artefacts. Anderson (2006: 1) mentions the presences of cenotaphs and tombs of unknown soldiers in modern nationalism. Anderson (ibid) observed that even if these tombs are void and without material remains of people, they are saturated with ghostly national imaginings. There is a nexus between the idea of religion and the idea of the state as imagined and this is why it was necessary for colonial scholars who misrepresented precolonial Africa as lacking religion to also portray the continent as without states. In short, to be portrayed as lacking [imagination] religion is also by extension to be misrepresented as lacking [imagination] states. The ideas remain unintelligible outside their incarnations in material expressions. If the state is imagined as Anderson says, then all civil religion is a product of imagination in much the same way the statue can be a product of imagination. This means that both religion and the state are consciously created works of art and therefore merits this study. In the words of Gramsci (1999: 441) there is a certain kind of "fetishism" here that binds civil religion to the state. For Gramsci (ibid), the fetish is in that no individual part that constitutes the organism can exist on its own. In the same way, the state cannot exist without materialities of civil religion. In other words, one cannot possess and own materialities without the presence of a transcendental state and religion that serve to underwrite ownership and possession: materialities are not merely defined by immanence or an immanent religion as posited by some scholars like Deleuze and Guattari (1987). In the third place the chapter will examine how materialities have been transformed into symbols that convey meaning and value to the adherence of this religion. The chapter will conclude by highlighting how materialities and symbols of civil religion have been used to construct and sustain the ideal unified nation state.

The term materialities refers to mere things that tend to last and these might be stones or important objects such as manuscripts, porcelain, vestments, discarded papyri, writings on tombs and temples. A study of the material objects does give us an insight into the past and the present. A careful study of artefacts such as tombs of the unknown soldiers, tombs of the fallen heroes and other material objects tell stories of how the living human beings interact with the objects and what value they place in what these objects stand for. The contemporary discourses on materiality studies is taking the direction of studying the lives of material objects as subjects and that ideas and beliefs begin in material reality. I do not propose to delve far into the issue but to examine how the material objects of civil religion have been used to unify a nascent state. The material study of civil religion will enable us to find out how civil religion happens materially and how it is expressed in material form (Meyer *et.al*, 2010:209).

Material objects have a symbolic function in civil religion. The objects are also symbols themselves. Geertz (1973) defines symbols as things that point to someone something else as in the case of a sign post showing that one has arrived in town. They both have a denotative and a connotative meaning, although postmodernists and poststructuralists would want to argue for the effacement of binaries between signifiers and signified. The symbols themselves become sacred. The tomb of the Unknown Soldier in civil religion becomes a real tomb (denotative) but it covey the feeling and emotions about those whose graves were not located (connotative meaning). In another sense, symbols are used for conventional signs of one sort or another as in red flags which might be a symbol of danger whilst the white cloth might be a symbol of peace. In the third sense, it refers to something that is confined to something which expresses in oblique and figurative manners that which cannot be stated in a literal and direct way. The fourth definition is that the word symbol is used for objects, events, acts or quality which serves as a vehicle for a conception. The conception becomes the meaning of the symbol (Geertz, 1973:91).

Defining Civil Religion

In his classical definition, Bellah (1967: 12)) defined Civil Religion as a genuine apprehension of universal transcended religious experiences of the American people. In another book entitled "The Habits of the Heart: Individualism and Commitment in American Life", Bellah (1985: 142) argued that whatever the differences among American people and the resulting differences in understanding individualism, there are some things they share, things that are basic to American identity. Bellah further argues, in the same book, that most Americans share common religious characteristics expressed through rituals and symbols. They share the idea of the deity, the idea of memorial sites such as Arlington cemetery, America as a chosen race, giving meaning to the American secular symbols such as the Flag, Presidential inaugurations and national holidays (Wimberly and Christensen, 1981: 91).

Materialities of civil religion that we are going to look at relate to state actors, the Kalashnikov split in two lying back to back at the national hero's acre, the statues such as the tomb of the Unknown Soldiers and a host of murals depicting the colonial tortuous path that the people of Zimbabwe trod till independence. In a chapter, 'Civil religion unpacking the concept on unpacking,' I made an exploration of colonial Rhodesian material objects of civil religion (Ruzivo, 2010: 1-18). That chapter presents a detailed study of colonial Rhodesian material objects of civil religion. These constitute the materialities of the Zimbabwean civil religion on the national level. After gaining independence in 1980 the nascent postcolonial Zimbabwean state embarked on a process of consolidating political and economic power. There was need to unite all the different ethnic groups of people as well as thousands of white people that colonised Zimbabwe and settled in the country. Whilst Zimbabwe has many religions such as Christianity, African Traditional Religion, Islam, Hinduism, and Buddhism one way of uniting the nascent postcolonial state was by crafting a cult of the state elevated above a variety of religions. It is a cult of the state insofar as it is a program of the state that is organised by it with the president as the high priest of the nation. The cult of the state would transcend ethnic rivalries and differences between the Shona, Ndebele and ethnic groups speaking different languages. In this sense, the absence or disappearance of the [African] state and its cult of civil religion would result in chaos and anarchy which anarchy is sadly being celebrated by some postmodernist and poststructuralist scholars who are keen to hack down African sovereignty and order as well as to pre-empt African struggles for restoration and control over their resources.

Holidays and Materialities of Civil Religion

After independence, the winning party ZANU PF constituted a government and this government instituted certain fundamental tenets that make-up what we may call civil religion. Like all governments in the world, the postcolonial Zimbabwean government instituted national holidays such as the celebration of the formal political Independence Day annually, on the 18th of April. Presidential speeches encoded in texts prepared for the occasion become sacred material for the Independence Day celebrations. The text itself embodies images of the liberation struggle. The presidential motorcade accompanied by motor bikes, the police vehicles and other state security systems are all symbols and objects of civil religion. The paraphernalia and trappings of power that accompany the president show how material objects, paradoxically in a country that has not had material economic independence, communicate the sacredness that surrounds the office of the president. There is an appropriation of the sacredness, which is usually associated with religion, into the office of the president. Here the sacredness serves the secular purpose. They, without question, speak to the nation that the day in question is a special day that is distinct from all other days. In this sense, Zimbabweans like all other people in the world make conscious decisions to separate things, including days and objects:

objects that are sacred are separated or distinguished from objects that are not sacred; citizens who are national heroes are separated or distinguished from citizens who are not heroes. Thus, contrary to postmodernist and poststructuralist postulations – binaries, distinctions or separations are functional in society.

The presence of the president as the chief priest of the nation and a coterie of government functionaries may be considered as also materialities of Zimbabwe's civil religion. The presidential speech becomes a sermon, in the sense that the president takes the opportunity to direct the nation and the state in areas that may affect the cohesion of the nation. The singing of liberation songs, the inspection of the guard of honour by the president, the lighting of the independence flame and all other ceremonies and pomp accompanying the celebrations constitute symbolic rituals of the cult of the state. The flame is a symbol of the aspirations of the Zimbabwean people: the aspiration of enjoying this independency forever. The flyby by mig21 fighter jets saves to show the military power and sanctity of the state as an institution with ultimate earthily authority within the jurisdiction/territory. In fact, Independence Day celebrations proceedings can be rightly paralleled to church liturgy. Every the state has its holidays that have been set apart to commemorate certain events with a bearing to that state. The United Nations has its special days such as Remembering the Rwandan Genocide, Remembering the Transatlantic slavery and commemorating the World War II, to observe certain events that are considered to be important to the United Nations body.

The National Heroes Acre and Civil Religion in Zimbabwe

The nascent state of Zimbabwe came up with a plan to build a national heroes acre in 1980 and it was opened in 1981. The purpose was to honour the fallen heroes. The burial ground is regarded as a sacred shrine. It is regarded as sacred because the sacredness that is generally associated with tombs has been appropriated into the civil religion of the state. This validates Morgan's (2009) observation that a site becomes sacred when people ritually mark the site where the person disappeared or is buried. Among the Shona people,

157

cemeteries are believed to be places frequented by the dead. Morgan (ibid) reifies this belief by stating that those that have disappeared as in the case of those whose remains have not been recovered may come back to the marked sport at the tomb of Unknown Soldier. There is a forty-metre tower that is significant and symbolical. It holds the eternal flame that was lit on Independence Day in 1980. It symbolises the spirit of independence as opposed to the spirit of (neo-)colonial servitude (The Patriot, 2011 3 July). A cave behind the tomb of the Unknown Soldier symbolises remembrance of the disappeared so that they may not be dead in a memorial sense (Morgan, 2010:23). The heroes' acre is the last sedimenting place for the remains of heroes. It is here that their bodies rest and their souls go to the ancestral world or *nyikadzimu* (see Nhemachena, 2017). It is the last position that is associated with the bodies of the heroes. The burial places generate, in the minds of the living, a reinvigorated memory of the departed. It evokes the spirit of sacrifice as a virtue among the living, as the highest ideal. The souls of the departed, through regular commemoration, frequent the living. The repeated stories of their involvement in the liberation struggle keep them alive in the memory of the living. The bones of the fallen heroes buried at the shrine symbolise the story of the liberation struggle. They symbolise the story of unity which serves to unify the state. The materials connect the living and the souls of the dead heroes into one community. The narratives of the dead heroes are narratives, indeed, of material religion. Through the presiding high priest of the nation, the president, a connection is established between the realm of material objects with that of the souls of the departed and with the Heavenly God. This connection is celebrated and performed using the fallen bodies of heroes, flowers wreath in memory of the dead. On the part of rulers, the bodies of the dead like those of the saints in churches are used to obtain divine power and to demonstrate authority and continuity. Here the bodies of the dead symbolise that those interred at the heroes' acre have played a special role and deserve preferential treatment. In African traditional religion death is not the end of the road. The deceased become the living dead in the ancestral world. They die only when no one can remember them. The significance of the heroes' acre and heroes' graves have often been used by the state to discredit opponents who are perceived to be its rivals or competitor in politics. Reference to 'fallen gallant fighters' sets the souls of the dead apart from all other dead figures (Hutchings and McKenzie, 2017:3-4).

The materials on the National Shine tell a story to generations of Zimbabwean citizens that have no idea of what went on in the anticolonial struggles of the past. Civil religion happens materially and 'society happens materially through material religion' (Meyer, 2010:209). Thus, on both sides of the tomb of the Unknown Soldier are murals that illustrate the history of Zimbabwe's liberation struggle from the period of occupation to independence in 1980. The surfaces are made of hard substance to show that Zimbabwe's independence was not given on a silver platter. The struggle for the independence of Zimbabwe was a contested affair between the white minority government and the various political groups that we have looked at above. On the right side of the tomb of the unknown soldiers are murals that show the period the 'pioneer column' entered the country. The Whiteman's brutality to Black people is well illustrated on the murals. The use of dogs, whips and guns depicted on the murals is meant to justify why the Blacks had to resort to armed combat to free themselves from the disinheritance, dispossession, exploitation and tyranny of colonialism. The climax of the struggle is the independence, since 1980, that is enjoyed by men and women as well as children within the country. The President of Zimbabwe is clearly depicted in the murals leading his people to victory. He is not only the President but the high priest of the nation who stands like Moses the lawgiver between his people and God.

As we have observed that materialities at the national shrine tell a history, the heroes' acre, as we have said above, has the Kalashnikov shape (AK 47 rifle). It is like two rifles with their backs to each other. The Kalashnikov rifle is a symbol for the independence not just of Zimbabwe but of Africa. When observed from the air the terraces on which people sit are the butt of the gun whilst the steps that lead to the tomb of the Unknown Soldier are nozzle of the barrel. The murals that we have been describing above resemble the handle and the terraced graves resemble the magazine of the rifle. Although the depiction is without contestation, it is a well-known fact that the narrative that carries the day is normally that of the victors. The tomb of the Unknown Soldier stands for the trigger of the Kalashnikov. The conical tower stands for the bayonet of the gun (The Patriot, 3 July 2011).

The National Flag and its Importance

The national flag is part of the materialities of the national shrine. Its colours are, green, yellow, white, red and black. The flag conveys the idea of national identity, geographic location and the collective aspirations of the people of Zimbabwe. Green symbolises the idea of the green vegetation and that the people of Zimbabwe are agriculturalists. Yellow conveys the idea of minerals that the African ancestors and the Heavenly God have graced the country with. Red represents the blood that was shed from the first uprising to the second uprising against colonialism. It is a reminder to the generations of today and tomorrow that the sovereignty and independence they have has been fought for. Black represents the Black majority of the country. Last, white stands for peace that was brought about because of the armed struggle. The Zimbabwe bird represents the builders of the Great Zimbabwe stone monument, a symbol of the civilisation of the Zimbabwean people (www.povo.co.zw/poster/zimbabwecourt of arms).

Fontein (2016) observed that early archaeologists conducting scientific excavations at Great Zimbabwe from 1889 to 1902 looted the Zimbabwe soapstone birds. Tombs were desecrated by these Euro-American fortune seekers some of whom are currently refusing to repatriate the looted artefacts to Africa. Some human remains were also stolen by the colonist and other Western looters. The soapstone birds were an important symbol of the earliest Black people to inhabit the place. The birds were discovered all facing to the Eastern direction. The significance might be that those who first settled there were of the *Shiri* clan who might have migrated from the great lakes region. The Hungwe soapstone bird is associated with water. The birds symbolised the direction that the Hungwe clan had migrated from. The Hungwe people were the first people to settle in the area and were therefore approached by the African new comers to intercede with God for rain on their behalf (Mufuka, 2012).

The Court of Arms as Materiality of Civil Religion

Another feature whose materialities speak to the present and to the future of the Zimbabwean state is the court of arms. A careful study of this iconic materiality will reveal what it embodies. The socialist aspirations of postcolonial Zimbabwe are symbolised by the star on the court of arms. The hoe shows the agricultural nature of most of the Zimbabwean people. In the newly independent Zimbabwe there is a transition from the gun to the hoe, **a symbol of the African work ethic**. Two kudus are symbolic of ethnic unity that abides in the country as shown by the emblazoned strip with words unity, freedom and work. The mound that the kudus are standing on represents the earth from which the Zimbabweans should eke out their survival by working and not, as encouraged by some in the contemporary era, by merely receiving Non-Governmental Organisations' hand-outs in the so-called global sharing economy. There is a green shield with a striped top. Green is a symbol of the fertility of the country. The strips which are white and blue are fourteen in number. Inside the shield is a symbol of the Great Zimbabwe. The strips of silk gold and green are a depiction of the financial activities and protection of the economy from the country's enemies. The red star as in the flag conveys the socialist ideology of the early post-independence government and the sense of equality among the citizenry. Blue and white strips represent the majestic wonders of Mosia Tunya (Victoria Falls). The Zimbabwe bird is an iconic symbol that symbolises the migration of the ancestors of the Zimbabwean people from the area of the Great Lakes region to Southern Africa.

The material objects of civil religion that we have looked at above have become part of the Zimbabwean national memory. Thousands of people that throng the National Heroes Acre every year during the burial of heroes express their loyalty to the country as the monuments speak to the sacrificial role played by those who are buried in the national, provincial and district hero's acres. Orsi (2010:

161

XI) observed, "Remembering is a devotional act. These objects make real and visible what hurts or preoccupies the petitioners by putting into material form their hopes for healing and expressions of gratitude for the Madonna's intercession. So, do the letters to me". The material objects in a way add something to the past, a sure sign that the story of the past is never final.

Materialities of civil religion are images of that which we do not see. John of Damascus in the 8th century, the iconodulist, observed that even divine scriptures "clothe" both God and the Angels. He even went further to argue that creation itself is the image of the invisible God. In John's view, images are also inscribed in the writing itself. John's argument is applicable to materialities of religion (Damascene, 1898). If both the images that are visible and those images contained in the inscriptions like those one would find at the Heroes Acre or on the Court of Arms are removed, then there is a disenchantment, to use Max Weber's term (Grosby, 2013), between the living and that which they can no longer behold. Generations that did not witness the Zimbabwean liberation struggle learn through images what went on before them. This is exactly what television images do. We believe what has happened elsewhere by watching representations that have been made by human technology. Plate (2005) observes that the focus of sense perception is on how we perceive our world through vision, taste, touch and hearing. Sensation arises when stimuli from the outside world are received through the bodily senses. The brain using its grid reference interprets and give meaning to the data received. Sense perception is a primary component of our interaction with religious myths, rituals, symbols and memories and it's the fundamental nexus for understanding religion and art and a bridge between the two. Sense perceptions do link the inner world to the world outside. The human body is linked to material objects that are in proximity to it. The society and community are by-products of the activities of perception (Plate, 2005:2). As we have shown, perception is not perception of the void. It is a perception of the materialities.

Conclusion

The Materialities of civil religion that we have looked at have served to unify the nation. The paraphernalia and trappings of power do show the connections between sacred offices and the material objects that point to their presence. Without these material objects the aura of sacredness is disenchanted. Material objects such as the national flag have been used as a rallying point for national unity. Rituals such as the lighting of the Independence flame at Independence Day celebrations point to what is beyond the material. The flame itself is an embodiment of the aspirations of the Zimbabwean people to remain sovereign and enjoy their independence forever. The material objects act as the connecting link between the material world and the spirit world. The Zimbabwean National Heroes' Acre and other smaller shrines dotted throughout the country, as we have observed, are rallying points of unity during Independence Day celebrations. These objects themselves sum up the history of the country from colonization to independence. We have also seen that, in the gatherings, the narratives of the bygone decades are used to reinforce unity. Those who sacrificed their lives in liberating the country are praised whilst those who betrayed the liberation struggle are chastised. This is a device meant to unify the nation. The material objects are reinforced by other non-material objects such as the singing of ideological liberation war songs to remind the nation where it came from, and national anthem that embodies the values, potentialities and aspirations of the Zimbabwean people. Material objects are not only symbolical but are narratives of dramas that we can no longer participate in but re-enact through rituals carried out during memorial days, important holidays such as Independence Day celebrations. In as much as great global religions like Christianity, Judaism, Islam and African Traditional Religions just to mention a few have their own materialities whilst the cult of the state has its own materialities that make it comprehensible.

References

Allies, M. H (trans.) (1898) *St John Damascene on Holy Images: Followed by Sermons on Assumption,* London: Thomas Baker.

Anderson, B. (1991) *Imagined Communities: Reflections on the Origin and Spread of Nationalism,* London: VERSO.

Bellah, R. (1967) 'Civil religion in America' *Daedelus: Journal of American Academy of Arts and Science* Vol. 96.

Bellah, R., Madisen, R., Sullivan, W. M., Swidler, A., and Tipton, S. M. (1985) *Habits of the Heart: Individualism and Commitment in American Life,* New Delhi: Tata McGraw-Hill Co. Ltd.

Chitando E. (2010) *Prayers and Players: Religion and Politics in Zimbabwe,* Harare: SAPES Trust.

Deleuze, G. and Guattari, F. (1987) *A Thousand Plateaus: Capitalism and Schizophrenia.* Minneapolis: University of Minnesota Press.

Fontein, J. (2016) Rain, Power, Sovereignty and the Materiality of Signs in Southern Zimbabwe, in Beardsley, J. (ed) *Cultural Landscape Heritage in Sub-Saharan Africa.* Harvard: Dumbarton Oaks.

Geertz, C. (1973) *The Interpretation of Culture: Selected Essays,* New York: Basic Books.

Gramsci, A. (1999) *Selections from Prison Notebook,* London: Elec book.

Grosby, S. (2013) Max Weber, Religion, and the Disenchantment of the World, in *Society* Vol 50 (3): 301-310.

http://www.financialgazette.co.zw/secrets-of-the-hungwe-clan/

https://www.thepatriot.co.zw/old_posts/insight-into-national-heroes-acre/

https://www.thepatriot.co.zw/old_posts/struggle-for-zimbabwe-the-internal-settlement-of-1978/

Hallencreutz, C. F (1998) Religion and Politics in Harare 1890-1980, Uppsala: Swedish Missionary Institute of Research.

Hutchings, T. and Mckenzie, J. (eds.) (2017) *Materiality and the Study of Religion: The Stuff of the Sacred,* New York. London: Routledge.

Meyer, B. (2010) 'The Origin and Mission of Material Religion', *Material Religion* Vol. 40.

Morgan, D., (ed.) (2009) *Religion and Material Culture: The Matter of Belief,* London: Routledge.

Murdoch, N. H. (2015) *Christian Warfare in Rhodesia-Zimbabwe: The Salvation Army and African Liberation*. Cambridge: Lutterworth Press.

Nhemachena, A. (2017) *Relationality and Resilience in a Not So Relational World: Knowledge, Chivanhu and (De-)Coloniality in 21st Century Conflict-Torn Zimbabwe*. Bamenda: Langaa Publishers.

Orsi, R. A. (2010) *The Madonna of the 115th Street: Faith and Community in Italian Harlem*, Yale: Yale University Press.

Plate, B. S. (2005) *Walter Benjamin, Religion and Aesthetics: Rethinking Religion through the Aesthetics*. New York, London: Routledge.

Sadomba, Z. W. (2011) *War Veterans in Zimbabwe's Revolution Challenging Neo-colonialism and Settler and International Capital*. Harare: Weaver Press.

Wimberly, R. C. and Christensen, J. A. (1980) 'Civil Religion and Church and State', *Sociology Quarterly* Vol. 21.

www.povo.co.zw/poster/zimbabwecourtofarms Accessed 01/08/2017

Chapter Six

Un-naming the Nameables: An Ecocritical Perspective of Operation *Murambatsvina* in NoViolet Bulawayo's We Need New Names

Juliet Sylvia Pasi

Introduction

The chapter incisively analyses the unjustifiable "connections" between the environment and humans in NoViolet Bulawayo's (2013) *We Need New Names*. Premised on the ecocriticism and ecofeminism lens, this chapter reveals that Bulawayo's narrative addresses social injustices such as land, environmental degradation, and impoverishment. Bulawayo's novel suggests a different historical trajectory; rather than seeing the roots of the people's suffering in colonialism, she points to the new environmental themes such as resource "grabbing", capitalist patriarchy, immigrants and mal-development. A reading of the novel reveals that supposed [African] human greed for domination and possession of land, and inappropriate development policies are primarily responsible for the less privileged Zimbabweans' plight. A close examination of the representation of Operation *Murambatsvina* in the novel reveals how the earth's basic life systems are endangered and demolished in the name of progress. Operation *Murambatsvina* was a government of Zimbabwe execution to demolish urban nonformal settlement and activities. Furthermore, the chapter contends that nature is an archetypal image of serenity and harmony. As such, its disruption is considered by some thinkers as analogous to the exploitation of humans. Nature is portrayed in the book as a disputing metaphor of regeneration where women and children struggle to attain new [postmodern] identities. Not only are these new identities localised, but they transcend borders to affect the female [African] immigrants in as far as the United States of America. In an animistic sense,

167

operation *Murambatsvina* is used analogously and inaccurately to represent the supposed discontinued "relationship" between humans and nonhuman nature. Thus, as a subject, the environment is perceived as a part of a whole, a biocentric world-view in which humanity, the nonhuman and the environment are deemed to exist. This chapter posits that by depriving the people of the land and the materialities that sustain them, Operation *Murambatsvina* destroyed their wholesome and sustainable lifestyles. Hence, an examination of the devastated environment in Bulawayo's (2013) *We Need New Names* leverages a critique of all forms of destruction of humans and nature. The chapter will conclude that in Bulawayo's (2013) *We Need New Names*, environmental destruction is considered as perpetuating the "domination" of women, children and nature in a patriarchal society. In short, I argue that putting women, children and nature on the same plane, as some authors do, perpetuates enslavement and colonial era renditions of [African] women as indistinct from beasts/animals of burden. In this sense, portraying women, children and nature as indistinct from each other is not necessarily decolonising but it replicates colonial portrayals of [African] women as indistinct from "things", "animals" or "beasts".

We Need New Names (abbreviated herein as WN) is set in the twenty-first century and in a post-independent African state where material resources are supposedly owned by and belong to all. The novel reflects new environmental themes such as resource "grabbing", capitalist patriarchy, immigrants and mal-development, taking its cue from minority traditions of resistance to injustice. The chapter situates Bulawayo's narrative in terms of socio-environmental justice and argues that *We Need New Names* redefines the environment and materialities by "connecting" political and social injustice issues with environmental issues. The novel focuses on the metaphorisation of environments riddled with social problems such as HIV and AIDS, migrant workers, lack of food, racism and above all the immigrants in America. This chapter thus, sets out to demonstrate the impact the environment has on the black female, male and children characters in the narrative. Highlighting this intricate "relationship", the chapter will illustrate how domination by race, sex and nation are seen as ills themselves, as well as practices that contribute to the destruction of the environment. An analysis of this web-like symbiotic "relationship" reveals the "interconnections" between the oppression of women and the destruction of the rest of nature (Ruether, 1992; Birkeland, 1993; Warren, 1997). Hence, an examination of the devastated environment in *We Need New Names* leverages a critique of all forms of violence against women and destruction of nature and its imbrications with new forms of [global] scrambles for and political-economies of materialities in contemporary Africa.

The analysis of the novel also critiques forms of development that do not take environmental degradation and their ramifications on the low-income groups, the disinherited and dispossessed women and children into consideration. The above perspective is anchored in the view that resistance discourses around the figuring of the environment are "shaped by accelerating processes of globalisation, exploitation and monopolisation of natural resources" (Harrison, 2012: 4). Resource "grabbing", capitalist patriarchy and mal-development are used to exploit resources in the novel *We Need New Names*. This chapter argues that, what is construed as development and growth in Bulawayo's novel deprives the disinherited and dispossessed of the vital resources of their lives and livelihoods (Shiva, 2014). Hence, this chapter reveals that Bulawayo's narrative addresses social injustices such as land and environmental degradation, and impoverishment of Africans. The chapter further argues that the narrative should also have looked at matters of dispossession and disinheritance of [African] others. It also shows the negative impact such social injustices have on humans, specifically, women and children.

Furthermore, the chapter contends that nature is considered, by some writers, as an image of serenity and harmony. As such, its disruption is derogatorily and animistically considered by such writers as analogous to the exploitation of women and children. Bulawayo uses Operation *Murambatsvina* or Operation Restore Order to demonstrate the symbiosis or living "interconnectedness" between nature and human society. Bulawayo chooses to un-name this operation by referring to it as "The Bulldozers." Metaphorising and un-naming this historical event, enables the child narrator, Darling to

169

describe the "brutal" impact of the bulldozers on both the people and the environment. Once the life-sustaining environment is destroyed, the human society is also denied its basic and fundamental needs of food, shelter, clothing, love and so on. Operation *Murambatsvina's* main project was to 'develop' or improve the well-being of all but unfortunately, it "affected hundreds of thousands of impoverished urban residents (Potts, 2006: 273). The government viewed it as an operation to restore order in the country's urban areas. Its main agenda was to eradicate illegal housing structures and activities from the cities (Potts, ibid). The Zimbabwean President, Robert Mugabe reaffirmed this agenda on 25 June 2005, during the opening of the 22nd Zimbabwe African National Union Patriotic Front (ZANU PF) National Consultative Assembly in Harare. He told the delegates that this was a clean-up operation or a reconstruction programme designed to "weed out hideouts of crime and grime, filthy stalls and encourage the construction of orderly, planned and tidy residential and business structures in their place" (Makamani, 2013:176).

However, what this development did not indicate was the environmental destruction and the impoverishment of Africans that is associated with development processes" (Shiva 2014). In spite of the fact that all development processes, including international development projects necessarily have side-effects on Africans, much critique focused on the side-effects of the Zimbabwean government's Operation *Murambatsvina* or the urban clean-up campaign. Hence, in the novel *We Need New Names,* the child narrator, Darling laments that they live in a tin house, where everything is unreal; her parents' bed is made up of "plastic and chicken's and duck's feathers and old pieces of cloth" (WN, 63). Mother also complains about the tinned house in Paradise and the scarcity of food. Both the social and the economic orders of their lives are changed completely and what remains is an impoverished ecosystem which can no longer sustain the people. Shiva (2014: 73) further contends that the "scarcity of water, soil fertility, and genetic wealth are considerably diminished as a result of the development process." Such natural resources form the bedrock of the people's productive economy. Although their scarcity impoverishes men, women and children in *We Need New Names*, an ecocritical and ecofeminist analysis of the text reveals that it has more of a detrimental impact on women and children than on men. Momsen (1995) also notes that as household managers, women are the first to suffer when disinherited or dispossessed and when access to sustainable livelihoods is unbalanced. Hence, the environmental destruction, a result of Operation *Murambatsvina* helps us understand why Mother must go to the boarder to sell and why she has a secret relationship with another man. Darling says she doesn't know what the man looks like but he comes in like a ghost and sneaks away at night (WN, 64).

Plot Summary: *We Need New Names*

NoViolet Bulawayo's debut novel, *We Need New Names*, is narrated by a young protagonist, Darling. The ten year old Darling chronicles her life experiences from the imaginary city of Paradise where she lives with her friends, Bastard, Chipo, Godknows, Sbho and Stina. She narrates the violence, the poverty and the struggles that they face in the shantytown of Paradise. The early chapters of the novel are narrated through the unapologetic and honest voice of a child as she navigates her way through the poverty stricken, diseased and violent world of which Zimbabwe is situated in. She describes how through Operation *Murambatsvina*, her first ramshackle home was demolished under President Mugabe's rule. After their homes are destroyed, Darling and her friends resort to stealing guavas from the affluent suburb of Budapest where most of the white people live. The two distinct worlds of Paradise and Budapest show the different life-styles between the blacks and the white community. The names given to Darling's friends, Bastard, Chipo, Godknows, Sbho, and Stina allow the reader to identify with their pain, suffering and struggles in the impoverished environment of Paradise. The unnaming of the disease HIV/AIDS, Operation *Murambatsvina* and Chipo's pregnancy also enables one to imagine and creatively contextualise the novel in Zimbabwe's history, political and economic struggles of the affected people. Darling moves to America to join her Aunt Fostolina. As an immigrant, she is confronted by different challenges that she has to overcome to survive, for example, the change in climate, racism, segregation and missing home. Her journey from Paradise to Michigan enables her to understand the complex nature of the ambiguous meaning of what upward mobility and life as an immigrant feels like. The ideals that she had about America, human rights and democracy are dismantled in the process. The ending of the novel is not conclusive as Darling is torn between going to college and memories of her life in Paradise and her friends.

Un-naming the Nameables: An Ecofeminist Perspective

We Need New Names gives new names to a number of known events and features, and it affords one distinct grammars of articulation to qualitatively spell out that which is unrepresentable. Darling's father suffers from AIDS, referred to as "The Sickness." Chipo's friends refer to her pregnancy as the "the stomach", which are euphemisms which enable the characters to live with and thereby give agreeable linguistic markers to their environment. The Operation *Murambatsvina* event is not named as such but is described through Darling's experiences. Darling's narration reveals how the women and children are affected by the destruction of the environment. It is an account that reveals that what hegemonics do to the environment parallels these hegemonics' dispossession, disinheritance and domination of the marginalised, women and children. In the novel, some of the British Broadcasting Corporation and Cable News Network presenters compare the destruction of the people's homes by the bulldozers to a tsunami and they say, it is like "A fucking tsunami walks on water, […] it came out of the water and left all those people dead in that other country (WN, 67-68). The metaphor of the tsunami reflects the magnitude of the environmental destruction. A tsunami is merciless "as it erupts from a ferocious quake within the earth and ferociously gushes onto land and destroys everything in its path…" (Fitzpatrick, 2015:11). The tsunami obliterates the environment, displaces people and leaves them houseless. Further, the earth that sustains their livelihood is stripped bare and they are left with nothing to eat, and with no place they can call house; with no clothes and no hope. Getting through the crisis requires an understanding of the effect that humans have on nature, owning and possessing it, affecting it and being affected by it. Specifically, environmental issues have to be seen as human issues since the ecosystem is positioned at the centre of everything. The "connection" between humans and the environment intensifies as both are violated by the actions of those in political and economic power. Thus, the earth's basic support life systems are destroyed, not just through 'development' but through some humans' actions. The bulldozers have "metal teeth" (WN, 65) and when they finally leave, "everything is, everything is smashed, everything is wrecked [...] broken bricks everywhere, tears on people's faces everywhere" (WN, 66). The government ordered steel jaws to destroy houses and informal ramshackle in the clean-up campaign but this sadly also shattered some citizens' lives, and their dreams were shattered, leaving behind painful memories. Also implied in this destructive process is that, the force of the government was presented as akin to a force of nature, like a tsunami, beyond the people's control (Fitzpatrick, 2015:11).

The nature of the "connection" between humans and the environment as presented in Bulawayo's literary text is a major concern of ecocriticism. Hence, the argument proffered here is that Bulawayo uses the girl-child voice to conscientise the readers about human activities and policies that lead to destruction of houses. Darling is given a voice when she renames this historical event. Thus, the girl-child is made visible as she recounts the incident from an insider's view, after having been silenced through the West's media reports. Hence, the "connection" with the environment affords her a platform to speak and name the un-nameable.

The view that nature holds an important place in the lives of these people as they relocate to Paradise is reflected in Bulawayo's descriptions of their movements. Their movements are "animalised" and such **personification** not only vitalises the role of **fiction** in articulating issues which are central to African materialities and symbolisms but also shows the structures and dynamics of aesthetics in an ecologically evolving Africa. The novel records how they appeared single file, "like ants; in swarms, like flies and in angry waves, like a wretched sea" (WN, 73). The **metaphor** of "ants" and

173

"flies" demonstrates and reinforces the inferior status of the people, and noteworthy is that the setting of the novel is in "independent" Africa which is still situated in the structuring resilient global matrix of economic and political power. In fact describing Africans as "ants", "flies" and so on dates back to the colonial dehumanisation and caricaturing of Africans (Nhemachena, 2016; Magubane, 2007).

Operation *Murambatsvina* reduced the victims to nothingness, stripped them of their remnants of dignity and individual existence and this form of dehumanisation is beyond mere quantification of deprivation and materiality measured in numerical terms. Their shared and common experience of anger at their loss and their brokenness gives them a singular identity as they all look the same. The government planned Operation *Murambatsvina* increased the vulnerability of the victims. It worsened the pauperisation of the victims, inferiorising them into "ants" and "flies" (WN, 73). Women, children and men are homogenised, in the narrative, into the singular "swarm" (ibid) identity which renders them powerless. They are portrayed as targets of oppression and exploitation by the Zimbabwean government's "maldevelopment" (Shiva, 2014: 79) programme. Their anger, portrayed in the narrative as the "angry waves" is reflected by Rigby (cited in Gaard *et al*, 2013: 129). Rigby (ibid) also observes that, "homogenization is intrinsic to the logic of colonisation, whereby the Other is not regarded as an individual," but as a "member of a class stereotyped as interchangeable, replaceable, all alike […], the colonised are stereotyped as 'all the same' in their deficiency" (Plumwood, 2002: 102). However, it is also necessary to note that colonisation also thrived on individualistic ideologies that were used to generate and sustain colonial divide and rule tactics. Therefore, this **symbolisation** and **metaphorisation** through literary criticism affords us more viewpoints to think about and think through the much needed processes of decoloniality which puts at the fore the need to understand ecological and restorative material concerns in present day Africa.

However, one also observes a subversion of this homogenisation in which the age and gender stereotypes are debunked. For instance, MotherLove is not just portrayed in the narrative as inherently nurturing and close to nature, but she is an epitome of resistance as she creates survival strategies that help sustain the 'broken' community. Her affinity to nature facilitates a strong link between the people and the nonhuman environment. Also, Darling and her friends show how, despite the destroyed environment, Paradise is a beautiful, peaceful and heavenly habitat. Despite the lack of health and educational facilities, the people can survive. The imaginary habitat of Paradise is also described as "all tin and stretches out in the sun like a wet sheepskin nailed on the ground to dry; the shacks are the muddy colour of dirty puddles after the rains" (WN, 34). The metaphor of the sheepskin suggests that besides being endangered by the hot sun and being weathered like a sheepskin, the soil still sustains a lot of people. The Biblical allusion therefore hints at the sense of innocence the people living there have, the same quality that is found in the natural environment that they occupy. This Biblical metaphor and allusion is further corroborated by the name "paradise". What makes Paradise a "paradise" is that it is a home to many. Although the land may be flawed, and may not be the ideal city home, Paradise is a beautiful haven for the disinherited, dispossessed and for those with demolished homes. Darling and her friends are able to identify with it because of its supposed heavenly and inherent beauty. However, portraying shacks as heaven for disinherited blacks can amount to naturalising the shacks as the ideal place for blacks. It misrepresents blacks as incapable of imagining their lives beyond shack settlements. The narrative proceeds to present, places like Budapest and Michigan as lacking this "innate" beauty because of their racist tendencies and the extremely cold weather, in the global north, that destroys all plants in the environment.

Ecofeminism and Operation *Murambatsvina*

The destruction of houses and other facilities through Operation *Murambatsvina* is presented as environmental "domination" and degradation in *We Need New Names*. Bulawayo dialogues implicitly with the Operation *Murambatsvina* but never engages with it in a substantial manner. The traumatic operation is chronicled from the perspective of a girl-child, Darling Nonkululeko Nkala. The girl-child's lens is used by Bulawayo to examine the "relationship" between the environment and society, in particular women and children. Paradise, the shanty residential area is where Darling and her friends, Bastard, Chipo, Stina, Sbho, and Godknows live. Although Bulawayo does not refer to the bulldozing of the houses in an explicit manner, through deft understatements and innuendoes, Darling conjures memories of the horrors of Operation *Murambatsvina*. Darling says that "the men knock down our house and Ncane's house and Josephat's house and Bongi's house and Sibo's house and many houses. [...] men driving metal, metal slamming brick, brick crumbling" (WN, 66). And when the bulldozers finally leave, "everything is broken, everything is smashed, and everything is wrecked. It is sad faces everywhere, choking dust everywhere, broken walls and bricks everywhere, tears on people's faces everywhere" (WN, 66). Through this heinous act, men, women and children are emotionally and psychologically broken. Significant to note is that the people in Paradise are made physically homeless. From an ecocritical stance, they are "uprooted from the soil of [their] ancestors" (Shiva, 2014: 99). Part of their lives is smashed by the steel jaws of the bulldozers and what is significant is the author's diction, where the use of the word "steel" denotes something that is devoid of feelings, something lifeless, without breath and without any capacity to empathise and or have a heart. More significantly, the environment that sustains the people is also demolished, which could be a mark of the possible extent of heartlessness in the world. The "connection" between people and their environment is disrupted through human action. This environmental crisis recalls Glotfelty and Fromm's (1996: xviii) definition of ecocriticism as an "earth centred-approach to literary studies". Glotfelty's (ibid) definition suggests that the environment provides for and sustains human beings and therefore that the interests of human beings must be subsumed under those of the environment. Using the same logic, Shiva (1994) asserts the interdependence of the human and nonhuman environment. Shiva (1994) underscores the belief that the causes of environmental degradation simultaneously cause a hegemonic culture of domination and the oppression.

In a bid to restore order in Bulawayo's (2013) *We Need New Names*, the earth's basic life systems are endangered and demolished in the name of progress and restoration of cleaner urban environments. The land that provided food and shelter for the people is desecrated in a bid by the Zimbabwean government to get rid of impoverished housing communities. As in other [including international] development projects, the "interconnectivity" between the people and nonhuman nature is sacrificed in the name of development. The people become "victims of progress" (Shiva, 2014: 99) as they are disinherited of the very soil "that provides the very essence of their being" (ibid). The people in Paradise are affected by this environment of harsh brutality and in such an environment all things begin to break down. To attest to this, Darling in *We Need New Names* points out that, "We didn't always live in this tin though. Before, we had a house and everything and we were happy. It was a real house with bricks, with a kitchen, sitting room, and two bedrooms. [...] Everything real" (WN, 62). Implied in Darling's utterance is that the government was responsible for the great imbalance enacted against the people and their environment. Such an imbalance suggests that the environment is part of a system in which humanity exists (Glotfelty & Fromm, 1996). The destruction of the people's homes simultaneously affects the environment and humans. However, despite their struggles and challenges, Bulawayo gives subjectivity and agency to her female characters and draws attention to important environmental issues that affect black women.

Operation *Murambatsvina* is depicted as being vicious to women. The women pay a disproportionately heavy price in the aftermath of Operation *Murambatsvina*. Mai Tari and Nomviyo offer a visual record of the devastation caused by the Operation. Mai Tari throws herself down in front of a bulldozer to protect her house. But one policeman hits her on the head with a gun and blood gushes out. Nomviyo had left her son Freedom sleeping in the house. They search for him in the rubble. When they find him, "his small body is so limp and covered in dust you think it's just a thing and a baby" (WN, 67). Such violence not only portrays the lack of sympathy by the ruling elite, but represents a threat to the social fabric and physical survival of a community. The destruction is just deplorable as Godknows points out later, that "There is nothing but trees and dry grass and brown earth […] and emptiness" (WN, 69). In the same vein, the operation leaves men, women and children with nothing but emptiness. The "dry grass and brown earth" represent the lifeless condition of the environment and the people in it, and through the use of pathetic fallacy, the author demonstrates the "connection" between humans and the natural environment. The pain is unbearable as people are left with no other form of urban accommodation. By giving centrality to the child's voice, Bulawayo is able to combine the environment, the feminine condition, the social and the political to give a holistic picture of the impact the destroyed had on the people.

The objective of Operation *Murambatsvina,* "to remove dirt" and cleanse the city of Harare, supposedly implies that Mai Tari's house and others, and Nomviyo's son, Freedom are part of the dirt that the ruling authorities need to get rid of. Chimedza (2008:89), refers to this dirt as the "crawling mass of maggots" […] "overwhelmingly composed of the economically weakest groups of all: women, children, the unemployed and underemployed, recent migrants from the rural areas trying to escape droughts and hunger […]" These marginalised people do not warrant consideration when the hegemonic [political and economic] elite makes decisions and policies. Nevertheless, because of the destruction, Darling and her family move to Paradise where her Mother complains about the tinned house, the food that is not there, the clothes and everything else. It is also significant to note that, as a direct consequence of the *Murambatsvina* Operation, the people in Paradise are deprived of the basic commodities such as food and [urban] shelter. As such, both the life-giving processes and human life are devalued. Hence, the violence against human beings, including women and children intensifies. The women are displaced and alienated from their livelihoods and the "natural resources on which their livelihoods depend – their land, their forests, their water, their seeds and biodiversity" (Shiva, 2014: xv). Bulawayo's account of *Murambatsvina* shows that the most vulnerable people are the women and children and experiences such as these shaped their livelihood. The ultimate devastation of the environment; including food crops and soils is a result of the so-called dirt-cleansing revolution.

Darling's account of *Operation Murambatsvina* reveals how the livelihood of the impoverished communities is destroyed. The impoverished people's history is erased. For instance, the black stool (WN, 74), passed on from generation to generation; representing Mzilawulandelwa's "whole history" (WN, 75) is also destroyed during *Murambatsvina*, and this ultimately affirms that what people do to the environment directly affects them. Apparent also is the important realisation of the "connectivity" between the environment and the woman and girl-child's livelihood in *We Need New Names*. In the narrative, there is no clear dividing line between the Operation *Murambatsviva* crisis, the Paradise environment and the women's livelihood. In fact, far from destroying the environment, the women's struggles are struggles for restoration and (re-)possession of land and houses, and significantly, of resistance. Such struggles are understood in line with ecofeminism philosophy; as a practical movement, which aims at addressing urgent mundane social concerns ranging from health, sexual abuse, political issues, restoration, reclamation, ownership and economic development. MotherLove's resilience keeps the community; men, women and children strong despite having lost their belongings, history and identity during Operation *Murambatsvina*. In Darling's dream, MotherLove's voice is likened to a swinging ripe fruit that one can put in one's mouth, and taste its sweetness (WN, 68). By naturalising MotherLoves' voice, the "connection" between women and nature is reinforced. Hence, Twine (2001) cements this view that women are connected to the environment. MotherLove's voice is therapeutic; it heals and soothes the wounded community and hence it brings peace to the community.

Paradise, the impoverished stricken residential township, with the tin shack dwellings, provides slums as shelter for many people. However, it is noted that Paradise is a diseased township as seen in Darling's father and the woman who hangs herself; both also have HIV/AIDS. The destruction of the environment affects the impoverished people in a deplorable manner. Darling's voice confirms that they own nothing except the deplorable memories of Operation *Murambatsvina*. With the environment destroyed, the community fails to get the essentials: food and [urban] shelter.

Though the men appeared to be strong in the presence of their women and children, alone "they fell apart like crumbling towers and wept with the wretched grief of forgotten concubines" (WN, 76). Displaced from their land and [impoverished] history, the community has to depend more on the environment for survival.

In scenario like the Operation *Murambatsvina*, what seems to be at stake is not just the people's lives but the safety of the whole; the ecosystem, the community and [urban] local knowledge (Shiva, 1994). Amidst the numerous challenges, it is the women's epistemological knowledge that keeps the [urban] community afloat. It is the women who, "gently rose from the hearths, beat dust off their skirts, and planted themselves like rocks in front of their men and children and shacks, and only then did all appear almost tolerable" (WN, 77). For example, it is MotherLove who engages in sustenance and activities to help people to forget their miseries. She "appeared with enormous barrels in which to brew a potent liquor that would make people forget. She also appeared with songs in her throat and the most colourful dresses in her sacks. Despite the circumstances, she refused to appear like something coming undone" (WN, 76). She engages her knowledge of the environment to challenge the situation. Thus, one might argue that through their environmental knowledge women are productive and reproductive. They also realise that environmental hazards are intricately linked to human hazards, hence they are inseparable. Thus, they turn to the environment for survival. Usher (1994:40) summarises this argument: "This crisis of ecological collapse demands that to survive, we move instead towards healing, towards the whole. As women, we must learn to become the measure of ourselves, in body and in mind. We must find strength within that is so deep and so rooted that it cannot be undermined".

Given the ecological collapse of the "local natural economy" (Shiva, 2014: 71), the infrastructure and the health system in Bulawayo's *We Need New Names*, MotherLove is seen as an "activist" and "symbol" of resistance. A new perspective to survival is created through women's inner strength; a creation of the whole, the biosphere. Her shebeen is not just a drinking place; it epitomises hope and a spiritual rebirth for the people in Paradise. They come together in MotherLove's shack to embrace the hope and joy of winning the elections. The bond that is created by the men and women could be perceived as a restorative strategy. Men and women are 'temporarily liberated' from their pain by coming together and helping each other, thus rendering fuzzy the male/female dualistic relationship.

The Forest and Mountain Spaces

The forest and the mountain space in *We Need New Names* gives a voice to the girl-child. One may argue that Bulawayo reclaims the forest and mountain space by asserting the girl-child's existence. Darling and her friends Godknows, Stina, Chipo, Sbho and Bastard live in a world where they are silenced and made invisible because of their age, gender and race. According to Bukenya (cited in Kaschula 2001: 33), the African girl-child is a "conspicuously 'silenced' person in a conspicuously 'silenced' continent" and the marginalised girl child's position in society is a result of this "silencing or de-oracisation" (ibid). As such, Bulawayo's re-naming of these children in the forest space is an attempt to draw attention to their visibility in a society that is riddled with political, social and economic problems. Fitzpatrick (2015: 3) reinforces this view by noting that, "Bulawayo's (2013) use of naming draws attention to the status of Darling as a subaltern, an individual that is usually one who was colonised and/or a female of colour that is rendered completely powerless because of their social status." The oppressed and subaltern status of the girl-child is represented by Bulawayo's renaming of Chipo's pregnancy and the rape.

Nonhuman nature (the forest) is presented as an archetypal image of serenity and harmony in *We Need New Names*. The forest space is transformed into an Emergency Room (ER) to save Chipo from her "stomach." A social transformation is already taking place as Darling and her friends obtain new names and new identities. In the forest, they become part of the ecological web of life, not as "masters, conquerors and owners of the Earth's resources" (Shiva, 2014: xxi) but as "members of the Earth family" (ibid). Thus, such strands of ecofeminism paradoxically deprive women of the right to possession and ownership of land and houses. Deemed to be merely part of the ecological webs of life, women are placed at the same level as animals and other freaks of nature much like during the colonial era. Darling and her friends take responsibility to care for the other weaker and disinherited members of the community like Chipo. They reject given "binarisms" and promote "reciprocity" with the environment when they use the forest space as an ER. A similar reciprocity is also evident in Mother's efforts to sustain the family. When Darling and Mother take care of Father, the values associated with the "dualistic" or "hierarchical" relationship are polarised. Hence, reading Bulawayo's (2013) novel this way underscores critical features of feminist ecology. An interrogation of Mother's and the children's "connection" to the environment reveals how ecofeminism is an "anti-dualistic" and "anti-hierarchical" form of thought but sadly one that neglects postcolonial [African] women's quest to reclaim, mastery, sovereignty, ownership and possession of their resources.

The downside of ecofeminism's theoretical exhortation for Africans to relinquish mastery, sovereignty, ownership and possession [in preference to flat ecological relationships] is underscored in matters of rape where ownership and possession of one's body should be at the core. In this sense, the crime of rape is premised on ownership, possession and mastery of one's body yet paradoxically ecofeminism exhorts giving up claims to mastery, sovereignty, ownership and possession. Chipo is raped by her grandfather at a very tender age. Bulawayo (2013) describes the sexual abuse without naming it per se as 'rape.' The rape is alluded to through Chipo's description of the rape act. She says, "He did that, my grandfather ... he got on me and pinned me down like that and he clamped a hand over my mouth and was heavy like a mountain" (WN, 41). Her pregnancy is not talked about. To the adults in Paradise, her condition is invisible. At the age of eleven, no one questions the pregnancy and the rape. Rather, the society in Paradise reinforces the silencing of the girl-child. Chipo is faced with a system which is based on unequal societal power relations; a system that is a part of the hegemonic agenda and conceives rape as normal. However, an examination of the woman-nature "relationship" in the novel reveals that Bulawayo seems to question the hegemonic [political and economic] hierarchical structure. By implication, she questions the functionality of both her family and society that has consistently and systematically denied her a voice or the "facility of oracy" (Bukenya in Kaschula, 2001:33). Amidst an insecure and sterile situation as a girl child in a patriarchal Zimbabwean society; a situation that is further aggravated by the harsh economic climate as well as the HIV/AIDS pandemic, thus the mountain space restores the girl-child's voice.

Chipo suffers emotional trauma. She has this confusing look; "this look of pain" (WN, 41). After the rape, Chipo stopped talking and if she really needed to say something, would use her hands (WN, 3). The African girl-child is heavily de-oracised yet ecofeminist likening the African girl child to nature further burdens her with images of animality and lack of culture as well as orality (Nhemachena, 2016). Her power of oracy is stifled by her family and the hegemonic [political and economic] milieu in which she finds herself in. In this regard, she becomes invisible and powerless. Bukenya in Kaschula (2001: 33) reiterates that, "productive oracy would entail self-definition, self-assertion, negotiation of relationships, resolution of conflicts, claiming of rights and indictment of their violation". While ecofeminism seeks to collapse the binary between humans and nonhumans, the exigencies of self-assertion and self-definition of the girl child and African women require exercise of autonomy and sovereignty. Lack of this productive oracy deems Chipo vulnerable and powerless in the face of men like her grandfather. Sharma (1993:88) argues that, "The human child is the most helpless and weak being". Thus, children are accorded a lower status to that of women and men. As such, their powerlessness, vulnerability and low status has meant that their suffering is invisible and unheard.

The children's lack of control, possession and ownership of the land and environment by virtue of their age, race and class shows their vulnerability. The impoverishment and lack of essential commodities makes the children and women more vulnerable to other forms of violence and abuse such as rape. This claim is supported by Shiva (2014: xvi) who argues that the "rape of the Earth and rape of women are intimately linked ... in shaping women's everyday lives." It is in this context that these "connections" are viewed as ecofeminist issues. An analysis of "violence" towards women and nature from an ecofeminist perspective thus emphasises children's and women's simultaneous struggles against hegemonic elite's abuse and environmental impacts as a result of Operation *Murambatsvina*. Hence, the metaphor of the "eyes of children," in telling their stories of conflict, pain, HIV/AIDS, poverty, trauma and desperation is a telling remapping of the condition of women and nature in contemporary Africa at the crossroads. By using the voice of the Zimbabwean girl-child, the complex roots of pain and trauma in the country assume new meanings and significance.

For instance, believing that the pregnancy will kill Chipo, Darling and her friends attain new names and statuses to help Chipo get rid of her stomach. What is of importance in this strategy is that the boys, Bastard, Godknows and Stina are left behind because this is a "woman thing" (WN, 78). The girls re-define the forest space and thus re-establish and reconfigure the hegemonic order. The setting of this dramatic event is entirely the natural environment. A connection is established between the forest landscape and the children. The landscape is the "dominant character" and it provides the resources that the children need for the abortion process. They plan to carry out the procedure in the forest, "in the mphafa" tree (WN, 79) because it has a "nice big shade" (WN, 79). The eco-function of the tree shows their dependence on nonhuman nature. Also noted is that the patient, Chipo, lies on the ground, as if to "connect" with the earth. The forest, where the procedure will take place, is also renamed an Emergency Room (ER). Within the forest space, the children are able to get all the instruments that they need for the procedure; the hanger, the rocks, twisted metal cup, a leather belt and a purple round thing. In the forest environment, the girls attain new statuses of change agents and decision makers concerning Chipo's fate. Darling is renamed Dr. Bullet, Sbho is Dr. Roz and Forgiveness is Dr. Cutter. In order to redeem Chipo, the girls have to undergo this metamorphosis. Thus, an explicit connection is established between the forest environment and the girl-doctors. Each girl tries to discover a new self or identity in the forest space.

Predicated on the ecofeminist theory, this chapter therefore posits that the hardships that Darling and her friends have to endure are illuminated by the natural setting as a "connection" between the girls and the forest is established.

Problematising the girl's naming process becomes imperative at this juncture. At a glance, the renaming from African names to English names is a metaphor that reveals how black people had been colonised and at the same time made houseless by their own government. One may argue that the girl-children fail to transcend the "Other" boundaries by reinforcing the dichotomy through their new names which [mistakenly] reflect the ideals that they have about America, that it is a land of, human rights, democracy, freedom and bounty. As such, the girls' American names imply a continuation of the colonisation process (Shiva, 2014:71). Such a naming process also invariably contests this type of development that is premised on the hegemonic Western patriarchal worldview that thrives on inferiorising and Othering the black woman. Both the American doctors' names and the ER infuse a political dimension in the human and nonhuman connection. This suggests that connections between environmental issues and the unjustified dispossession and subordination of women and other disinherited groups should be taken seriously (Warren, 1997). Of significance to this chapter is that the renaming process represents a feminist response that is ecological; that "reactivates a conscious awareness of… nature, lifting it out of its patriarchal definition as something passive and inert - a definition that has also been extended to women" (Shiva, 2014: 4). Thus, we are compelled to recognise "connections" and continuity of life within an organic, evolving, dynamic nature (ibid). Durkheim (cited in Plumwood, 1993: 50) supports this idea by pointing out that "dualism denies continuity, treating its pairs as comprising 'two worlds between which there is nothing in common', worlds between which there is a vacuum." With ecofeminism, separation is challenged as it emphasises ecological "interconnectedness" of human and nonhuman natures. In *We Need New Names*, such "connections" between the girl-children, their environment and their society are deemed to be inseparable. The boundaries between them are considered to be porous and flexible, allowing interchange and influence (ibid).

The "intertwined" issues reveal how the girl-child and the women in Paradise carry an "environmental burden disproportionate to that of their male counterparts" (Crawford, 2013: 87). The forest ER represents a failed public health system which in turn impacts on the Black woman, a point that is further articulated in their relegation to invisible spaces in the novel. Hence, using the forest as an ER represents nature as a congenial site to critique Operation *Murambatsvina* and subsequently, the policies of the hegemonic elite. The forest space "generates bonds of affinity that enable the [children] to awaken to new political possibilities about themselves as agents protective of a natural world" (Smith and Watson, 2010:190). Not only do the children protect the natural world, but they believe that they are saviours of the girl-child's, Chipo's life. Ironically, to achieve this, the girls' new names are associated with the United States, a "land they consider knowledgeable and full of resources, just like ER" (WN, 21), since "ER is what they do in a hospital in America" (WN, 84). The ideals that are upheld are those which associate America with success and the availability of resources. By implication, Africa is the "Other", the undeveloped continent that needs to be civilised by the American continent. Amidst the horrific and traumatic effects of Operation *Murambatsvina* and the steel and massive jaws of the bulldozers, the forest gives the children purpose and meaning. They are able to relocate themselves to a different world, the States. They provide a strong statement of ecofeminism by establishing a functional ER in the forest. The children are "connected" to one another and to the environment in a manner unknowable to the adults in Paradise. By so doing, they escape the invisibility and oppression of hegemonic elite by creating their own ER and new names for themselves.

Furthermore, practical and liberatory "connections" are a significant agenda in *We Need New Names*. MotherLove is one of the agents who advocates for social reform, social change and security for the children. She saves Chipo from Darling and her friends' plan to remove her bulge. She exudes power and authority over both the environment and the children. Arguably, the open forest space symbolically shows the porosity or the non-existence of once-assumed stable borders (Grewe-Volpp, 2013: 223) in both Budapest and Paradise. It is in the forest space that the girl-children and MotherLove assume new identities, go for healing and find sustenance and reassurance. To achieve this, MotherLove and the girls challenge culturally fixed notions of the forest space. However, Darling and her friends connect with the natural environment to "transform the public space to give it meaning and significance. They reinterpret the local public space making it more conducive to female subjectivity and gender vision (Comer, cited in Grewe-Volpp, 2013). This realisation is reaffirmed through the symbol of the butterfly, representing freedom and spiritual rebirth. Significant to note is that the purple butterfly sits on Chipo's head and when it flies away, they chase it screaming out for luck (WN, 88). The children "connect" with the butterfly within the forest space. For Chipo, the butterfly represents a new form of strength and potential that would enable her to have the baby that she is carrying. The butterfly symbolically asserts their freedom and visibility. At the same time, the forest space allows them to create "more democratic relationships with ecofeminist values of equality, care, and responsibility" (Grewe-Volpp, 2013: 227).

The validity of this position is premised on the fact that the children sometimes find peace and harmony in environment. However, one notes that the appearance of MotherLove in the forest ER comes as a surprise to the children. She does not scold the children, instead she allows Chipo to embrace her. Hence, both MotherLove and the girls are not confined to boundaries of femininity. Instead, they deconstruct and challenge the disinheriting frameworks that circumscribe socially sanctioned responsibilities.

Ecocriticism and Ecofeminism in Relation to Gender and Development

The mall that is built by the Chinese, and Operation *Murambatsvina,* is a form of development in Bulawayo's (2013) text that is analysed in this section. An analysis of 'development' and women issues in *We Need New Names* reveals the unjustified disinheritance, dispossession, exploitation and domination of women through "the agenda of 'economic reforms' set by capitalist patriarchy" (Shiva 2014: xvii). Thus, one may argue that Operation *Murambatsvina* is such an agenda, hence, the endeavour to interrogate how the resulting environmental crisis "intertwines" with gender issues in *We Need New Names*.

When resources are wantonly used for Western 'development,' sustainable lifestyles are also destroyed. For example, the building of the mall in Shanghai by the Chinese means that essential resources such as land and water are also appropriated. The Chinese mall metaphorically represents the link between the "rape" of the earth (wastage of resources to selectively advance society) and the rape of women. This point is very important with regards to ecological threatening situations in which resources are expropriated but there seems to be no conscious effort to replenish them. Darling narrates that before the Chinese brought their machines, they burned the grass (WN, 43). The machines with their terrible jaws, mauled the earth, "machines grind rocks, machines belch clouds of smoke, machines iron the ground" (WN, 42). This process involves the erosion of the resource base for existence thus denying large numbers of people the means of survival. This is so because the Western notion of development is based on dispossession and disinheritance of Africans and the exploitation of nature for the satiation of global hegemonic elite's wants.

With ecological instability, new forms of impoverishment are created (Shiva, 2014: 72) and children and women are the most affected. For instance, as Darling and her friends peep into the tent to see what is inside, they see "two black girls in skinny jeans and heels and weaves walk out" (WN, 45). The Black girl-child thus, learns that providing sexual favours was the route to survive (Stein cited in Gaard *et al,* 2013: 191). The appropriation and destruction of the land and the resources by the Chinese parallels the exploitation of the black girls as they engage in sexual relationships to survive.

The mutual inferiorisation of women and the environment is also reinforced yet paradoxically the colonial inferiorisation of African women was premised on caricaturing them as freaks of nature (Nhemachena, 2016). Both women and the environment are exploited by the dispossessive and destructive hegemonic systems. Viewed in this light, ecofeminism reveals the "interconnectedness" of various social and environmental issues that may not, upon first glance, seem related" (Crawford cited in Gaard *et al*, 2013: 88). As Warren in *Feminism and Ecology* argues, "It is only when we dive deep and see the interconnections between various systems of oppression that our feminist theories will hold much water." Such deep diving will perhaps transform human and nonhuman "connections" (Gaard *et al*, 2013: 197). However, Eurocentric exhortations for "biocentric" approaches are intended to ultimately result in postanthropocentric and anthropocene worlds that deny African men and women ownership, possession and control over their land and environment. With postanthropocentrism and anthropocene, the interests and needs of African women, children and men will be subordinated to the purported interests of the environment which is itself monopolised, owned, possessed and controlled by Western transnational corporations that are currently promoting ideologies of "biocentrism" (Nhemachena, Warikandwa and Mtapuri, 2017). In this regard, African scholars need to be careful about Eurocentric ideologies that collapse [African] human beings and nature, and ideologies that efface distinctions between nature and human-owners of the nature (Nhemachena, 2016).

The construction of the Chinese mall also reveals how the black men are impacted by environmental injustice. Whilst the Chinese believe that the mall with "all nice shops inside, Gucci, Loui Vuitton, Versace" (46) will benefit the people, Darling and her friends believe that China is a "red devil looking for people to eat so it can grow fat and strong" (WN, 47) and "should be a dragon [...] that way, it will be a real beast, always on top" (WN, 48). The children are aware that they will not benefit from the mall because they are impoverished. They are also aware that the Chinese are depriving them of their land as they shout that they should leave their country and go build where they came from. A closer examination of the Chinese development agenda reveals that they present themselves as saviours and guardians of the community in Paradise while in fact their project is to exploit local ecology for capital accumulation. They merely seek easy access to natural resources as well as to human labour. The Gucci, Loui

Vuitton, and Versace foreign labels are just names for a "system which promises a better life for all but ends in killing life itself" (Mies, 2014: xxiv). Darling and her friends seem to realise that nature sustains life. Hence, the children's feeble shouts are an expression of their anger and at the same time, a sense of responsibility to end the earth's destruction. Okuyade (2013: ix) also points out that, "Mankind continues to make concerted efforts to ensure that the other worlds are kept alive since the human world solely depends on them for sustenance and existence."

In the novel, the children also realise that both their land and the men who are shovelling earth into wheelbarrows are exploited by the Chinese men. The latter have protective clothing while the black men work in regular clothes - torn T-shirts, shorts, trousers cut at the knees, overalls, flip-flops, tennis shoes" (WN, 42). In addition, Darling says that they "look like they've been playing in dirt all their lives - it's all over their bodies, their clothes, their hair" (44). A value hierarchy relationship is established between the Chinese men and nature, black women and men. As such, one may argue that Bulawayo's (2013) *We Need New Names* shows how colonialism, capitalist patriarchy, racism and gender intertwine and directly link to the environment.

Conclusion

Operation *Murambatsvina* is used analogously to represent the "connection" between humans and nonhuman nature. It also reveals the significant role that the environment plays in the people's lives. The novel focuses on environments riddled with social problems such as HIV and AIDS, migrant workers, impoverishment, lack of food, racism and post-colonial disillusionment due to resilience of unjust structural systems. As the environment fails to sustain the people, the political implication is apparent when the people leave the country in masses for the so called greener pastures. The diasporic realities of the Zimbabwean immigrants; men, women and children are used to illuminate the social, political and economic crisis that occurred in Zimbabwe. The construction of malls by the Chinese in *We Need New Names* not only destroys the environment but also the people's livelihoods. Thus, as a subject, the environment is perceived as a part of a whole, a biocentric world-view in which humanity, the nonhuman and the environment exist. However, sadly biocentrism implies postanthropocentrism and anthropocene meaning that the interests of [African] humans whether male or female are subordinated to the environment which is itself monopolised, controlled and possessed by the Western transnational corporations. In this regard, likening [African] women to nature or effacing distinctions between them is ultimately counterproductive because it animalises [African] women and prepares them for on-going (re-)colonisation by transnational corporations that still monopolise ownership and control of African land, and environments to which women are reduced in the representations.

References

Birkeland, J. (1993) "Ecofeminism: Linking Theory and Practice." In *Ecofeminism: Women, Animals, Nature*, (ed.) Greta Gaard. Philadelphia: Temple Univ. Press.

Bulawayo, N. (2013) *We Need New Names*. London: Chatto & Windus.

Chimedza, T. (2008) "Bulldozers Always Come: 'Maggots', Citizens and Governance in Contemporary Zimbabwe" in Vambe, M, (ed.). *The Hidden Dimensions of Operation Murambatsvina* in *Zimbabwe*. Harare: Weaver Press.

Chirikure, C. (1994) *Chamupupuri*. Harare: College Press.

Crawford, C. (2013) Streams of Violence: Colonialism, Modernization, and Gender in Maria Cristina's "John of God, the Water-Carrier," in Gaard, G. (ed.).. *International Perspectives in Feminist Ecocriticism*. New York: Taylor and Francis: 87-100.

Fitzpatrick, D. R. (2015) "From Paradise to Destroyedmichygen: An Analysis of the Function of Names in *We Need New Names* by, NoViolet Bulawayo". University of Colorado, Boulder *Undergraduate Honours Theses*. Paper 874.

Gaard, G. (ed.). (2013) *International Perspectives in Feminist Ecocriticism*. New York: Taylor and Francis.

Garrard, G. (2004) *Ecocriticism*. London: Routledge.

Glotfelty, C. and Harold, F. (eds.) (1996) *The Ecocriticism Reader: Landmarks in Literary Ecology*. Athens and London: University of Georgia.

Glotfelty, C. (2007) "What is Ecocriticism?" *ASLE: The Association for the Study of Literature and the Environment* n.d. Web. 10 Nov. 2007.

Grewe-Volpp, C. (2013) "Keep Moving: Place and Gender in a Post-Apocalyptic Environment". In Gaard, G. (ed.) *International Perspectives in Feminist Ecocriticism*. New York: Taylor and Francis: 221-234.

Harrison, G. S. (2012) Environmental Justice Metafiction: Narrative and Politics in Contemporary Ethnic Women's Novels by Louise Erdrich, Linda Hogan, Ruth Ozeki, and Karen Yamashita. PhD Thesis. University of Wisconsin-Madison.

Kaschula, R.H. (Ed.) (1998) *African Oral Literature: Functions in Contemporary Contexts*. Claremont: New Africa Books.

King, Y. (1983) "Toward an Ecological Feminism and a Feminist Ecology," in Rothschild, J (ed). *Machina Ex Dea: Feminist Perspectives on Technology*. New York: Pergamon.

King, Y. (1989) "The Ecology of Feminism and the Feminism of Ecology", in Plant, J (ed). *Healing the Wounds: The Promise of Ecofeminism*. Santa Cruz, California: New Society Publishers.

Magubane, B. M. (2007) *Race and the Construction of the Dispensable Other*. Pretoria: University of South Africa Press.

Mies, M. & Vandana S. (1993) *Ecofeminism*. Halifax: Fernwood Publications.

Mies, M. and Shiva, V. (2014) *Ecofeminism*, London: Zed Books.

Momsen, J., (1995) *Women and Development in the Third World*. London: Routledge.

Nhemachena, A. (2016) Animism, Coloniality and Humanism: Reversing the Empire's Framing of Africa, in Mawere, M., and Nhemachena, A. (eds.) *Theory, Knowledge, Development and Politics: What Role for the Academy in the Sustainability of Africa*. Bamenda: Langaa Publishers.

Nhemachena, A; Warikandwa, T. V. and Mtapuri, O. (2017) Transnational Corporations' Land Grabs and the On-going

Second Mad Scramble for Africa: An Introduction, in Warikandwa T V; Nhemachena, A. and Mtapuri, O. (eds.) *Transnational Land Grabs and Restitution in an Age of the (De-)Militarised New Scramble for Africa: A Pan African Socio-Legal Perspective*. Bamenda: Langaa Publishers.

Okuyade, O. (ed.). (2013) *Eco- critical Literature: Regreening African Landscapes*. New York: African Heritage Press: 15-30.

Plumwood, V. (1993) *Feminism and the Mastery of Nature*. New York: Routledge.

Plumwood, V. (2002). *Environmental Culture: The Ecological Crisis of Reason*. New York: Routledge.

Potts, D. (2006) "'Restoring Order'? Operation Murambatsvina and the Urban Crisis in Zimbabwe." *Journal of Southern African Studies* 32 (2): 273-291.

Rigby, K. (2013) The Poetics of Decolonisation. In Gaard, G. (ed.) *International Perspectives in Feminist Ecocriticism*. New York: Taylor and Francis: 120-136.

Ruether, R. R. (1975) *New Woman/New Earth: Sexist Ideologies and Human Liberation*. New York: The Seabury Press.

Ruether, R. R. (1992) *Gaia and God: An Ecofeminist Theology of Earth Healing*. San Francisco: Harper San Francisco.

Sharma, R. N. (1993) *Urban Sociology*. New Delhi: Surjent Publications.

Shiva, V. (ed.) (1994) *Close to Home: Women Reconnect Ecology, Health and Development*. USA: Capital City Press.

Smith, P. A. (1998) "Green Lap, Brown Embrace, Blue Body: the Ecospirituality of Alice Walker." *Cross Currents* 48 (4): 471–87.

Stein, R. (2013) "Sex, Population and Environmental Eugenics in Margaret Atwood's *Oryx and Crake and The Year of the Flood*," in Gaard, G. (ed.) *International Perspectives in Feminist Ecocriticism*. New York: Taylor and Francis: 184-202.

Twine, R. (2001) 'Ecofeminisms in Process' *Journal of Ecofeminism* [online] available at http://www.ecofem.org/journal

Usher, A.D. (1994) "After the Forest: AIDS as Ecological Collapse in Thailand". In Shiva, V. (ed.). *Close to Home: Women Reconnect Ecology, Health and Development Worldwide*. Philadelphia: New Society Publishers.

Warren, K. J. (1987) Feminism and Ecology: Making Connections, *Environmental Ethics* 9(1): 3-20.

Warren, K. J. (ed.) (1997) *Ecofeminism: Women, Culture, Nature*, Bloomington: Indiana University Press.

Chapter Seven

Gendered Experiences: Land Grabs and the De-Feminization of Africa's Agrarian Futures

Martin Uadiale & Anirejuoritse Awala-Ale

Introduction

Since 2008, there have been increasing land grabs by transnational corporations on the African continent. These transnational corporations are involved in land grabs that are dispossessing and disinheriting African peasants but they use the pretext of boosting world food production (Doss *et al*, 2014: 1). Along with growing demands for biofuels, there has been speculative demand for African land by transnational "investors" and these speculations have largely influenced the increasing transnational land grabs in Africa (Bomuhangi *et al*, 2011: 1). According to an estimate, the volume of land grabbed, by transnational corporations posing as investors, since 2009 stands at 227 million hectares (Oxfam, 2011: 5). Out of the ten largest land grabs between the years 2007-2011, six of them have taken place in sub-Saharan Africa (LaFrancesca, 2011: 16). Startlingly, the area that has been grabbed in Africa is roughly the size of the United Kingdom (UK) and Germany (Narula, 2013: 106). It is worth noting that land grabs do not occur in isolation, and in many instances, there is a concomitant water grab (Taylor, 2015: 4). These grabs are lamely justified as necessary for "global" food and fuel security.

The current spate of transnational land grabs is made easier by market reforms foisted on Africa, since the 1980s, by the neoliberal World Bank and IMF as part of loan conditionalities in Africa. These structural adjustment programmes proposed by these international financial institutions (IFIs) had the effects of initiating liberalisation policies, export oriented economies and reduced government regulations on wages and prices, thus setting the stage for present day land grabs in Africa. The efforts of some African governments in making these vicious resource thefts possible should not be forgotten or neglected. These land grabs are made easier by the aspirations of some African governments that uncritically yearn for 'foreign direct investment' (FDI). There is an uncritical belief in Africa that the so-called foreign direct investment is a necessary precondition for national development (Kachika, 2010: 8). Hence, some African governments collude with foreign "investors"; thus suffering from misapprehensions about the benefits from transnational corporations, the African governments assist the transnational corporations in grabbing land from African peasants (The International Land Coalition, 2011: 2).

The damage however outweighs the anticipated advantages that are hoped to accrue to African states. The implications of such land grabs include the dispossession of peasant farmers who have historically being the underwriters of Africa's food security. The African peasants are disinherited and displaced from their land, rendering them landless independent wage workers in a world where, paradoxically, transnational corporations are busy manufacturing and preferring to employ humanoid robots (Nhemachena, 2017). Thus, land that is grabbed by the transnational "investors" is farmed using robotic technology rather than using the services of human employees. These Euro-modern techniques which use pesticides and insecticides hamper environmental sustainability, leaving the soil degraded. Ultimately, this prevents the achievement of food security for the African continent (Altieri and Toledo, 2011: 590; Altieri, 2012: 2; Ambalam, 2014: 125; Donkers, 2014: 92; Fitzpatrick, 2015: 20).

However, to completely understand the implications of land grabs for inequalities, livelihoods, food security, and Africa's agrarian futures, there is a need for an examination of the gendered impacts of the transnational land grabs. Research into this theme has been stifled by scholarly focus on the size and spread of land acquisitions in Africa. Hence, women are disregarded as insignificant social groups in the land grab discourse (Zetterlund, 2013: 1). This is surprising - women are the most important element for the achievement of food security in Africa. An assessment of the implications of land grabs in Africa without including women will be flawed. When writing on the implications of land grabs, it is impossible and erroneous not to acknowledge the effect that transnational land grabs have on African women farmers. Female employment in agriculture is about 40% in sub-Saharan Africa, it is about 55% in South East Asia, about 25% in Latin America and the Caribbean (Akanji, 2013: 6).

Ultimately, by examining the impacts of transnational land grabs on women, it will become clear that the 'impacts' of land grabs on women is an historical phenomena that has been recurrent since the origin of capitalism. These contributions also highlight striking gaps in our knowledge of gendered effects of land grabs and their policy implications.

Understanding Modern Day Land Grabs: Theoretical Perspectives

On the heels of the 2008/2009 Triple F (food, finance and fuel) crisis came the unprecedented massive transnational land grabs (The International Land Coalition, 2011: 10; Doss *et al*, 2014: 2). The phenomenon of land grab has elicited intense debate, with civil society organisations, non-governmental organisations (NGOs) and academics condemning it due to its negative social impacts (Borras and Franco, 2012; De Shutter, 2011). In contrast, supporters of the transnational land grabs [such as the World Bank (WB), the Food and Agriculture Organisation of the United Nations (FAO), governments and global corporations] regard land grabs as the solution to the triple F crisis (Cotula *et al*, 2009). Hence, they facilitate and oversee vicious transnational land grabs of supposedly, underutilized or empty African lands (Borras and Franco, 2013: 1723).

The land grabs occurring today must be understood in the context of the dispossessive nature of transnational [global] capitalism (Magdoff, 2013). Constructing a complete understanding of the nature and purpose of land grabs necessitates an understanding of Karl Marx's theory of primitive accumulation and Harvey's (2003) notion of accumulation by dispossession. Primitive accumulation was the concept employed by Marx in Capital Vol.1 'to characterize the European historical process upon which the development of capitalist relations was premised'. The features of this historical process include changes in economic and social relations necessary for the origination of [global] capitalism. These changes and conditions encapsulated as primitive accumulation include: concentration of capital and labour; dispossessing workers of their means of production - their land. This in turn paved the way for the creation of free independent wage workers (Vasudevan *et al*, 2008: 161). In other words, the term primitive accumulation as employed by Marx describes the methods through which capital became concentrated in fewer hands and a mass of independent wage workers was created for exploitation during the transition from feudalism to capitalism in Europe (Ruddy, 2011: 3). Marx treated primitive accumulation as a foundational process of capitalism, laying the structural conditions for the consolidation of a capitalist society. However, in relation to Africa, it is necessary to note that transnational corporations are not merely involved in primitive accumulation but in (neo-)colonial dispossession and disinheriting of Africans.

Harvey (2003) takes account of the theory of primitive accumulation and revises it, asserting that primitive accumulation was not just the foundational process for capitalism's origin; rather it is an ongoing and recurring feature of capitalism. He conceptualises these new forms of [transnational] capitalist accumulation as 'accumulation by dispossession' and the forms of modern day capital accumulation include: the dispossession of peasant populations in Asia, Africa and Latin America (Whitehead, 2015). With respect to this chapter, we argue that the term "accumulation" is imprecise to describe what is happening in Africa-the most appropriate term to use is **'theft by dispossession'** or **'primitive stealing'** rather than primitive accumulation because the transnational corporations are not merely accumulating but stealing land from African peasants.

These processes of accumulation, according to Harvey (ibid), represent capitalism's attempt to overcome its 'crises of accumulation' emanating from internal contradiction inherent in the capitalist system (Harvey, 2005: 145-150). 'Overaccumulation' signals a situation in the capitalist system where reinvestment of capital does not incur returns. There are no avenues for profitable investment anymore. Surpluses of devalued capital exist concurrently with devalued labour with no way to utilise both together. A strategy employed by capitalism to arrest the 'crises of accumulation' is through a spatial-temporal fix (Harvey, 2009: 65). Spatial fix entails the alleviation of the 'crisis of accumulation' by moving capital or labour to a different territory and beginning new production regimes. Hence, for Harvey (2001: 24) land grabs represent a spatial fix for the 'overaccumulation' crisis.

By utilising the spatial-temporal fix, the crisis of capitalism can be temporarily assuaged and this forms a common pattern within capitalism. Even more significant than capitalism's ability to temporarily fix its inherent contradictions is its intrinsic and unparalleled ability to manipulate and exploit crises for its benefit. In its origination, capitalism developed as a response to the feudal crisis (Federici, 1998: 61). In other words, it was unsurprising that on the heels of the 2008/2009 triple F crises, large scale unprecedented land grabs occurred on a global scale with its justifications. The triple F crisis may have been viewed as an obstacle to capitalist development, this is far from the truth, and this crisis has proved to be an opportunity for the continued transnational corporations' dispossession and exploitation of the African people and their continent.

Harvey (2005) has argued that the contradictions of capitalism and its inherent crisis will be the end of this system. However, we are witnessing the power of capitalism to not only scale its crisis, but to expertly manipulate it for more intense dispossession of Africans. The debt trap of the 20th century made way for the change in the land tenure situation in Africa (Federici, 2001: 1). Now Western crises of the 21st century have paved the way for the transnational land grabs that are occurring at a more rapid rate and which will exceed, in volume and impacts, the land dispossession in colonial history (White et al, 2012: 624).

The Gendered Implications of Land Grabs

A focus on the experience of [African] women with respect to land grabs is an acknowledgement of the importance of land to

199

women (Behrman *et al*, 2011: 1). African women farmers are 'the operatives and custodians of food and the food system' (Akanji, 2013: 6). In Africa, they produce 80% of the food that people consume (Federici, 2011: 5). Thus, Wandia, (2009) states that:

> In Sub-Saharan Africa, agriculture accounts for approximately 21 per cent of the continent's GDP and women contribute 60-80 per cent of the labour used to produce food both for household consumption and for sale. Estimates of women's contribution to the production of food crops range from 30 per cent in the Sudan to 80 per cent in the Congo, while their pro-portion of the economically active labour force in agriculture ranges from 48 per cent in Burkina Faso to 73 per cent in the Congo and 80 per cent in the traditional sector in the Sudan.

African women are core members of the world's agricultural regime; 'they produce more than half of all the food grown in the world' (Oxfam, 2013: 2) and roughly 1.6 billion women depend on agriculture for their livelihoods (Oxfam, 2013: 2). They feed their families and provide for the education of their families. Over 60% of Africans survive by subsistence agriculture spearheaded by women (Federici, 2001: 2). For this reason Emeriti Professor Silvia Federici states that:

> In every part of the world, before the advent of capitalism, women played a major role in agricultural production. They had access to land, the use of its resources and control over the crops they cultivated, all of which guaranteed their autonomy and economic independence from men. In Africa, they had their farming and cropping systems, which were the source of a specific female culture, and they were in charge of the selection of seeds, an operation that was crucial to the prosperity of the community and whose knowledge was transmitted through the generations (Haiven, 2009).

Although women underpin the local food economy of African states, their interests are not represented in ongoing discourses about transnational land grabs. There are several ways in which land grabs undermine the rights of women peasant and smallholder farmers in

Africa. A recent Action-Aid report (2010b) also highlights the erosion of women's livelihoods in Ghana that results from the direct impacts of biofuels investments:

> ...many of these decisions were made without the consultation of local communities, which in several cases were deprived of their land being classified as "marginal", despite women use them for the cultivation of the Karite nut trees, an important source of income for the local population in the rainy season. (Action-Aid, 2010b: 28).

As a result of this, women are dispossessed of their lands without any compensation. This loss of land is a loss of their source of livelihood. The situation in Ghana is a pertinent example of this as shea trees used for making shea butter are destroyed by transnational corporations (Kachika, 2010: 10). Proponents of transnational land grabs arrogantly argue that the lands that are grabbed are marginal and idle lands. The notion of idle marginal lands is misleading because they are rarely as they are described. Women use these lands for non-agricultural purposes such as for small-scale farm production, for fuel, medicines, dietary diversity including fallowing to manage soil fertility, pastoralism as well as shifting cultivation (Vhugen, 2012: 7; McMichael, 2011: 3). Nevertheless, following the loss of their traditional source of income, they are often simplistically promised compensation and employment opportunities (Kachika, 2010: 10).

Regarding employment opportunities, women are at the losing end and their position is increasingly undermined. Granted, employment on large scale plantations owned by private interests rarely offer appropriate working conditions and are not enviable positions. The fact that women are dispossessed and deprived of their roles as underwriters of food security in Africa suffices to show the risks, for indigenous people, of the ongoing transnational land grabs. In any case even where they are employed, women assume very low positions. Arguments that are often made to justify the low positions for employed women include allegations about their physiological or morphological features, their alleged fragility and nimbleness meaning they cannot partake in physically demanding tasks. For this reason, women are subjected to simpler tasks such as pruning, spraying, thinning, and tying, thereby excluding them from better-paying, less strenuous, or less dangerous activities (Behrman *et al*, 2011: 2).

Apart from challenges resulting from transnational mechanisation of agriculture, women are less likely to obtain available employment positions by virtue of limited educational background (Oxfam, 2013: 9). Women do not possess the prerequisite qualifications to hold positions within transnational agricultural facilities.

Disempowerment of Women

The value of land to women is beyond its yield possibilities or its acreage. It is the backbone of their agricultural livelihood; it is a source of cultural and social value as well as spiritual value and, most importantly, it is a store of wealth and a source of collateral security. One woman who was dispossessed of her land told Oxfam: 'When you lose your land, you have lost your value and even your body, because the body adds value to the land. You see us talking [but] we are moving corpses' (Oxfam, 2013: 7). Action-Aid (2010a: 23) also recorded the voices of women farmers in Mozambique who have lost their land to transnational corporations involved in jatropha plantations:

> What we want is to get our farms back, because that is what our livelihood is dependent on...we are dying of hunger and there is nothing that we have that is actually our own.
> I don't have a farm, I don't have a garden, because the only land that I have has been destroyed...We grew maize, groundnuts, beans, pumpkins, watermelons...I have given up: I am staying helplessly, because we don't have anything to eat. We are just suffering with hunger, because even if I go to look for another farm, they will just destroy it again.

These statements are not exaggerative, the effect here is that women are disempowered as they lose their ability, as a disinherited class, to challenge and change existing [global] political-economic power relationships that create and sustain structures of disinheritance (Agrawal, 1995 in Meinzen-Dick, Brown, Feldstein and Quisumbing, 1997).

Consequently, women find themselves without access to land and water. For survival, they are forced to engage in humiliating and degrading activities such as prostitution, pornography and lesbianism which compromise their health, their moral values and customs. They may also seek early marriages or pledge their children to try and remedy the hardships (Tandon, 2011; Oxfam, 2013: 2).

Gendered Outcomes of "Primitive Accumulation" and "Accumulation by Dispossession?"

The invidious situation of African women peasant farmers is not new. Within the ambit of capitalism, women have been exploited and denigrated. As it shall be shown, historically, capitalism has fostered gender differentiations within the world proletariat, confining women to unpaid domestic labour of the home and stripping them of every right that may empower them. Indeed, capitalism thrives on class differentiations, enabling racism and sexism in the world proletariat. This is a precondition for capitalism's continued "accumulation" and survival.

Marx believed that conquest, slavery, theft, enclosures and ultimately the use of force characterised the transition from feudalism to capitalism in Europe. However, Federici's (2004) analysis of primitive accumulation includes a set of historical phenomena or preconditions, absent in Marx, which have been extremely important for capitalist "accumulation". The phenomenon was the development and consolidation of a new sexual division of labour, wherein women's labour and women's reproductive functions are subjugated and function for the reproduction of the male work-force (capitalist labour power) (Federici, 2004). Federici (ibid) analysed the European witch-hunt terror in the sixteenth and seventeenth centuries as a manifestation of the capitalist class intention to control the reproduction of labour necessary for European transition to capitalism (ibid: 12, 22).

This reproduction of labour (the male work force) that Federici (ibid) writes about occurs through three interconnected processes. Firstly, through activities provided almost exclusively by the women that help regenerate the waged worker outside the reproduction process and these include: shelter, food, bed and physical care. Secondly, through activities which maintain and regenerate non-workers outside the reproduction process. This refers to activities taken by mothers on behalf of children (future waged workers) and thirdly, through childbirth, producing new wage workers (Bhattacharya, 2017).

Hence, in the new capitalist regime, women were turned into 'instruments for the reproduction of the labour and the expansion of the workforce' (Federici, 1998: 91) - a fact that Marx never acknowledged or explored. In other words, during the transition from feudalism to capitalism, women 'suffered a unique process of social degradation that was fundamental to the accumulation of capital' (Federici, 1998: 75; Vogel, 1995). This blindness by Marx to the significance of women's unpaid reproductive work in the process of capitalist accumulation limits Marx's understanding of the true extent of the capitalist exploitation of labour (Federici, 2008).

At this point, it is seen that the original phase of "primitive accumulation" (origin of capitalism in Europe) required the subjugation of women's bodies, 'the devaluation of their reproductive and caring labour and knowledge, their exclusion from waged work and their forced reliance on the male wage for survival, the production of new forms of gendered subjectivities, and the erasure and appropriation of alternative and oppositional political imaginaries' and the confinement of women's productive capacity to domestic labour (Ruddy, 2011: 5). The question worth asking at this juncture is, does the current era of 'accumulation' by dispossession, as outlined by Harvey (2005) involve similar processes of disinheriting of [African] women.

Indeed, today, in the face of a new process of dispossession, women still have similar experiences (Federici, 2011: 5). Today, only 1% of women in Tanzania have legal land titles. In Zimbabwe, up to 20% of women have land titles, but despite this relatively higher number, "women rarely profit" from their land (AWID, 2012). This can be traced to the advent of the colonial land grabs which influenced the establishment of gender differentiations in Africa. Large arable lands were seized by the colonialists and were earmarked for the production of cash crops. Heading this production were some African males who also employed the services of the women, although they were given menial tasks like weeding. (Delius, 2008; Thipe, 2013: 490).

Furthermore, men were favoured with respect to land allocation, equipment and training because of the mechanisation of agriculture. Kenya is an important example of the negative influence colonial settlers had on land registration and titling (Gray and Kevane, 1999: 12). Precolonial Taita women in south-western Kenya had well-developed land use rights after marriage, and the rights of widows were particularly strong. They could sell, lease or pawn these lands (Fleuret, 1988: 140). However, following the colonial introduction of land registration, their rights were limited as these lands could only be registered in the husband's name (Gray and Kevane, 1999: 12). According to Davison (1988b:165) these policies gave 'precedence to individual ownership invested in male heads of households and in turn marginalized the usufruct rights of women formerly guaranteed under lineage tenure.'

Colonialism introduced and perpetuated the patriarchal land ownership system. Prior to colonialism, ownership of land was collective, and through customary rights, women had access to land, unimpeded. However, with colonial control, individual land ownership and land titling was rigidified. Tracts of land which had to be registered to a family were in fact registered in the name of the head of the family who was invariably a male. This was the beginning of this patriarchal transfer of lands (Schmidt, 1992; Parpart, 1995: 8; AWID, 2012).

This dispossession of women continued after the end of colonialism. Following the independence era of African states, many African countries faced "debt" crises which were in fact the legacy of colonialism. Dispossession and disinheritance of Africans under colonialism set the stage for the debt crisis that was to come. Also, the economic systems of African states were anchored 'to a narrow export base with a concomitant weak industrial sector and anemic rates of growth' (Wengraf, 2016). In short, African states inherited an underdeveloped economic infrastructure, bereft of industrialisation but with the sole aim of being suppliers of raw materials to developed metropolitan states (Cooper, 1940: 16). Furthermore, studies have shown that an aspect of French colonialism was the disproportionate allocation of the colonial expense burden. African states carried the weight of the French colonial expenses through taxation.

The debt crisis ushered in the structural adjustment era on African states which saw the introduction of atrocious neoliberal policies: thus the World Bank and IMF helped to further denigrate women by visiting them with hardship emanating from neoliberalism. The debt crisis offered international capital an avenue for further gender differentiations (Federici, 2001: 5). Naturally, it is difficult to offer a generalised assessment of the impacts that structural adjustment programmes (SAP) had on African women because policies varied slightly from country to country. However, some effects of SAP policies which were implemented, included reduced government expenditure in social services such as health and education. This affected African women extremely as they assumed the roles of 'shock absorbers', increasing their workload to compensate for lost income as well as the loss of the social services they had been dependent on (Altomore, 1991).

In addition, SAP introduced land tenure reforms concentrating on the registration of individual titles and accentuation of private ownership of lands (Bruce and Tanner, 1992: 102). These changes in land tenure systems and land use jointly limited women's land entitlements (Kachingwe, 2012: 5). The impacts of SAP were so hurtful, that in Nigeria, following negotiations with the IMF, women and workers took to the streets to protest the end of free education, unemployment and removed subsidies (Federici, 2001: 10).

If women had land use and transfer rights they would not sell it off to foreign "investors". Foreign "investors" would naturally have a difficult time negotiating with a group that understands the need for land and water resources. Women would not agree with the capitalist argument that land cannot create wealth when used for just subsistence agriculture and shelter. Women know the value of land

and are known to use any type of land, even if it is considered as arid or infertile land. They gather firewood and resources from there. Neither would they accept the argument that it is only productive when given to the bank in exchange for credit. To them, such an argument cannot be valid considering that for centuries, land has been the source of African women's wealth and sustenance (Haiven, 2009).

A question can be posed by proponents of capitalism - how can capitalism work to continuously denigrate women when the World Bank, (a capitalism serving neoliberal institution) helps to empower women by integrating and accommodating them in the global economy? World Bank president Robert Zoellick even attested to the need of investing in women: "[a]t this time of economic turmoil, investing in women is critical" and a "host of studies suggest that putting earnings in women's hands is the intelligent thing to do to aid recovery and long-term development" (Roberts, 2012: 87). Indeed, gender mainstreaming, gender budgets and women's empowerment have become key policy goals in the United Nations (UN), the International Financial Institutions (IFIs) (Roberts, 2012: 100). Its justification is anchored on the developmental narrative that investments from Western governments, individuals and private corporations is necessary for developing the 'human capital' of impoverished women in African states (World Bank, 2012; World Bank, 2014; Roberts, 2012: 92).

The following section shall address the question of the World Bank's gender initiatives, showing that the actions of the World Bank and other neoliberal institutions purporting to be promoting women's empowerment is nothing more than an attempt to hide their true intentions

Women's Revolt against Housework, the World Bank's Response and the Post-Feminist Order

The actions of the World Bank are a response to a crisis; a crisis which it will further manipulate for capitalism's consolidation. This crisis is a product of feminist critique of Marx's inability or blindness in recognising and acknowledging the significance of women's unpaid reproductive work in the process of capitalist accumulation. Marx recognised the importance of 'labour power', that is our ability to labour which is a necessity for the capitalist machinery to keep churning. Thus, according to Marx, the labour power was a source of value because through it, we create commodities and value for capitalism. However, Marx never addresses the question of how labour power is produced and sustained (Vogel, 1981: 197; Gimenez, 2005: 12).

This is where Feminist-Marxist scholars seized the gauntlet and expanded on this question. These scholars noted that labour power, 'is actually itself produced and reproduced outside of capitalist production, in a "kin-based" site called the family'. These feminist scholars, unlike Marx, further recognise that 'capitalism must rely on both an immense amount of unpaid domestic labour for the reproduction of the workforce and the devaluation of these reproductive activities (Federici, 2008; 2011: 3).

The above is indicative of the relationship between capitalism and the oppression of women. In an excellent passage, Vogel explains clearly the connection between class struggle and women's oppression:

> Class struggle over the conditions of production represents the central dynamic of social development in societies characterised by exploitation. In these societies, surplus labour is appropriated by a dominant class, and an essential condition for production is the constant presence and renewal of a subordinated class of direct producers committed to the labour process. Ordinarily, generational replacement provides most of the new workers needed to replenish this class, and women's capacity to bear children therefore plays a critical role in class society. From the point of view of social reproduction, women's oppression in class societies is rooted in their differential position with respect to generational replacement processes (Vogel, 2013: 4-6).

These feminist scholars have recognized that the labour of women which forms the basis of capitalism is performed free of charge, for the system, by women who in addition are continually oppressed and exploited. Outside of the workplace environment, women provide the main support for capitalism by their unpaid reproductive labour. This gives an understanding that any progress with respect to gender rights is only temporary and false. The disinheritance, dispossession and oppression of women is tied to the current global system and thus any serious discussion on achieving sustainable gender equality is a discussion on the dismantling of the present system altogether (Kachingwe, 2012: 11; Bhattacharya, 2017).

This contemporary understanding of the role of dispossessed and exploited women within the ambit of capitalism has been the basis of activists' campaigns against domestic slavery such as the Campaign for Wages for Housework, fostered by activists such as Maria Rosa Dalla Costa, Selma James, Leopoldina Fortunati, Ariel Salleh, Maria Mies, Claudia Von Werlhof, Veronica Benholdt-Thomsen (Federici, 2009: 1). A further manifestation of these activists' movement 'asserting the economic value of women's reproductive work, and declaring "welfare" a women's right' was 'the Welfare Mothers Movement that, inspired by the Civil Rights Movement, led the first campaign for state-funded "wages for housework" (under the guise of Aid to Dependent Children)' (Federici, 2008; Roberts, 2012: 95). There has been an increased repudiation of the sexual division of labour inherent in capitalism and its consequences consisting of economic dependence on men, social subordination, confinement to an unpaid, naturalized form of labour, a state-controlled sexuality and procreation (Federici, 2008).

There have been responses such as the World Bank's gender initiatives in Africa. An example of one such initiative is *The Women Entrepreneurship Development Project for Ethiopia*. This programme aims to increase the earnings and employment of female-owned micro and small enterprises (MSEs) in Ethiopia (World Bank, 2017). While it can be stated that these are positive advances, this chapter argues that these actions are insidious, following a capitalist pattern of responding to crisis and exploiting it. In this case, the purpose for the World Bank's response is to give credence to the proclamation that gender equality and women empowerment is being achieved or has been achieved (Baker, 2010: 2). The implication is that feminist critiques are no longer relevant as their demands or criticisms have been met. Such a notion is alarming because the fact is that gender equality can never be achieved in a system that relies on entrenched gender disparities for its survival. The actions of the World Bank can thus be described and understood as post-feminist in nature.

The term — post-feminism does not refer to a period after feminism. It 'refer to a complex cultural politics in which (limited) feminist successes are celebrated and taken for granted so as to repudiate the continued need for feminist politics' (Ruddy, 2011: 2). Angela McRobbie (2004: 4) suggests post-feminist discourses: "… actively draw on and invoke feminism as that which can be taken into account in order to suggest that equality is achieved, in order to install a whole repertoire of meanings which emphasize that it is no longer needed, a spent force".

In other words, according to McRobbie (2004: 5-6), post-feminism is complex political and socio-cultural terrain whereby liberal feminist ideals are adopted, substituted or manipulated within neoliberal culture and eventually displaced as irrelevant as the demands of feminists have been met.

These views about feminism's demise are already being established in the West as reflected in the 2006 decree by Beverly Oda (Minister of Canadian Heritage) who asserts that having achieved gender equality in Canada, any reference to gender equality or feminist language is to 'be excised from the Status of Women Canada's mandate' (Brodie, 2008). Thus, showing that in the West, feminism is taking little or no space in public policy and policy discourse. This transition to a post-feminist perspective is what neo-liberal institutions like the World Bank are trying to achieve on the African continent.

From the above, postfeminism can be theorized as a crucial aspect of "accumulation" by dispossession. For contemporary process of enclosures and its successes involves first of all a postfeminist enclosure of feminist ideals, followed by gendered political neutralisation, disavowal of feminist 'imaginaries' which would have been the source of political struggles against oppressive relations (Ruddy, 2011: 3). This way, women are incorporated into neoliberal capitalism but divorced from critical feminist politics. Having become redundant, women are encouraged to 're-make their lives according to the model of the self-reliant market citizen' (Ruddy, 2011: 7).

The insidious nature of this state of affairs is that while the modern woman is called by the postfeminist discourse to take her rightful place among men as citizen workers, engaging in equal pay, post-feminism has not and will not challenge the gendered division of domestic labour and social reproduction (Ruddy, 2011: 10). The post-feminist discourse masks the re-intensified gender and broader (neo-)colonial equalities in today's world. A fact is that while women participation in the paid labour force has increased, there is still existing inequalities within the context of the family. As Roberts (2012) notes, 'the roots of gender inequality are not found in the 'inefficient' use of women's labour *per se,* but rather in the systemic devaluation of women's work' (Roberts, 2012: 94). In short, in the modern era, women are now doubly burdened by paid and unpaid labour, often utilising paid labour of women of colour and foreign domestic workers (Baker, 2010: 2; Ruddy, 2011: 11). An excerpt from a poem by Marge Piercy (2014) provides a powerful review of the post-feminism, noting the unfair situation of the modern women, expected to be successful career wise and further expected to raise a stable family alone:

> There is no oppression. Just lean in to the corporate machine, become part of its vast personhood. You too every one of you can be a millionaire if you just try harder, gaze upward.
>
> And you can win a lottery or two, give birth to or father a perfect plastic child who will become an even richer millionaire with no teen problems [or you have failed].

In sum, it is impossible to associate the actions of the World Bank with gender equality and empowerment. At its core, as a neoliberal institution, it is tasked with opening up new markets for capitalist investment through privatisation and deregulation of the market. In this context, the actions of the World Bank, while seeming to be well informed and well-intended responses to feminist demands for gender equality they are actually undoing feminism, consigning it as a vestige of the past (McRobbie, 2004: 255). Indeed, Harvey (2003) considers neoliberalism as representing the restoration of class power under conditions of an "accumulation crisis".

Conclusion

The purpose of this chapter was the examination of the gendered effects of ongoing transnational land grabs. It was revealed that transnational land grabs have the effect of dispossessing, disinheriting and disempowering African women. Characteristically of [global] capitalism, it has responded to these critiques by introducing an era of post-feminism. Through the efforts of the World Bank and its gendered initiatives, capitalism has simultaneously lulled women into the capitalist system, pacifying criticisms, while at the same time ensuring that the existent gender disparities within the world proletariat remains. The implication for feminism is that the presumed notion that women can assume human liberation during a capitalist era is false. Capitalism's survival is not hinged on its ability to satisfy human needs. For its survival, capitalism divides and conquers the world's proletariat as it perpetuates racism, ethnicity, 'tribalism', class differentiations and gender disparities for its survival. As a socio-economic system, capitalism is committed to racism and sexism. In order to do this, capitalism always 'denigrates the nature of what it exploits' (Federici, 1998: 17): in this case, the women. History shows that even when men may enjoy freedoms, women will always be regarded as socially inferior, only with the task of social reproduction and production of labour power. The gender, racial, class divisions that capitalism creates only serve to intensify and conceal exploitations.

References

Action-Aid (2010a) *Meals per Gallon – The Impact of Industrial Biofuels on People and Global Hunger*, London: Action-Aid UK.
Action-Aid (2010b) *Her Mile – Women's Rights and Access to Land: the Last Stretch of Road to Eradicate Hunger*, Italy: ActionAid.

Altieri, M. A. and Toledo, V. M. (2011) 'The Agroecological Revolution in Latin America: Rescuing Nature, Ensuring Food Sovereignty and Empowering Peasants', *Journal of Peasant Studies* 38 (3): 587-612.

Altomore, M. (1991) *Gender and Adjustment*, Washington DC: Agency for International Development.

Akanji, B. O. (2013) 'Structural Transformation and Gender Rights in African Agriculture: What Pathways to Food Sovereignty and Sustainable Food Security?', Paper Presented at the International Conference 'Food Sovereignty: A Critical Dialogue', Yale University, 14-15 September.

Altieri, M. (2012) Convergence or Divide in the Movement for Sustainable and Just Agriculture, In Lichtfouse, E. (Ed.) *Organic Fertilisation, Soil Quality and Human Health* (pp. 1-9). Dordrecht: Springer Netherlands.

Ambalam, K. (2014) 'Food Sovereignty in the Era of Land Grabbing: An African Perspective' *Journal of Sustainable Development* 7 (2): 121-132.

AWID (2012) Africa's Latest Land Rush: The Effect of Land Grabs on Women's Rights [Online] Available at https://www.awid.org/news-and-analysis/africas-latest-land-rush-effect-land-grabs-womens-rights [4 August 2017].

Behrman, J., Meinzen-Dick, R. and Quisumbing A. R. (2011) *The Gender Implications of Large-Scale Land Deals*, Washington DC: International Food Policy Research Institute (IFPRI).

Bomuhangi, A., Doss, C., and Meinzen-Dick, R. (2012) *Perspectives from Rural Ugandans and Implications for Land Acquisitions*. Washington DC: International Food Policy Research Institute (IFPRI).

Borras, S. and Franco, J. (2012) 'Global land Grabbing and Trajectories of Agrarian Change: A Preliminary Analysis', *Journal of Agrarian Change* 12 (1): 34–59.

Brodie, J. (2008) 'We are All Equal Now: Contemporary Gender Politics in Canada', *Feminist Theory* 9 (2): 145-164.

Bruce, J. W. and Tanner, C. (1992) 'Structural Adjustment, Land Concentration and Common Property: The Case of Guinea

Bissau', Paper Delivered at Meetings of Association for the Study of Common Property, Washington DC, 18-20 September.

Cooper, F. (2002) *Africa Since 1940,* New York: Columbia University Press.

Cotula, L., Vermeulen, S., Leonard, R. and Keeley, J. (2009) *Land Grab or Development Opportunity. Agricultural Investment and International Land deals in Africa,* London: IIED, FAO and IFAD.

Davison, J. (1988) Who Owns What? Land Registration and Tensions in Gender Relations of Production in Kenya', In Davison, J. (Ed.) *Agriculture, Women and Land: The African Experience* (pp. 157-176). Boulder: Westview Press.

Daley, E. and Park, C. M. (2012) *The Gender and Equity Implications of Land-related Investments on Labour and Income-generating Opportunities: A Case Study of Agricultural Investments in Northern Tanzania,* Rome: FAO.

De Schutter, O. (2011) 'How Not to Think of Land-Grabbing: Three Critiques of Large-Scale In-vestments in Farmland', *The Journal of Peasant Studies* 38 (2): 249-279

Delius, P. (2008) Contested Terrain: Land Rights and Chiefly Power in Historical Perspective, In Claassens, A. and Cousins, B. (Eds.), *Land, Power and Custom: Controversies Generated by South Africa's Communal Land Rights Act* (pp. 211–37). Cape Town: UCT Press.

Donkers, H. (2014) 'Sustainable Food Security, a Paradigm for Local and Regional Food Systems'. *International Journal of Humanities and Social Science* 4 (12): 89-102.

Federici, S. (2001) *The Debt Crisis, Africa and the New Enclosures,* The Commoner, [Online] Available at http://www.commoner.org.uk/02federici.pdf [6 August 2017].

Federici, S. (2004) *Caliban and the Witch,* New York: Autonomedia.

Federici, S. (2009) *The Reproduction of Labour-power in the Global Economy, Marxist Theory and the Unfinished Feminist Revolution,* [Online] Available at https://www.womin.org.za/images/the-alternatives/ecofeminism-social-reproduction-theory/S%20Federici%20-%20Labour%20Power,%20Marxist%20Theory%20and%20Feminist%20Revolution.pdf [4 August 2017].

Federici, S. (2011) Feminism and the Politics of the Commons, In Hughes, C., Peace, S. and Van Meter, K. (Eds.), *Uses of a World Wind, Movement, Movements, and Contemporary Radical Currents in the United States.* Oaskland: AK Press.

Fitzpatrick, I. (2015) *From the Roots Up: How Agroecology Can Feed Africa,* London: Global Justice Now.

Fleuret, A. (1988) Some Consequences of Tenure and Agrarian Reform in Taita, Kenya, In Downs, R. E. and Reyna, S. P. (Eds.), *Land and Society in Contemporary Africa* (pp. 136-158). London: University Press of New England.

Gimenez, M. E. (2005) 'Capitalism and the Oppression of Women: Marx Revisited,' *Science and Society* 69: 11-32.

Gray, L. and Kevane, M. (1999) 'Diminished Access, Diverted Exclusion: Women and Land Tenure in Sub-Saharan Africa,' *African Studies Review* 42 (2): 15-39.

Haiven, M. (2009) *Silvia Federici, on Capitalism, Colonialism, Women and Food Politics* [Online] Available at https://politicsandculture.org/2009/11/03/silvia-federici-on-capitalism-colonialism-women-and-food-politics/ [1 August 2017].

Harvey, D. (2001) "Globalization and the 'Spatial Fix'," *Geographische Revue* 2: 23–30.

Harvey, D. (2005) *A Brief History of Neoliberalism,* Oxford: Oxford University Press.

Harvey, D. (2009) "The 'New' Imperialism: Accumulation by Dispossession", *The Socialist Register:* 63-85.

Huillery, E. (2012) *The Black Man's Burden: The Cost of Colonization of French West Africa,* [Online] http://piketty.pse.ens.fr/files/Huilery2013JEH.pdf [7 August 2017].

Kachika, T. (2010) *Land Grabbing in Africa. A Review of the Impacts and the Possible Policy Responses,* [Online] Available from https://www.oxfamblogs.org/eastafrica/wp content/uploads/2010/11/Land-Grabbing-in-Africa.-Final.pdf [1 August 2017].

Kachingwe, N. (2012) *From Under their Feet: A think Piece on the Gender Dimensions of Land Grabs in Africa,*' Johannesburg: ActionAid International.

Kawewe, S. M., and Dibie, R. (2000) 'The Impact of Economic Structural Adjustment (ESAP) on Women and Children: Implications for Social Welfare in Zimbabwe,' *Journal of Sociology and Social Welfare* 27(4): 79–107.

LaFrancesca, J. (2013) 'Land Grabs and Implications on Food Sovereignty and Social Justice in Senegal', Unpublished MSc thesis, University of San Francisco.

Tambiah, S. (1989) 'Bridewealth and Dowry Revisited,' *Current Anthropology* 30(4): 413-427.

Magdoff, F. (2013) Twenty-First-Century Land Grabs: Accumulation by Agricultural Dispossession, *Monthly Review* [Online] Available at https://monthlyreview.org/2013/11/01/twenty-first-century-land-grabs/ [7 August 2017].

Meinzen-Dick, R. S., Brown, L. R., Feldstein, H. S., and Quisumbing, A. R. (1997) 'Gender, Property Rights, and Natural Resources', *World Development* 25 (8): 1303-1315.

McMichael, P. (2011) *Interpreting the Land Grab,* Uppsala: Uppsala Centre for Sustainable Development.

McRobbie, A. (2004) Notes on Postfeminism and Popular Culture: Bridget Jones and the New Gender Regime, In: Harris, A. (Ed.) *All About the Girl: Culture, Power and Identity* (3-14). New York: Routledge.

Narula, S. (2013) 'The Global Land Rush: Markets, Rights, and the Politics of Food', *Stanford Journal of International Law*: 101-175.

Nhemachena, A. (2017) Hearing the Footfalls of Humanoid Robots: Technoscience, (Un-)employment and the Future of Development in Twenty-First Africa, in Mawere, M. (ed) *Underdevelopment, Development and the Future of Africa.* Bamenda: Langaa RPCIG.

Oxfam (2011) *Land and Power: The Growing Scandal Surrounding the New Wave of 45 Investments in Land,* Briefing Paper 151, Oxford: Oxfam.

Oxfam (2013) *Promises, Power, And Poverty: Corporate Land Deals and Rural Women in Africa,* Oxford: Oxfam International.

Parpart, J. L. (1995) *Gender, Patriarchy and Development in Africa: The Zimbabwean Case*, Michigan: Women in International Development Publication.

Piercy, M. (2014) 'Welcome to Post Feminism and the Left is Obsolete', *Monthly Review* 66 (6) [Online] Available at https://monthlyreview.org/2014/11/01/welcome-to-post-feminism-and-the-left-is-obsolete/ [21 July 2017].

Roberts. A. (2012) 'Financial Crisis, Financial Firms... And Financial Feminism? The Rise of 'Transnational Business Feminism' and the Necessity of Marxist-Feminist IPE', *Socialist Studies* 8 (2): 85-108.

Schmidt, E. (1992) *Peasants, Traders, and Wives: Shona Women in the History of Zimbabwe, 1870- 1939*, Portsmouth: Heinemann.

Tandon, N. (2011) 'From Under their Feet. Women and the Land Grab Threat. Findings from Malawi, Mozambique and Zambia', Unpublished Research Report for ActionAid.

Taylor, A. (2015) 'Large-scale Land Acquisitions in Tanzania: A Critical Analysis of their Implications on Water Security', Unpublished MA thesis, Dalhousie University Halifax, Nova Scotia.

Thipe, T. (2013) 'Defining Boundaries: Gender and Property Rights in South Africa's Traditional Courts Bill', *Laws* 2: 483–511.

Vasudevan, A., McFarlane, C. and Jeffrey, A. (2008) 'Spaces of Enclosure', *Geoforum* 39(5): 1641– 1646.

Vhugen, D. (2012) 'Large-scale Commercial Investments in Land: Seeking to Secure Land Tenure and Improve Livelihoods', *Haramaya Law Review* 1 (1): 1-30.

Vogel, L. (1981) Marxism and Feminism: Unhappy Marriage, Trial Separation, or Something Else?', In Sargent, L. (ed.) *Women and Revolution*. Massachusetts: South End Press.

Vogel, L. (1995) *Woman Questions: Essays for a Materialist Feminism*, New York: Routledge.

Vogel, L. (2013) *Marxism and the Oppression of Women: Toward a Unitary Theory*, Chicago: Haymarket Books.

Wandia, M. (2009) 'Safeguarding Women's Rights will Boost Food Security', *Pambazuka News* 439, [Online] Available at http://pambazuka.org/en/category/features/57225 [1 August 2017].

White, B., Borras, S. M., Hall, R., Scoones, I. and Wolford, W. (2012) 'The New Enclosures: Critical Perspectives on Corporate Land Deals', *Journal of Peasant Studies* 39(3–4): 619–647.

Wengraf, L. (2016) Legacies of Colonialism in Africa: Imperialism, Dependence, and Development, *International Socialist Review*, 103 [Online] Available at http://isreview.org/issue/103/legacies-colonialism-africa [Accessed 6 August 2017].

World Bank (2012) *World Development Report 2012: Gender Equality and Development*, Washington DC: The World Bank.

World Bank (2014) *Improving Gender Equality in Africa*, [Online] Available at
http://www.worldbank.org/en/region/afr/brief/improving-gender-equality-in-africa [Accessed 6 August 2017].

Zetterlund, Y. (2013) Gender and Land Grabbing: A Post-Colonial Feminist Discussion about the Consequences of Land Grabbing in Rift alley Kenya, Unpublished MA Thesis, Malmo University.

Chapter Eight

Reconfiguring the African *Jindwi* Traditional Drums in a Post- colonial Mutare Museum Setting, Zimbabwe

Njabulo Chipangura & Pauline Chiripanhura

Introduction

In this chapter, we will examine Mutare Museum's long history of asportation and "collecting" ethnographic objects rooted within colonial classifications and we argue for the inclusion of African communities in museum activities in a post-colonial milieu. We will begin by carefully examining how the placing and displaying of traditional drums *(ngoma)* in one of the museum's galleries was influenced by colonial assumptions that source community interactions with their asported and dislocated objects should go no further than visual observation. More so, Africans were not allowed to perform their rituals which were feared by colonialists who were apprehensive of African prophets that stirred and led rebellions across the continent. We thus argue that museumising was a tool of capture that did not only serve colonial curiosities but was also a mode of dispossessing and disinheriting Africans from their sacred religious objects that could potentially influence future anticolonial uprisings. Subsequently, African songs were also banned during the colonial era as they were used together with African drums to stir insurrections, rebellions and resistance to colonial subjugation (Ranger, 1967; 1970). We also see that once the drums were asported and placed in museums they served a dual function in that they became objects of colonial ethnographic investigations and captured 'trophies' meant to block rallying points of African anticolonial insurgencies. Thus, within this discourse, the museum was overwhelmingly used as an institution to propagate the colonial ethnographic gaze, in a context where ethnography and anthropology were used to buttress colonialism, contrary to the socio-cultural histories of the objects which hinged on certain African community values and beliefs. Using the example of ritual drums forcibly seized from the *Jindwi* community in Zimunya, Mutare in the late 1960s we argue that the African sacred ritual and secular uses of the drums were thereafter overshadowed because of the museumising process. However, we also recognised that in part, this discourse was a secular ritual performed by the colonialist to shut down dissenting voices speaking against colonial subjugation and dispossession.

Finding Mutare Museum and the African Ethnographic Objects

Located in Eastern Zimbabwe, Mutare Museum is one of the five museums under the administration of the National Museums and Monuments of Zimbabwe (NMMZ). This museum was established in 1964 [just at about the time when the anticolonial liberation war started] and is a by-product of colonisation which started in 1890. Zimbabwe, formerly called [Southern] Rhodesia, obtained its political independence from Britain in 1980. The other museums in the country are; the Zimbabwe Museum of Human Sciences in Harare which specialises in archaeological and ethnographic "collections", the Natural Museum in Bulawayo looks after natural history "collections", the Military Museum in Gweru is assigned with the role of looking after military "collections" and the Great Zimbabwe Museum in Masvingo which specializes in the conservation of dry stone structures. Whilst we agree that Mutare museum's system of displaying ethnographic collections was shaped by colonialism in a way that resulted in the dispossession and marginalisation of certain communities, in this chapter we maintain that these "collections" can still be reconfigured to convey new meanings by using ethnomuseological approaches. A possible association between the ethnographic objects with the source communities can thus be established because they are eager to repossess their objects and be involved in museum activities and to challenge the legitimacy of curators in their self-proclaimed exclusive right as guardians and interpreters of the material past (Comaroff and Comaroff, 1992).Thus, contemporary insights resulting from reflexive and critical engagements with living communities is of immense value in constituting the field of ethnomuseology.

Fig 1; Showing Mutare Museum (picture by Paul Mupira)

Numerous ethnographic objects asported and collected during the colonial period are housed at Mutare museum and are exhibited in a manner that conforms to the traditional and colonial practice of dispossessing Africans [taking the objects away from the African visual observation] and then presenting their objects exclusively for European and American visual observation. The objects are displayed on the floor in a derogatory way, presenting the objects as if they were strange and exotic, and devoid of any social and historical significance (See Fig 2). This chapter will therefore illustrate how we managed to interpret the socio-cultural functions of the drums using referential analogies drawn from our participant observation in contemporary *Jindwi* ritual practices. Overall, we argue that by removing the objects from their cultural setting and inserting them into the visual symbol system of the museum, their dynamic web of physical and social use and meaning was broken.

Fig 2; Sledges displayed on the floor in the transport gallery without any labels or accompanying text

A Short History of the Mutare Museum

The history of Umtali Museum is inextricably interwoven with that of the Umtali Society (Broadley, 1966). The Umtali Society came into being as a committee of the Southern Rhodesia Hunters and Game Preservation Association in October 1953. This society was established for inaugurating and fostering interest in the establishment of a museum in Umtali. A subcommittee was set up with Captain Boultbee as Honorary Curator who then initiated the "collection" of objects for the new museum. The society accumulated and displayed the first "collections" of historical and natural objects, which persuaded the municipality to provide a temporary home for the museum. As they still had to obtain a building, their first exhibition was shown in an empty showroom in January 1956 inspiring colonial public interest in the proposed museum. It was only in November 1957 that the Umtali Municipality granted the association some space in an old hostel, allowing them to exhibit on a semi-permanent basis (Broadley, 1966). Captain Boultbee contributed pistols alongside specimens obtained in Rhodesia. By mid-1958, about 500 people were visiting the museum each month but the museum had no funds for maintenance and development leading the association to approach the trustees of National Museums and Monuments of Rhodesia to takeover. Sir Edgar Whitehead officially opened the museum in November 1958 and, having secured grants from the government and Umtali Municipality, in August 1959 the trustees took over the Umtali Museum as the third one under their control Captain E.F Boultbee was then appointed Honorary Curator of the Umtali Museum Society on 1 September 1959.

The trustees realised that the existing building was unsuitable and with the help of the Umtali Museum Society it raised funds for the new museum building. The new museum building was officially opened by Sir Alfred Beit on 13 September 1964. When it opened its doors to the public, the museum had displays in antiquities, transport, botany and geology. Later, additional displays of ethnographic and archaeological objects were put in the Beit Gallery. Therefore, as can be deduced from this historical narrative, the formation of Mutare Museum and many other museums throughout Africa are closely linked with the phenomenon of colonialism (Bvocho, 2011). These museums share a common history in terms of their development in that they were by-products of colonialism and are 20th century creations; a period in which their formulation came because of European imperialism. They were created in specific socio-political contexts that sought to denigrate and disinherit the local populace, diminish self-confidence and to reduce pride in their past achievements. Similarly, we can argue that ethnographic displays at Mutare Museum have been stagnant ever since independence in 1980 and biased towards colonialism such that many socio-cultural aspects of source communities from which these objects were obtained have been ignored. As a result, indigenous populations have roundly criticised museums for being alien, imported, elitist, urban-based and serving colonial interests, decades after colonialism ended in Africa (Nzewunwa, 1994). Murambiwa (1999), writing on the history of Mutare Museum, argues that between 1965 and 1979 there were deliberate attempts to use this museum to undermine African culture while at the same time highlighting the positive impact of colonisation.

The Authorised Museum Discourse in the Beit Gallery

Mutare museum has five permanent display galleries namely; Eastern Districts, Mezzanine, Transport, Boultbee and Beit. The Beit gallery measures approximately 224 square metres and it contains a wide range of exhibitions that cover themes related to the traditional aspects of the Shona culture in Zimbabwe. Shona is the name widely given to the indigenous population in Zimbabwe and is constituted by people who speak one similar language also called *Shona*. However, the *Shona* language itself is not homogenous because within it are different dialects that vary from region to region. Eastern Zimbabwe is constituted by the *Manyika, Ndau, Jindwi, Hwesa* and *Karanga* speaking people. Our focus is on the *Jindwi* traditional drums that are housed in this gallery. The Beit Gallery has two entrances. The first entrance is in front close to the main museum entrance and the other is situated just adjacent to the Boultbee gallery. The gallery in its old format before it was revamped in 2016 comprised of transport accessories in glass case on the immediate left side of the first entrance. Opposite this display were zoological displays comprising animal, tree and two cases with different kind of insects. Next to this was a display of traditional beehives with one containing live bees. Along the length of the gallery, there were a variety of mixed objects including geological displays, different types of traditional artefacts, such as drums and games such as *tsoro*. Coupled to these, was a display case with beads, head rests, snuff boxes and a portrait of a traditional chief adorned with symbols of chieftainship, such as badges and ceremonial artefacts (Mareya, 1999). In this old set up the exhibitions in the Beit gallery did not represent any meaningful story and visitors could easily mistake it for a storeroom. This is because the gallery had a mixture of a lot of different types of exhibits having no clear-cut objectives and or specific themes. The problem was worsened by an improper and almost derogatory presentation of ethnographic artefacts which were dumped on the floor displayed as strange, exotic and devoid of any social and historical significance to the way of life of the African people (see fig 2).

Thus, since the inception of political independence in 1980, Mutare Museum has failed to reorganise these misconstrued ethnographic exhibits that wrongly depict the indigenous population. For example, the *Jindwi* traditional drums were acquired during the colonial period as part of a broader trajectory ostensibly in the colonial scientific study of the cultures of the African 'other'. Archaeologists and ethnographers were given the responsibility to amass the objects which they later displayed in the Beit gallery after completing the inquiries. The objects were subsequently displayed without contextual information or showing an appreciation of where they came from as they were only serving the documentation, conservation and presentation function. However, in as much as the museum prioritised the physical protection of the objects, museum communities valued their sacred and secular ritual functions more than anything else. They recognised the socio-cultural practices that ensured the survival of the objects since time immemorial before they were asported from their original contexts and placed in a museum. Thus, the authorised museum discourse excluded contemporary values of museum communities which were centred on both tangible and intangible use, secular and sacred values. We borrow our use of the Authorised Museum Discourse (AMD) concept from Smith (2006) who describes a similar process she termed the Authorised Heritage Discourse (AHD) as a set of practices and performances that populate expert constructions of heritage knowledge by "obscuring" the social and cultural practices that are the precursors to this materiality. However, it is also necessary to note here that museumisation did not necessarily obscure the African socio-cultural practices, rather museumisation replaced Africans' social cultural practices with European colonists' socio-cultural practices [including the ceremonial commissioning of the museums] within which the asported African objects were implanted. We, by extension, argue that while the *Jindwi* community appreciate the physical structure of the drums, their religious uses also mattered particularly in relation to rain petitioning ceremonies. Thus, we also note that by museumising, the colonists did not merely obscure African social and cultural practices, they also foregrounded their own social and cultural practices including those that constituted foundations of colonisation and dispossession.

In our study of *Jindwi* drums, we used an analytical approach developed by Karp and Kratz (2000) to examine the political-economy and materiality of ethnographic representations in museums. Of fundamental importance to this approach was a careful consideration and examination of the word 'ethnography' as central to exhibitions of people's cultures. In analysing this term, Karp and Kratz (2000 :19) concluded that "ethnographic displays are not only confined to natural history museums, ethnographic museums or culture history museums" as "they are part of almost all cultural displays, including displays of the ethnographic, and other displays in art museums and outside museum contexts altogether". Furthermore, they also classify ethnographic displays as emerging out of complex histories and ideological contexts that include at least four elements. These four elements cover aspects of enlightenment, imperial and colonial expansion history, the actual history of representation itself, and, finally, the history of exhibiting exotic cultures (Karp and Kratz, 2000: 19). Similarly, the displaying of *Jindwi* drums in the Beit Gallery somehow fits within the premise of exhibiting supposedly exoticised cultures by the colonial authority when the museum was opened to the public in 1964. However, Africans cultures were not necessarily exotic in Africa although colonists sought to exoticise such cultures. As a matter of fact, it was the colonists who were exotic in Africa and not the African cultures.

The AMD as a concept can then be used to explain such irregularities in ethnographic representations. First, as we have argued earlier on, the history of asportation, "collecting" and displaying ethnographic objects in colonial museums was intricately interwoven with colonial scientific inquiries on the cultures of the 'other' [erroneously deemed to lack their own science]. Thus, colonial and utopian desires to classify the indigenous populace as the 'other' through the ethnographic gaze and the longing for a primitive timeless African past were the harbingers to the formation of most African museums (Chipangura, 2014). Henceforth, museum curators were endowed with tremendous authority in configuring ethnographic displays thereby 'othering' indigenous knowledge

226

systems within the premises of the AMD. Disciplines such as ethnography, archaeology and anthropology were used in this discourse not only to cement racial binaries but *a fortiori* to disinherit Africans whose objects were subsequently exhibited in museum displays. For example, ethnographic "collections" were exhibited in the Beit Gallery in a manner that conforms to the traditional practice of presenting objects exclusively for colonialists' visual observation. Yet, some argue that this type of scenography does not do justice to objects which, it is argued, cannot be understood in terms of a single unchanging identity, but rather, by tracing the succession of meanings attached to them as they move through space and time (Edwards, Gosden and Phillips, 2006).

The placing of asported objects in a museum created the exhibitionary complex; - a visual gaze that undergirds colonial practices of exhibiting ethnographic objects in African museums. According to Bennett (1995:13) the exhibitionary complex "… perfected a self-monitoring system of looks in which the subject and object positions can be exchanged, in which the crowd comes to commune with and voluntarily regulate itself through interiorising the ideal and ordered view of itself as seen from the controlling vision of power- a site of sight accessible to all". In this way, not only was a new 'public' formed within the narratives of national progress through and toward civilization, but it was also placed in "new relations of sight and vision" as well as "new relations of power and knowledge" (Bennett, 1995:14). However, we note here that the colonial exhibitionism and display of African objects privileged the vision and ocular senses of the colonists while denying Africans, from whom the objects were seized, the same privilege to be visibly and contiguously with their objects. In other words, rendering African objects visible in the colonial museums had a corollary, which is, that its other side was the denial of the value [dispossessed] Africans placed on seeing their own objects in their own communities. Mutare Museum thus occupies a distinctive niche in the development of Euro-modern scientific enquiry, as a site of dispossession and accumulation where objects were arranged in specified colonial orders even as the dispossession of Africans [of the same objects] created disorder in their communities and cosmologies.

227

This is the reason why today, the *Jindwi* community still regard the museum as an institution laden with colonial associations, cultural repression, and disruption of their religious and secular community order and loss of their heritage. Thus, the onus was on this museum to change ethnographic displays which had been static for a long time in which indigenous societies were frozen in a kind of timeless past (Chipangura, 2014). Museums thus have a distinctive role to play in (re-)configuring geographies of (neo-)colonial power, dispossession, space and the de-construction of knowledge that endorsed imperial policies (Rassool, 2006).

The Post-colonial Museum and Knowledge Production

In most African countries, the notion of a museum in its totality is still regarded as Eurocentric with a lot of people regarding the museum as an 'appropriator' of their important cultural objects that were stolen and looted by (neo-)imperialists. Harrison and Hughes (2010: 250), writing about the role of museums in post-colonial societies, argue that "post-colonies are connected in terms of their heritage by the need to forge new national identities in the wake of decolonisation". Identity has emerged as one of the most important issues for postcolonial nations and as such [postcolonial] museums plays an important role in helping people to identify both who they are as individuals and the collectives to which they belong (Harrison and Hughes, 2010). Similarly, the *Jindwi* community regard the drums that are at Mutare museum as symbols of identity and as a result are critical on the authorised ways by which the objects are displayed in the glass cases. Within a post-colonial museum setting, the ways in which colonialism structured dispossession policies and ideologies associated with the displaying of ethnographic objects are challenged. This is because colonialism was the precursor to the imposition of the western model of the museum in the early twentieth century and as a result the indigenous people lost cultural objects and were marginalised from the colonial and imperial museums. Ethnographic objects were simply looted from local communities without a proper understanding of their socio-cultural uses and various associations with their makers. Thus, rethinking of old dispossession policies which facilitated the looting of drums belonging to the *Jindwi* community should be critically examined from postcolonial lenses which allow us to cognise the subsequent misrepresentations of exhibitions under the pretext of colonial scientific research. Displaced from their original context and re-placed in museums, they became drums of colonial ethnography and were assigned with new colonial meanings derived from colonial scientific, historical and aesthetic paradigms of western knowledge (Gimblet, 1991).

The post-colonial museum also advocates for a movement away from Western traditional object oriented approaches in museums into becoming spaces of interactive engagement between various cultures (Bruce, 2006). This is because many museums are rapidly transforming by aligning themselves to the demands brought about by community expectations. The value of an artefact does not reside in the artefact alone, but in its [African] social use and environmental context that foregrounded its making in a localised set up (Smith, 2006; Gimblet, 1991). More so, today with ever-changing expectations, museums are looking at the historical connections between the objects and source communities to ensure continued relevancy within the communities that they serve (Chipangura, 2014). Often, the objects stored and displayed by museums have deep socio-cultural meanings that transcend beyond the AMD. However, it is imperative not to only emphasise mere "connections" or cultural "meanings" of [African] objects but to also highlight the African ownership and possession of the objects. In other words, Africans are not merely connected to objects but they own and possess their objects.

Jindwi Ritual Ceremonies and Approaches in Ethnomuseology

The Eastern Shona comprise of several chieftainships and covers seven major districts which are Buhera, Mutasa, Makoni, Chipinge, Chimanimani, Mutare and Nyanga. During the colonial period, ethnographic objects were "collected" from these areas for scientific study stimulated by colonial desires to understand the cultural diversity of the natives. Our focus in this chapter is on traditional drums that were looted from Zimunya chieftainship under Mutare

District. We employed the ethnomusicological approaches to rethink the placement of the drums in the Beit gallery. This is because some scholars think that objects like the drums acquire a wide range of meanings during their use as they pass through the hands of individuals, embedded in different social strategies and networks before being dislocated from their original context by becoming museum "collections" (Gosselain, 1999; Appadurai, 1986; Hoskins, 1998). The *Jindwi* community of Zimunya used several instruments to give rhythm to their songs during the ritual ceremonies. They used drums, *mbira, marimba, hosho,* hand and leg rattles and flute type instruments. Each occasion had its own type of music and dances. *Chimaisiri* is one good example of a dance that was performed by the *Jindwi* punctuated by loud drum beats during the ceremonies. We gathered that originally this dance was associated solely with hunting ritual ceremonies but has now become a social dance for beer parties, other joyful occasions and funerals. In the past, *Chimaisiri* dance was performed before a hunting session as a way of asking for guidance and protection from various wild animals that hunters used to encounter in the forest. It was also performed after hunting as a way of celebrating a successful hunting session.

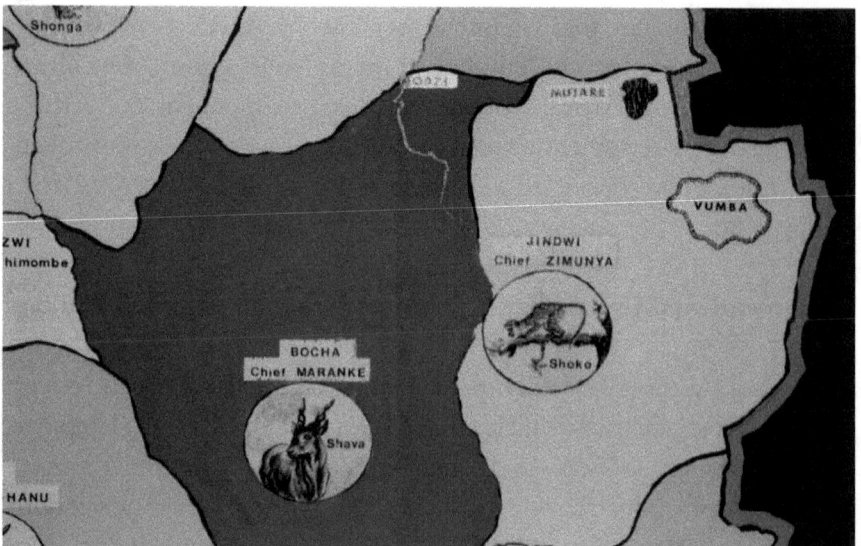

Fig 3; The *Jindwi* of Zimunya and their neighbours (picture by authors).

Mhande is another indigenous song –dance which was performed by the *Jindwi* during the annual ritual for rain and accompanied by the drum beat. The *mhande* repertoire consists of distinctive songs and rhythms used for communicating with the *majukwa* (spirits that intercede between Africans and God-for rain). The *majukwa* spirits in turn communicate with God (*Mwari*) the provider of rain on behalf of the people. Mhande performance involves singing, drum playing, hand clapping, dancing and ululation. It is generally believed and accepted by the *Jindwi* that religion is a medium through which some complex problems of this earth especially comprehension of the life after death or life **beyond the grave** can be addressed. Their social structure rests on religious beliefs and that *Nyadenga* (God) the Heavenly Supreme Being is responsible for everyone's destiny. Since God was said to be busy in the Heavenly spiritual world, he was not accessed by an ordinary man but through spirits - *Midzimu* which can be at family level or *mhondoro* which operates at broader cultural levels and across different families and communities. Thus, the *Jindwi* believe that when a person dies, his/her spirit wanders about until rituals are performed for the spirit of the deceased to come back and protect its children. Ceremonies are held by the *Jindwi* which give these spirits of the deceased leeway to come back to the family. Only a fully-grown person who bore children has such ceremonies performed for them. These ancestral spirits help and guide the families in their day-to-day lives. The spirits of the dead are believed to convey any message from the living to the Heavenly God and as such are central to the religion and belief of the *Jindwi*. The *Midzimu* was also the commonly used medium during the rain requesting ceremonies. Such hierarchical and well-structured religious beliefs by the *Jindwi* strongly refute colonial misconceptions and ideas about the supposedly animistic nature of African cultural beliefs.

Fig 4; The *mhande* ritual dance by the *Jindwi* during rain requesting petitions (picture by authors).

Against this background, we used ethnomuseology as a methodology to shed light on questions concerning material and ritual technologies used by the *Jindwi* relative to similar objects that were collected and placed in the museum. Unlike conventional museological conceptions of linear and sequential time in native perspectives here we argued that sometimes the past, the present and the future coexist. This is because for colonial beneficiaries of museums, objects can re-enact multiple temporalities that coexist and may become reactivated through human sensuous and sensory practices (Hamilakis and Anagnostopoulos, 2009). Thus, we essentially observed that the *Jindwi* are still using the same traditional drums, which are found in museum exhibitions, during their ritual ceremonies. Such kind of analogical reasoning underpins interpretations of the past developed within the context of personal knowledge of how individuals and communities interact with material culture (Iles and Childs, 2002:193). Moreover, contemporary communities generally exploit the same traditional objects just like their forebears with little changes. On this point, it is necessary to note Nhemachena's (2015; 2017) observation that African ancestors are not necessarily in the realm of the past because they are regarded by Africans to be ahead in the ancestral world-thus ancestors are not inhabitants of the past, as erroneously portrayed by colonial scholars and writers. The *Jindwi* drum *(ngoma)* is cylindrical in shape, open and narrower at the bottom than the top. The drum is made from hardwood and has its top covered by animal skin secured on both sides with wooden pegs (Ellert, 1984).

The other type of drum used by the *Jindwi* is semi-circular with a skin stretched over the opening and secured by wooden pegs (See fig 5). Ethnographic methods were used together with museological approaches to explore the contemporary relevance and meaning of the material past. Using ethnomuseology research we also managed to observe the ritual practices associated with the use of the traditional drums. Music accompanied most of the activities that the *Jindwi* engaged in. The drum was used during funerals, traditional ceremonies and festivities. Apart from the drum, the other instruments that were used are; thumb pianos, xylophones, hand and leg rattles and flutes to give rhythm to their songs and to make them more entertaining. By conducting this research, we aimed at bridging the gap between the static object displayed in the museum and similar objects that are being used in ceremonies. This method also enabled us to clarify issues of theory and epistemology that drives the AMD by directly observing the social dynamics associated with the use of the drums. Typically, it was also more of a participant observation in *Jindwi* ritual ceremonies with a view of producing a comprehensive and empirically based reconstruction of past behaviours that could inform us on the real uses of same objects which are displayed devoid of context at Mutare Museum.

Fig 5; The various *Jindwi* drums encased in a display in the revamped Beit Gallery

Ethnomuseology as a method can either use substantive or referential reasoning. Substantive analogical reasoning requires a close contextual similarity or direct historical continuity between the past and the present (McCall, 2012:163). It can thus be used in making a direct equation of an ethnographically known phenomenon with some material culture that is found in museum exhibitions. Referential reasoning is another mode of ethnomuseology which "…relies on the recognition of linkages between the dynamics of human behaviour, its organization into cultural systems, and the resulting patterns of material remains that were looted and placed in museum as displays (McCall, 2012:164). This method was used to link the characteristics of contemporary *Jindwi* uses of the drums with the systems of human behaviour that produced them. Subsequently, the same narratives that emerged from referential reasoning were used to assign African socio-cultural values to the drums that were encased in dioramas in the Beit Gallery. Thus, cultural practices have been undertaken using the drums even before the introduction of authorised conservation systems in museums by the colonialists.

The Revamped Beit Gallery

A new exhibition emerged from this ethnomuseology research in the revamped Beit Gallery which was opened in June 2016. This exhibition is the first wholesome post-colonial display at Mutare Museum which was designed with the full participation of the dispossessed communities. The main aim of the exhibition is to promote cultural tolerance and interaction in communities and an understanding of local cultures that are being threatened by changing [global] socio-political developments. Traditional music and dance is one of the subthemes that are focused on in this new exhibition which chronicles the traditional aspects of the Eastern Shona people in Zimbabwe. Our ethnomuseological research revealed that the Eastern Shona people are music lovers. They entertained themselves through music and dance hence music formed part of their tradition in their day to day activities such as cultivating, harvesting and during funerals. Although the coming of the western culture had an impact on the musical industry of the Eastern Shona, these traditional forms of entertainment still exist especially in the rural areas. In this exhibition, events and their specific songs and dances are explained and short video images of traditional musical performances are shown.

The new exhibition uses both audio and video depictions to illustrate the socio-cultural uses of the drums that were discursively collected when this museum was opened in 1964. We argue that the objects should not be separated from beliefs, values, ideas, attitudes and assumptions of the African society.

Conclusion

In this chapter, we looked at how colonialism informed the formation of Mutare museum together with its underlying ethnographic looting practices. In the colonial era, ethnographic objects were stolen from source communities, studied and exhibited in the museums. Curators were assigned the role of keepers with colonial "expert" knowledge in documentation, conservation and exhibition of the objects. We used the case study of the *Jindwi* of

Zimunya to illustrate how the authorised museum discourse further dispossessed communities that were keen to reclaim their drums which were encased in dioramas. However, with the advent of the post-colonial museum concept, communities began to critique the looting and exhibition practices that had for long failed to recognise the importance of their objects, haphazardly looted and stored in a colonial museum setting. For such communities, ideas structured around notions of spirituality, rituals, sacredness were the harbingers to materiality which manifested in the form of drums that were appropriated for scientific study and found home in museums. More so, we argued that by removing the drums from their cultural setting and inserting them into the colonialists' visual symbol system of the museum, their dynamic web of physical, economic and social meaning was broken. Museum communities continue to ascribe values to these objects in different ways from practitioners and their interpretations in most cases conflicts with the official museological narratives.

Acknowledgements

This chapter is based on a broad ethnographic fieldwork that we undertook in Eastern Zimbabwe between 2014 and 2015 under a project titled *'The traditional aspects of the Eastern Shona'*. The project received financial support from the Beit Trust with a view of reorganising of the old collections in the Beit Gallery at Mutare Museum. The new display which is a cumulative result of this research was opened in June 2016. Ethnographic interviews, audio and video recordings and photographing were carried out with the permission of the cultural groups under study.

References

Appadurai, A. (1986) *The social life of things, commodities in cultural perspectives*, Cambridge: Cambridge University Press.
Bennett, T. (1995) *The Birth of the Museum*, London and New York: Routledge.

Broadley, D.G. (1966) 'History of Umtali Museum', *Rhodesian Science News*, Volume 8, Number 5, 1966.

Bruce, C. (2006) Spectacle and Democracy: Experience Museum Project as a Post-Museum. In *New Museum Theory and Practice.* Martine, J., (ed), Oxford: Blackwell Publishing.

Bvocho G. (2013) 'Multimedia, Museums and the Public: Communicating Heritage Information', *Museum Memoir No. 3*, Harare: National Museums and Monuments of Zimbabwe.

Chipangura, N. (2014) Rethinking the practice of collecting and displaying ethnographic objects at Mutare Museum'. In *Museums and the Idea of Historical Progress.* Omar, R., *et.al* (eds), Cape Town: Iziko Museum Publication.

Classen, E. *et.al.* (2006) The Museum as Sensescape: Western Sensibilities and Indigenous Artifacts in *Sensible Objects; Colonialism, Museums and Material Culture.* Edwards, E., *et.al* (eds), Oxford and New York: Berg.

Comaroff J and Comaroff J. (1992) Ethnography and the Historical Imagination, Boulder Co: Westview

Edwards, E. *et.al.* (2006) Introduction. In *Sensible Objects; Colonialism, Museums and Material Culture.* Edwards, E., *et.al* (eds), Oxford and New York, Berg.

Ellert, H. (1984) The Material Culture of Zimbabwe, Harare: Longman.

Gimblet, B.K. (1991) Objects of Ethnography. In *Exhibiting Cultures: The Poetics and Politics of Museum Displays.* Karp, I., and Lavine, S.D., (eds), Washington DC: Smithsonian Institution Press.

Harrison, R. and Hughes, L. (2010) Understanding *the Politics of Heritage: Global Heritage Perspective.* Manchester: Manchester University Press.

Hamilakis, Y. and Anagnostopoulos, A. (2009) 'What is Archaeological Ethnography?' *Public Archaeology: Archaeological Ethnographies*, Vol. 8, No. 2-3.

Iles, L. and Terry, S. (2014) Ethnoarcaheological and Historical Methods. In *Archaeometallurgy in Global Perspective; Methods and Synthesis.* Robert B.W., and Thornton C.P., (eds). New York: Springer.

Karp, I. and Kratz, C. (2000) Reflections on the Fate of Tippoo's Tiger: Defining Cultures through Public Display. In *Cultural Encounters and Representing 'Otherness'*. Hallam, E., and Street, B.V., (eds.), London and New York, Routledge.

Mareya, B. (1999) Project proposal for the Beit Gallery New Exhibitions: The Traditional aspects of the Eastern Shona in Zimbabwe' Unpublished, National Museums and Monuments of Zimbabwe.

Mupira P. (2013) Storyline for the Proposed Reorganisation of the Beit Gallery Exhibitions, Unpublished, National Museums and Monuments of Zimbabwe.

Murambiwa, I. (1999) 'Reconciling the museum with its stakeholders: Mutare Museum's challenge', A paper presented at the Museums, Peace. Democracy and Governance in the 21 Century, Commonwealth Association of Museums' Triennial Conference, Barbados, May 5-12.

Nhemachena, A. (2015) Indigenous Knowledge, Conflation and Postcolonial Translation: lessons from Fieldwork in Contemporary Rural Zimbabwe, in Mawere, M. and Awuah-Nyamekye, A. (eds.) *Between Rhetoric and Reality: the State and use of Indigenous Knowledge in Postcolonial Africa*. Bamenda: Langaa RPCIG.

Nhemachena, A. (2017) *Relationality and Resilience in a Not So Relational World? Knowledge, Chivanhu and (De-)Coloniality in 21ˢᵗ Century Conflict-Torn Zimbabwe*. Bamenda: Langaa RPCIG.

Nzewunwa, N. (1994) The Nigerian Teacher and Museum Culture. In *The Presented Past: Heritage, Museums and Education*. Stone P.G, and Molyneaux, B.L, (eds), London: Routledge.

Prown, J.D. (1982) Mind in Matter: An Introduction to Material Culture Theory and Method, *Winterthur Portfolio*, Vol.17, No.1.

Ranger, T. (1967) *Revolt in Southern Rhodesia, 1896-1897.A Study in African Resistance*, London: Heinemann

Ranger, T. (1970) *The African Voice in Southern Rhodesia, 1898-1930,* London: Heinemann,

Rassool, C. (2006) Community Museums, Memory Politics and Social Transformation in South Africa: Histories, Possibilities and Limits. In Museum *Frictions: Public Cultures/Global*

Transformations. Karp, I., *et al* (ed), Durham: Duke University Press.

Smith, L.J. (2006) *Uses of Heritage.* London and New York: Routledge

Chapter Nine

A Contextual Analysis of Small-Scale Mining: Interrogating the Question of Materialities in Namibia

Paulus Mwetulundila

Introduction

Namibia is classified by the World Bank as an upper middle-income country with an estimated annual Gross Domestic Product (GDP) per capita of U$ 5293 (The Namibian, 1 January 2014). The county is rich in material natural resources ranging from marine resources to mineral resources that are influential in producing and driving most of the country's wealth (National Planning Commission, 2012). Since shortly after independence the Namibian government has, on the basis of misguided advice from the International Monetary Fund (IMF) and the World Bank, pursued atrocious free market principles in the hope of promoting commercial development and job creation to bring disadvantaged Namibians into the mainstream economic realm. It was thought that the rural population would also benefit from the implementation of the neoliberal free market principles which were erroneously regarded as capable of uplifting the material means of livelihoods of the citizens. Indicative of the lack of material means of subsistence among the Namibian citizens is the 2011 National Housing and Population Census which showed that the country's population stands at 2.1 million people (Namibia Statistic Agency (NSA), 2012) of which 278 245 people are unemployed (NSA, 2015) and a high proportion of these figures is likely to fall or has already fallen into a trap of the vicious cycle of impoverishment due to lack of material means of subsistence. These statistics necessitate sustained scholarly attention to the need for decolonising African materialities, in Namibia, including the dynamics of material means of subsistence among the majority of the impoverished and disinherited African population.

241

In Namibia, a large section [about 5 000 to 10 000] of the population, survives by small scale mining which provides their material means of livelihood. They mine high value semi-precious stones such as green, blue and multi-colour tourmaline, green and orange garnet and aquamarine found in central Erongo and northern Kunene (Mweemba, 2014). If well managed, small-scale mining can make a remarkable contribution to employment creation, which in the long run will help reduce impoverishment in the Namibian population. For example, in Tanzania it is reported that the government's support to the small-scale mining sector alleviated rural impoverishment on a scale far surpassing the impact of donor funded job creation efforts in the 1990 (Simonis Storm Securities, 2006). Small-scale mining is one of the sub-sectors in Namibia that is under-researched, thus a little is known about it despite being in existence for about 70 years (Nyambe and Amunkete, 2009). Overall, the mining sector in Namibia plays a significant contribution to the country's economy, accounting for about 9.3% of GDP (Mweemba, 2014).

While some scholars assume that the extraction of minerals in Africa started with colonisation, there is evidence that, in Namibia, there was mineral extraction among pre-colonial inhabitants who produced minerals such as copper and iron (Jourdan, 1990). Also while some writers like Latour (2005) presuppose that in traditional societies minerals were regarded as actors, subjects or gods and goddesses, in Namibia, there is evidence that minerals that were/are extracted and sold are/were considered to be objects and not subjects. In this sense, when Namibians extract and sell their minerals, they do not consider themselves to be extracting and selling subjects or gods and goddesses. For this reason, there is need to be careful about some theories which would be dangerously inaccurate if uncritically applied to African environments and to African philosophy on materialities. While some scholars like Smith (2011) argue against Africans exercising environmental sovereignty, Namibians need to exercise environmental and material sovereignty for them to extract their resources and sell them in order to have material means of survival. The examples of small-scale miners in Tanzania and Namibia are apt to show the importance, on the part of Africans, of exercising sovereignty over their environments. The critical question here is about how Africans can realise economic sovereignty if they do not exercise environmental and material sovereignty, that is, sovereignty over their environments and over their materialities? The argument in this chapter is that to deprive Africans of sovereignty over their materialities [whether by purveying ideologies about subject-subject relations, agency, animism or flat/protean ontologies] including their environments amounts to legitimising the dispossession and (re-)colonisation of Africans.

Mining activities are of two categories, namely; large-scale mining and small-scale mining. Larger-scale mining is usually undertaken by big transnational companies that also employ skilled workers. In large-scale mining, diamonds, gold and uranium are extracted. Because of the fact that large-scale mining employs skilled workers and due to the fact that the large-scale mining industries are believed to remit some taxes, the Namibian government's attention has been largely focused on large-scale mining, with very little attention to small-scale mining. As far as Namibia is concerned, small-scale mining is defined as mining processes that use low technology or mining with minimal machinery, low financial inputs and miners are generally [formally] unskilled (Mweemba, 2014). A similar definition that fits the Namibian context was coined by Hentschel *et al* (2002), who define small-scale mining as mining by individuals, groups, families or cooperatives with minimal or no mechanisation, usually in the nonformal sector of the market. The extraction is based on exploiting small ore-bodies that are uneconomical for large-scale mining. These mining areas [for small-scale mining] are called mining claims and are only granted to Namibians or individuals who are holders of non-exclusive prospecting licenses (NEPL). NEPL is a mining license acquired by small scale miners to prospect for any minerals or group of minerals on any land throughout Namibia. It is issued by the Namibian Ministry of Mines and Energy (MME) (Mweemba, 2014). The application process for NEPL and mining claims cost about US$ 4.50 for individuals and small companies enabling affordability to low income earners unlike the exclusive prospecting license (EPL) and mining license (ML) which are licenses for big organisations that requires rigorous processes and costly exercises to execute mining activities in Namibia.

Namibia's small-scale mining interest is on developing mineral deposits by exploring for mining in some of the numerous small minerals deposits that occur in some regions of the country. There are more than 35 different minerals and materials in small-scale mining operations throughout Namibia. Most of the mining activities in this sub-sector involve extraction of gemstones & mineral specimen, tin and tantalum and industrial minerals and dimension stones which are more prevalent in Erongo, Kunene and !Karas regions (MME, 2003).

The MME is working in partnership with the Ministry of Environment and Tourism (MET) in coordinating the application processes, issuing of claims and entering into environmental contracts with small-scale miners. The environmental contract compels the miners to adhere to policy that will protect the environment and ensure rehabilitation so that no severe and long term environmental damage will be caused by the mining activities. Specifically, MME coordinates the application process in ensuring the issuing of legal mining claims to the small-scale miners, whilst MET handles environmental contracts that are designed to promote adherence to environmental protection. According to Angula's (2007) study on the assessment of the environmental impacts of small-scale mining, eighty percent of the miners who were interviewed indicated that they know the process involved in acquiring the mining claims as well as the environmental contracts. The remaining twenty percent did not know how to become legal small-scale miners. In other words, they did not know the process of acquiring the necessary authorisation that enables one to mine lawfully. This is an indication of high awareness of procedures, among the small-scale miners, in acquiring mining claims in the country.

In some areas, small-scale miners are well organised in associations that advocate for the group benefits as witnessed in Erongo region where they founded Erongo Regional Small-Scale Miners Association (ERSMA). ERSMA is the mother body for the smaller associations for small-scale miners. According to the

Economist (2014), ERSMA was established in 2008 by The Rossing Foundation and is registered with MME with the primary objective to represent, protect and advance the interests of small-scale miners in Erongo region. The Rossing Foundation is a non-profit organisation that has been in partnership with the Namibian Ministry of Education, Art and Culture since Namibia's independence in 1990. The organisation further extended its support in other fields such as enterprise development where they supported small-scale miners in Erongo region, (Rossing Uranium, 2006). The Economist (2014) further reported that there are about 500 miners registered with the association. It is projected by the Economist (2014) that the total number of small-scale miners in the country is about 2000, suggesting that about 80% of the small-scale mining activities in the region are conducted "illegally". Each member in the association pays an annual fee of US$ 37. In the long run, ERSMA aims to regulate the sales and create an international market so that semi-precious stones mined by the association's members can be sold according to their actual value, and not for varying and arbitrary, negotiated prices. Miners get desperate when trying to sell their minerals, thus they end up selling their gemstones, to dealers, at very low prices. As a result, small-scale miners bring their gems for value addition and polishing to ERSMA who have machinery which positively result in miners being able to charge higher prices for their gems. ERSMA also helps small-scale miners by renting out mining equipment at discounted rates (Economist, 2014).

Another association with a mandate similar to ERSMA is the Kunene Small-Scale Miners Association (KSSMA) which is mandated to act as a focal point where the interests of small-scale miners are articulated and presented on matters pertaining to small-scale miners in Kunene region, Namibia, SADC and the world. Their aim is simply to ensure that their mineral products are not only sold within the country's boundary but penetrate the world market. Serving the interest of small-scale miners in Gibeon, Maltohoe, Rehoboth and Mariental districts of the southern part of the country, is the Geo-Capricon Minerals Developers. Like other associations for small-scale miners in other regions, it ensures efficient marketing of the small-scale miners' products in Hardap region. It represents about 25 small-scale miners in the region (Economist, 2014)

Collective coordination of economic interests by small-scale mining associations has been a success and community members in different parts of the country have been always urged to work in cooperatives for joint support. If the small-scale sector is well coordinated and properly managed, it has the potential of catalysing the development of a country, and improving the welfare of its people by collectively attaining the socio-economic uplifting of the local community. Thus, there are formations of various small-scale mining associations that are believed [and encouraged by the government] to have made significant contributions towards the optimal and sustainable utilisation of minerals, manage the activities of the miners and promote the socio-economic interests of members in the respective locations (The Patriot, 2016).

Benefits of Small-scale Mining

Mining is the backbone of the country's economy because a lot of the country's revenues are generated from its operations. The 2016 report on mining industry performance shows that about US$ 2.1 million was generated from the mining sector (Malango, 2016). According to the International Labour Organization (ILO) (n.d.), small-scale mining may be dangerous, disruptive and should be discouraged. Contrary to the ILO's views, although the contribution of small-scale-mining to the country's economy is still unknown, it plays a vital role in alleviating impoverishment and it supplements the income of those involved in the extraction industry. Small-scale mining is productive and profitable to some Namibian citizens who would otherwise lack material means of livelihood (Mweemba, 2014).

Thus, the government of Namibia has made provision for the registration of mining claims by Namibian nationals and Namibian registered companies. As the country has different types of mineral resources, its small-scale mining sector provides possibilities for economic growth through the creation of employment for many people who are directly or indirectly involved in the mining activities. Equally important is the fact that small-scale mining can also supplement income and alleviate impoverishment, which is one of the objectives enshrined in the Namibian Harambee Prosperity Plan (HPP). HPP is a government targeted action plan aiming to accelerate development in clearly defined areas. HPP lays the basis for attaining prosperity in Namibia (Government of Namibia, 2016). Small-scale mining constitutes a means of income generation, especially in rural areas and semi-urban areas where jobs are hardly available. So, small-scale mining adds a meaningful contribution to employment creation that results in income generation which is necessary in accessing essential needs and services such as food, water, electricity, clothing, shelter, health and education. The small-scale mining sub-sector employs between 5 000-10 000 miners who are involved in small-scale mining. Even though the exact contribution of the small-scale mining sector to the country's GDP is not known, Nyambe and Amunkete (2009) re-emphasise the importance and positive role which the sub-sector has.

If small-scale mining is sufficiently funded, properly organized and administered efficiently, it can reduce the prevailing unemployment rate which stand at 34.0% as indicated by the country's latest report on Namibia Labour Force Survey (NLFS 2016), NSA, 2017. This will eventually improve the quality of life for many people in remote areas where such small-scale mining activities are conducted. Since there are various households, in different parts of the country, whose incomes solely depend on income generated from small-scale mining, progress in the sub-sector will translate into prosperity of the households. Small-scale mining can also play a significant role in addressing economic development through empowerment of the indigenous people especially rural women who have been impoverished, dispossessed, marginalized and neglected for long. This will greatly assist in transforming the unfortunate norm of women's financial dependency especially on their male partners who often constitute the main income earners of the households. In such a manner, the promotion of small-scale mining will further strengthen and promote freedom and equality among women in the Namibian society.

Figure 1 below shows some of the minerals that are extracted by small-scale miners in Namibia

Different semi-precious stones mined and sold by small-scale miners at the T-junction of Henties Bay-Usakos road (Photo by Paulus Mwetulunila)

Figure 2 below shows jewelleries sold at Henties Bay by small-scale miners at the T-junction of Henties Bay-Usakos road (Photo by Paulus Mwetulundila)

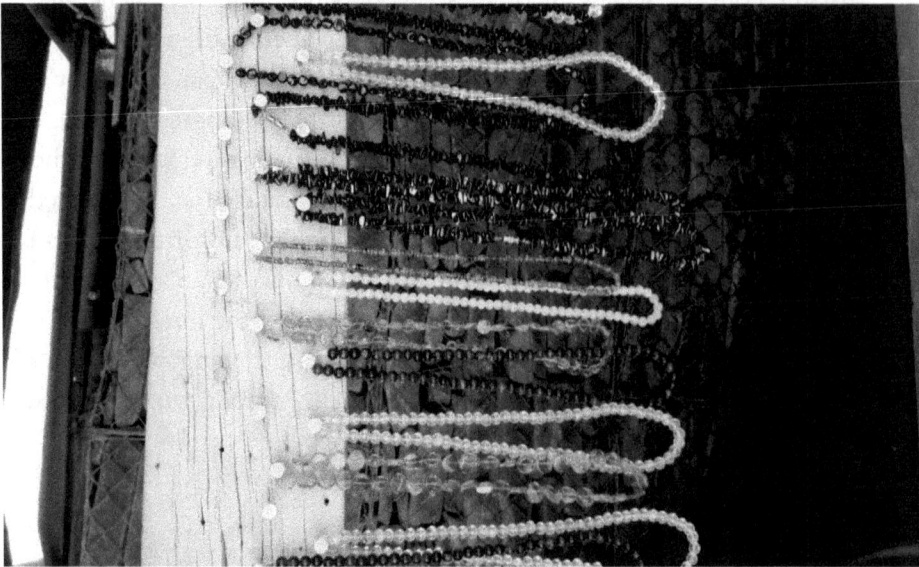

Level of Women's Participation in Small-scale Mining

According to the Namibian 2011 Housing and Population Census, rural women formed the largest demographic group in the population. Despite considerable official efforts in improving the living conditions of the rural population, rural women still face multiple predicaments in their daily lives. They are severely disadvantaged in terms of access to land and ownership of land as well as lack of access to rural employment opportunities. In their study, Nyambe and Amunkete (2009), interviewed Namibian women and men, and they found out that women are less engaged in small-scale mining. They further attribute this to the nature of activities involved in small-scale mining as one has to use manual labour and a lot of energy to harmer rocks when searching for precious stones, and this can deter women from participating.

Although a number of women are seen at market places selling mineral products, there are no available statistics on how many women are directly employed in the small-scale mining in Namibia. This lack of statistics could be a result of the Namibian government's lack of interest in the small-scale mining sector. Such lack of interest is also evident in many other Southern African countries. However, Zimbabwe is an example of a country with a high representation of women in small-scale mining. Many rural women in Zimbabwe have formed syndicates made of women only before applying for prospecting licenses and a national NGO was established in 2003 to safeguard their interests, and its members are mainly drawn from the ranks of the rural impoverished, the disabled, widows, single mothers and those living with HIV/AIDS (IRIN, 2013). Mweemba (2014) identified several challenges faced by women in small-scale mining, and these challenges include:

- Lack of technical skills
- Lack of credit facilities
- Bias and stigmatisation
- Lack of exposure to appropriate technologies
- Lack of exposure to markets

Challenges Faced by Small- Scale Miners in Namibia

If the small-scale mining sub-sector receives all the necessary resources and support, it promises to contribute significantly to the country's GDP as much as it generates income for individuals and households. However, despite its magnificent contribution in easing the economic hardships for individuals, the sector is prone to multiple challenges that hinder its growth and potential contributions to the socio-economic development of the country. One of the challenges faced by small-scale miners [and the most constraining one] is the lack of financial resources. Given that most of the miners are poorly educated [in a formal sense], they do not have access to credit facilities as financial institutions require collateral security in order for one to get a loan to finance one's mining activities. Therefore, banks consider small-scale mining as a risky business. Investment in the small scale mining sector is little and so there is lack of capital to purchase the required machinery/equipment for their mining operations. In instances where miners are able to rent machinery, they are usually faced with financial challenges of having to transport these machines to the mining sites, which are mostly located in mountainous areas (Mweemba, 2014).

According to The Patriot (2016) and Mweemba (2014) miners operate under harsh conditions and the working conditions in many countries' small-scale mining sectors are not favourable. There are no specific regulations within the small-scale mining sector regarding workers safety, unlike in the case of large-scale mining. Problems of low yields and under productivity also constitute constraints for the miners. Another identified challenge is the low level of mining and mineral processing skills and techniques among the participants in the small-scale mining industry. Due to lack of funds, miners execute their jobs using unsophisticated machinery, without or with limited knowledge of how such machinery operate. In many instances, this may result in the damage of the minerals being mined, as the manner of extraction might be inappropriate; also the results could be the destruction of machinery (Mweemba, 2014).

Mweemba (2014) further noted that some small-scale miners complained about lack of formal markets, both locally and internationally, in which to sell their products. At the moment, small-scale miners are coerced by the un-conducive markets to trade their semi-precious stones that they mine on a negotiated price instead of selling at the market value. Small-scale miners also lack laboratory equipment/instruments to analyse samples in order to improve on their mineral processing. The sector also suffers from lack of skilled labour force that can add value to the products. Value addition is very crucial on international markets as it increases the value of the minerals.

Small-scale miners also face physical dangers that can occur in the small-scale mining industry, such risks like accidents in the mining shafts. Some miners also live in health-hazardous areas without safe drinking water, sanitation and other basic services. This puts them at risk of contracting diseases such as cholera.

Many countries have recorded a high number of incidences of child labour within the small-scale mining sector whereby children between the ages six to seventeen are involved in processing and selling mineral products-one such country is Tanzania (Mahr, 2017). The majority of these children do not attend school and have very little or no education at all. According to the Labour Resource and Research Institute (LaRRI) (2004) there are no incidences of child labour in small-scale mining within Namibia. This implies that labour laws are well adhered to in Namibia and that children are not deprived of opportunities for education.

Land Ownership

In addition to other challenges faced by the small-scale miners in Namibia, there is a challenge from land owners. In their study, Nyambe and Amunkete (2009) found out that there are conflicts experienced over rights to mine in privately owned land. This is because most of the mining activities take place on the commercial farmland which is privately owned by some individuals. However, minerals found on privately owned pieces of land remain the property of the state and mining explorations require negotiation of contracts with land owners in order to be granted access as stipulated by the Mineral Policy of Namibian (MME, n.d.). However, there have been incidents where small-scale miners were denied access to these farms by the farm owners. Farmers who own the land cite various problems that are caused by the small-scale miners, such as damage to fences. The farmers are of the opinion that, when miners dig holes in their farms, at times animals fall into the uncovered pits. The farm owners further complain that small-scale mining activities have enormous repercussions on the farming activities as some animals may stray because some miners break fences around farms. Animals also fall in holes and they get injured. The farm owners also complain that they are adversely affected by small-scale mining because there will be need to renovate the damaged fences and buy medicines for their injured animals. However, the MME's small-scale mining division works hand in hand with the small-scale miners in situations where disputes arise between farmers and small-scale miners. Prospecting on the farms is the most difficult issue because getting permission to access the farm is subject to contractual agreements that are accompanied by payments of lots of money for prospecting Since many of the small-scale miners are poorly educated in the formal sense, not all of them are equipped with knowledge of the mining policies and this is to the advantage of farm owners who are against small-scale mining on their land. In terms of compensation to the farm owners, a fee of N$ 2000 is payable every month for the use of the land and N$ 10 000 once off fee is payable for rehabilitation of the land.

Namibia's small scale-mining sector has always been greatly disadvantaged by the remote geographical locations of rich diamond deposits and the early demarcation of the restricted diamond areas where miners are not allowed to mine. Namibian small-scale miners are principally involved in the extraction of gemstones mainly of the tourmaline group of minerals, and mostly located in and around Omaruru-Karibib-Usakos where most mining claims are held (Nyambe and Amunkete, 2009).

Environmental Impact of Small-scale Mining

Despite positive contributions from the small-scale mining sub-sector, Angula (2007) noted that it has also contributed to environmental degradation. These impacts of small-scale mining are classified as primary and secondary. Primary negative impacts are those that result directly from mining activities, such as water pollution, scars on the landscape, destruction of flora and fauna and other forms of damage on the environment. While secondary ones are those that result from the spin-offs of the mining activities such as littering, impacts on flora, the migration of people from other regions to the mining vicinity, and money generated from mining activities but not spent in the region (Angula, 2007).

Conclusion

The lack of organisation among small-scale miners reduces the likelihood of small-scale miners successfully growing into larger operators. Although the small-scale mining sector enables local communities to participate directly in the exploitation of their indigenous minerals, there are numerous challenges that the sub-sector faces. The lack of growth of the small-scale mining sector in Namibia can be attributed to the absence of a mineral development policy. Because of absence of such a policy, very little protection is provided for small-scale miners especially in places where transnational companies show interests in the same mineral deposits for which they would not want to compete with small-scale miners. In such cases politicians have tended to side-line the already disadvantaged small-scale miners. The small-scale mining sector remains one of the areas through which disinherited Black Namibians can be empowered.

The government in partnership with other private companies should financially support small-scale miners and they should purchase the required equipment that will be useful in the sustainable development of the sector. Funding can also be used to train miners to acquire the necessary knowledge of methods of mineral extraction that have little harm to the environment. Therefore, miners should be made aware that small-scale mining can be extremely environmentally damaging and that it often has serious health and safety consequences for workers and surrounding communities. Thus, it is very important for miners to take precautionary measures to safeguard their wellbeing and the sustainability of the environment. African small scale miners need to ensure that they sustainably utilise their material resources.

Whereas other scholars argue that in Africa there is animism in which human Africans are assumed to be indistinct from nature including minerals and animals, this chapter has shown that Namibians have got and yearn for sovereignty, ownership and control over their resources which were looted by colonists centuries ago. This chapter has also shown that whereas some scholars are seeking to promote animistic subject-subject relations in which human beings are assumed to be at the same level or plane of immanence with nature including minerals, Namibians are not necessarily at the same plane of immanence with their minerals. In fact Namibians consider minerals to be minerals, minerals are not necessarily like humans, they are not subjects and they are not gods. This is why minerals are extracted, processed and marketed- if the minerals were considered to be subjects or gods then they would not be extracted and sold. Whereas some scholars are against [African] environmental sovereignty, this chapter has shown that Namibians seek to have sovereignty over their minerals and material resources. Similarly, whereas some scholars posit that there are flat ontologies in Africa; Namibians are not necessarily on the same protean plane with their minerals and land, which constitute material objects rather than subjects. Thus, Namibians seek to and have transcendence as well as sovereignty over their material resources. In this regard, postmodernist, poststructuralist and posthumanist pretensions that there is erosion of distinctions between human [African] beings and nature/animals and minerals are not supported in Namibia.

References

Angula, S, L. (2007). *The Environmental Impacts of Small-Scale Mining in Namibia; A Case Study of Uis Small-scale Mining Site-Erongo Region.* Published Master Thesis. Windhoek. University of Namibia.

Economist Namibia. (2014). *Third Small-scale Mining Association on Cards*. https://econmomist.com. na/8604/mining-energy/third-small-scale-mining-association-on-card/.

Government of Namibia. (2016). *Harambee Prosperity Plan: Namibia Government's Action Plan towards Prosperity for All*. Windhoek.

International Labour Organization. (n.d.). *Facts on Small- Scale Mining*. Geneva. http://www.ilo.org/wcmsp5/groups/public/-dgreports/-dcomm/documents/publication/wcms_067582

IRIN. (2013).*Women Dig into Zimbabwe's Male-dominated Small-Scale Mining Sector.* http://www.irinnews.org/news/2013/10/29/women-dig-zimbabwes-male-dominated-small-scale-mining-sector.

Jourdan, P. (1990). *Mineral Industry of Namibia*. Institute of Mining Research. Harare: University of Zimbabwe.

Hentschel, T., Hruschka, F., Priester, M. (2003). *Artisanal and Small-Scale Mining: Challenges and Opportunities*. London. IIED Publications.

Labour Resources and Research Institute. (2004). *The Informal Sector in Namibia*. Prepared for the National Union of Namibian Workers (NUNNW), Labour Resources and Research Institute.

Latour, B. (2005) *Reassembling the Social: An Introduction to Actor Network Theory*. Oxford: Oxford University Press.

Malango, V. (2016). *Mining Industry Performance in 2016*. Chambers of Mines of Namibia. http://www.chamberofmines.org.na/files/8714/9322/5983/1._Mining_Industry_Performance__Challenges_2016.

Mahr, K. (2017). *Tanzania Struggles to End Child Labour from the Lure of Gold*. http://www.reuters.com/article/us-tanzania-mining-children-feature-idUSKBN176007.

Ministry of Mines and Energy. (2003). *Namibian Mining Claims, How to Apply for PEG and Register Claims*. Windhoek. Namibia Small Miners Assistance Centre.

Ministry of Mines and Energy. (n.d.). *Mineral Policy of Namibia*. Windhoek. http://www.mme.gov.na/files/pdf/minerals_policy_draft_final.pdf.

Mweemba, S, M. (2014). *Small Scale-Mining in Namibia: An Overview*. Windhoek. (Presentation at the 7th Conference of the African Association of Women in Geosciences).

Namibia Statistic Agency. (2017). *Key Highlights of the Namibian Labour Force Survey 2016 Report*. Windhoek.

Namibia Statistic Agency. (2012). *Namibia 2011 Population and Housing Census*. Windhoek.

National Planning Commission. (2012). *Annual Economic Development Report*. Office of the President. Windhoek.

Nyambe, J, M., Amunkete, T. (2009). *Small-Scale Mining Impact on Poverty in Namibia: A Case Study of Miners in Erongo Region*. Windhoek. NEPRU.

Rossing Uranium. (2006). *Rossing Foundation: Arandis*. www.rossing-com.info/arandis.htm.

Simonis Storm Securities. (2006). Namibian Mining: The Economic Stronghold. Windhoek
http://www.chamberofmines.org.na/files/2914/7092/7973/Namibian_Mining-The_Economic_Stronghold1.pdf.

Smith, M. (2011) *Against Ecological Sovereignty: Ethics, Biopolitics and Saving the Natural World*. Minneapolis: University of Minnesota Press.

The Namibian (16 January 2014) World Bank Sees Namibia's GDP at 4, 4 % in 2015/2016. https://www.namibian.com.na/index-php?id=archive-read.

The Patriot. (2016). *The Importance of Small-scale Mining in Namibia*. http://thepatriot.com.na/index.php/2016/07/01/importance-of-small-scale-mining-in-namibia/.

Chapter Ten

A Contrastive (Re)mapping of Blacks, Land and Nature in Colonial Rhodesian and Contemporary Postcolonial Zimbabwean Fiction.

Ruby Magosvongwe

Introduction

The chapter explores selected White female writing depictions of Blacks, land and nature in the Rhodesian novel versus similar depictions in selected post-2000 Zimbabwean fiction. The "interconnectedness" of Blacks, particularly women, land and nature in African cosmology makes for interesting reading. For example, reading the calendar among the indigenous Zimbabwean Shona very much depended and still depends on the lunar month that is "closely tied up" with the woman's monthly menstrual cycle, hence such expressions as: *"Ari kumwedzi; Ari kugeza; Mwedzi mutete"* or even *Mwedzi weMbudzi"*, November in Shona, busiest agricultural month that coincides with common rampant goats' calving. All the foregoing expressions are intertwined with the female fertility cycle. To this end, women's actions on and about land are sometimes not only deeply spiritual, but also phenomenological. The latter justifies examination of literary depictions that show women's involvement on the land and its productivity, as well as look at the general ecological implications on issues of sustainable development. The intertwined nature of colonial dispossession and commoditisation of African land and its carnage on human relationships, including ripple effects on environmental management is also worth exploring using literature as case studies. The foregoing approaches, as a contribution to eco-criticism, could help unlock some myths and contradictions surrounding post-2000 Zimbabwean attitudes and reactions to land, nature and ecological conservation efforts. It is in this light that in the present discussion, I do a contrastive critique of the depictions of Blacks, women, land and nature in Schreiner's *Trooper Peter Halket of*

Mashonaland (1897), Lessing's *The Grass is Singing* (1950) and Pauline Henson's *Case Closed* (2003) on one hand, and Memory Chirere's selected short stories focusing on land in Zimbabwe's post-2000 period on the other hand respectively. The critique appropriates the Human Factor Approach (Adjibolosso, 2017) on dealing with issues of dispossession, conservation and preservation of the environment. The latter is in response to the increasing demand to use holism that must include the human condition, indigenous knowledge, African traditional practices, historicity of the subject matter, and the general African populace's concerns with mundane existence in their quest for resource reclamation, sustainable livelihoods and development, including sustainable eco-preservation. Before I delve into the literary discussion on the depictions of Blacks, women, land and conservation, I give an exposition of the contradictions characterising the discourses of eco-criticism and ecological activism in Zimbabwe, most probably common and applicable to other Southern African countries.

I open my discussion with the assertion that any development agenda that downplays and ignores the colonial disinheritance, subsistence realities, environmental securities, yearnings and aspirations of the affected local African communities in colonial and post-independence Zimbabwe continues to perpetrate injustices and illegalities on the continent of Africa. Exclusion of the local African populations from ownership of resources and from participation in sustainable environmental management is self-defeating. Anthropological narratives like Vambe's *An Ill-fated People* (1972) give accounts of how the African indigenous populations used to own and possess African resources as well as to co-exist harmoniously with nature before the dispossession, disruption and disintegration ushered in by colonialism. The dire impact on the largely pariah-induced existence of the dispossessed and marginalised Blacks was not given serious consideration, as the disinherited Blacks were subsequently forced to become labourers in the colonial economy that dispossessed them of their land and other resources (Ramose, 2005). Land and other resources were robbed from Africans resulting in colonialists monopolising ownership and control of the

258

materialities in Zimbabwe. The dispossessed Blacks were then reduced to imperial chattel and beasts of burden.

Some portions of the land are considered to be sacred in the indigenous Zimbabwean worldview and therefore the *mhondoro* (territorial guardian spirits) and *Mwari* (God) who are deemed to be guardians, owners and sanctifiers of the land are revered. The practices helped to maintain the ecological balance that the world is generally bamboozled with about today. The dispossession, disruption and damage brought about by the Western notions of "development" have been monumental and at times irreparable. For example, in the Mashonaland East Province of Zimbabwe, Mutoko District, there is massive environmental degradation as a result of granite mining. The huge granite rocks are exported to Europe and to other granite industries elsewhere in Zimbabwe. Yet, ironically, all that accrues to the local communities in Mutoko are open pits, dongas and gullies. Nothing has also been ploughed back into the local communities that are directly disenfranchised, neither are there any visible efforts to rehabilitate the environment. Zimbabwe also has ghost towns like Kamativi, Kwekwe, Red Cliff, for example, where environmental damage occurred because of mining activities that have since stalled. Ecological activists have been quiet about environmental degradation in Penhalonga, Eastern Zimbabwe close to the Mozambican border. Instead of raising alarms about the environmental damage, including redirecting of water courses and cyanide poisoning, in Penhalonga, the ecological activists prefer to raise alarm only about the alleged destruction of forests on land which is now occupied by formerly dispossessed Black beneficiaries of recent land reclamation in Zimbabwe.

While we cannot unwind the clock of history and the attendant existential realities, positive principles can still be gleaned from the philosophies and principles that kept African traditional communities cohesive while exercising ownership and control as well as co-existing with nature. Ferris and Moitui (2011) discuss this co-existence with nature in African/Shona traditional communities as a phenomenological principle of life in African traditional religion. However, the emphasis on harmonious co-existence with nature ignore some moments in which African communities had conflicts with or were destroyed by wildlife for example. Although Taringa and Bishau (2016) similarly discuss how "green spirituality" and "its" taboos across the ages have helped to preserve the interdependence between humankind and nature, the Shona people explain their cosmologies in terms of *mhondoro* and *Mwari* rather than "green spirituality (see Lan, 1986). While Lan (1986), Chung (2006) and Lyons (2004) point out that the Shona [including freedom fighters] observed ancestral and *mhondoro* taboos, Taringa and Bishau (ibid) attribute the taboos to what they call "green spirituality". Taringa and Bishau thus assert that "green spirituality" and observance of "its" taboos helped to protect liberation war fighters who they hold co-existed with wildlife in forests, mountains, holes, caves and the natural habitat since they had neither homes nor barracks that could shelter them from the natural elements. However, it is imperative to note that the mode of life of the freedom fighters was much more complex that mere co-existence. The Shona people take medicines to neutralise the venom of snakes that would otherwise bite and kill them and they sought spiritual protection from *mhondoro*; also it is necessary to remember that the freedom fighters were not in the forests principally for purposes of co-existence but to fight and they were fighting - firing guns in ways that obviously would destroy vegetation, even if unintended. Also if human beings are part of nature, the fact that the freedom fighters were fighting colonists underscores the complexity, beyond simplistic co-existence, of the lives of the freedom fighters. In fact the Shona people have got a saying "*panorwa nzou huswa ndiwo hunoparara*" (when animals or people fight some things in the environment are inevitably destroyed). Kanengoni's (1997) *Echoing Silences* that explores how liberation war fighters depended on African *mhondoro* and *Mwari* and related taboos, has episodes that depict this interdependence in closer detail, including the psychological, physical and emotional securities obtained therefrom.

The interconnectedness of African *mhondoro* and ecological conservation is a fundamental sociological aspect that cannot be ignored in sustainable development and environmental management. Yet, some of these human factor issues as well as the moral geography undergirding people's life outlook seem not to be receiving the serious attention that they deserve (Maathai, 2010). Maathai (2010: 160) argues supporting respect for African cultural heritage on issues of collective understanding and community development:

> Culture gives self-identity and character. It allows them to be in harmony with their physical and spiritual environment...It enhances their ability to guide themselves...It's their reference point to the past and their antennae to the future... People without culture feel insecure and are obsessed with the acquisition of material acquisition and public displays which give them a temporary security...

Our scholarship has generally been either silent about these healthy life-conserving principles in traditional communities or paid lip service, choosing rather to focus on, and heightening the leeward side of some cultural practices using Western lenses. The (neo-)colonial economy that dispossessed Africans and then commercialised ownership of the African environment, excluding others from both access and beneficiation, has engendered devastating and complex problems. It dispossessed, disinherited, murdered, imprisoned, and robbed the Africans (Kincaid, 1988: 35), a sad reality that persists in the contemporary (neo-)colonial economy till today. Cumulatively, then, it is thus admissible that visible ecological activism as an emerging phenomenon in Zimbabwe is hegemonic, linked to a backlash associated with the new land politics cogently summarised in Hanlon, Manjengwa and Smart's book title, *Zimbabwe takes back its land* (2013). The binary approach to issues of land access and ownership, conservation and environmental management is regrettable. It subtly absolves huge chunks of the Zimbabwean population as well as transnational [mining] corporations from answerability, responsibility and ownership of ecological resources and programmes thereby undermining efforts to embrace more holistic approaches to sustainable development in the post-independence.

From the outset of Zimbabwean post-2000 land occupations, there has been an incessant outcry for conservation of the environment and preservation of the ecosystem. Nomenclature of book titling and the major linguistic patterns testify to this despondency. Titles like *Paradise Plundered* (Barker, 2007); *The Place of Tears* (Primorac, 2006); *African Tears* and *Beyond Tears* (Buckle, 2001) and *Jambanja* (Harrison, 2006) depicting the post-2000 land occupations linguistically project a massive ecological disaster on the Zimbabwean landscape. These narratives depict tears of a privileged minority clique that cannot imagine the idea of resources equity in a land formerly dominated by Whites alone. Yet, the same land redistribution process is widely embraced as emancipatory by most Blacks who perceived themselves materially and spiritually disenfranchised by the colonial land systems that were transposed wholesale onto post-independence Zimbabwe. In conjunction with this ecological activism has been a parallel avalanche of white auto/biographical and fictional writings against massive clearance of land and rampant killings of wildlife by the newly resettled land occupiers (Harrison, 2006; Barker, 2007; Buckle, 2001; 2009; Manase, 2016). This new wave of writing coincides with the era/environment characterised by increasing global calls against climate change and global warming arising from poor management of the ecosystems. Without downplaying the importance of such activism and calls, complications and complexities arise when the ecological concerns seemingly appear to be interventionism advancing the cause of disrupted privileged White farmer livelihoods on the mainly newly Black resettled farms. To this end, the critical approaches in the debate and policies about land and preservation of the ecosystem in and on post-2000 Zimbabwe, ironically in my view, remain blighted if focus is mainly on preservation of wild life, forests and tourist sites without bringing into the equation resource restoration and subsistence issues of a huge Black population that had been dispossessed, marginalised and subjected to pariah existence for close to a century in a country that is their ancestral heritage.

Therefore, the avalanche of White writings that are almost uniformly an outcry against the new Black land occupiers and owners of land outside the historicity of the land problems in Zimbabwe does not make the matter any simpler to manage because of the paternalistic attitudes and predictable racial binaries that it perpetuates. A-historical depictions/narratives pitying the 'conservation-conscious' Whites supposedly in love with nature on rolling estates and game parks/reserves against the Black wanton nature destroyer does not contextualise experiences, neither does it tell the full story about Black pariah existence and imbalances that huge populations have had to contend with for a long time. It therefore remains an unfortunate historical lie that scholarship continues to perpetuate. Eco-criticism that divorces the micro from the macro factors will render partial solutions and is therefore problematic.

White re-writing imaginaries of land, the environment and claims to belonging become problematic in this regard. Hughes (2007) and Pilossof (2012) discuss and critique white attachment to African land minus binding relationships with its peoples who were treated as chattel and as animals. Almost invariably, commercial White farmers occupying vast tracts of land with African labourers squashed in a small corner of the farm in compounds as sanctuary (Barclay, 2010), talk about 'my labour', 'my boys', 'nigger', 'kaffir', 'the hoodlums' (Barclay, 2010: 150f; Barker, 2007; Harrison, 2006; Buckle, 2001; Lessing, 1950; Schreiner, 1897). The unhealthy scenario that was historically designed and ingrained in anti-Black land and environmental policies/systems accounts for the antagonism evident in the violent evictions of commercial White farmers from the prime lands witnessed during the post-2000 land occupations. The unashamed attachment to land as primarily economic and commoditisation of the same (Buckle, 2001; 2009; Harrison, 2006; Barker, 2007; Rodgers, 2010) makes the matter even more difficult to appreciate, more so when issues of environmental degradation seemingly appear to absolve the colonial Manichean existence and its inherited land imbalances whose impact during land redistribution directly exacerbates the very degradation.

The latter is not a new motif/subject in criticism of Zimbabwean Literature in English. Black-authored fiction in Shona and English has been exploring the motif differently but similarly converging on environmental degradation and anti-life land tenure systems. In fact, the motif has actually become an overplayed and over-drummed tune to a point of predictability. Ironically, Black and White-authored Zimbabwean auto/biographical and fictional narratives coincidentally agree on the hegemonic forces at play. Politically and economically, the issue has been worsened by Zimbabwe's economic pariah condition that emanated from Euro-American punitive sanctions and isolation to beat the country back into line with White hegemony and restore the fortunes of former White minority land-owners (Raftopoulos, 2009). Eco-criticism as well as "perceptions on landscapes and ecological concerns" (Manase, 2016: 111) and "post-colonial ecological activism" (Manase, 2016: 113) that prioritise animal survival, including post-colonial outcries of perceived rabid decent into anarchy (Fanon, 1967; Manase, 2016; Sanders, 2006), capturing the "horror of devastation" (Manase, 2016: 117) ushered in by Black rule cast the cause in bad light, no matter how 'noble'.

Furthermore, conservation approaches and eco-criticism that ignore the African traditional indigenous philosophies towards ecological balance, particularly in view of the skewed land distribution and redistribution that is not cognisant of subsistence needs of the dispossessed Black majority are most likely self-defeating. There is need for a balance between the Euro-modern scientific approaches and the African traditional approaches to environmental management for a longer lasting solution (Mafongoya *et al*, 2016; Taringa *et al.*, 2016). This is why the Human Factor Approach is indispensable for a holistic and lasting solution to conservation of the environment and ecological balance in Zimbabweans' land management efforts. Not to ignore the massive mining operations, both legal and illegal, that the general population is witness to but are not directly benefitting from. The rabid emergence of vampire land barons that have sucked dry the destitute urban and peri-urban land seekers of their hard-earned money does not make the matter any easier to handle. Furthermore, local and urban authorities' post-2010 differential treatment of land-developers that prioritises capital interests of foreign investors despite the breach of the same environmental principles and laws makes the matter even more complex. The poisoned river systems affecting both livestock and humans downstream emanating from the post-2000 Chiadzwa diamond mining venture is a case in point. The outcry by the affected and displaced Marange communities has been repeatedly captured on the ZTV main news from the outset of diamond mining in Chiadzwa that displaced and disinherited locals of both tangible and intangible cultural heritage rooted in their traditions and the environment. No solution appears to be in sight in view of the Government's heightened efforts towards resuscitating a dying economy through increased production and exports (Mangudya, 2017), and diamond mining in Chiadzwa offers one such lifeblood.

Interdependence between Land and Shona Cosmology: A Cursory Phenomenological Expose

As already noted earlier in my discussion, though land is generally viewed as a characteristic male principle, the "interconnectedness" of women, land and nature in African cosmology makes for interesting reading. In my view, eco-criticism that ignores Black women's contribution to sustaining livelihoods, families and communities offers partial solutions to the quest for sustainable ecological balance that Zimbabwe needs. For example, though this is not the focus of the present discussion, reading the calendar among the indigenous Zimbabwean Shona very much depended on, and still depends on, the lunar month that is closely tied up with the woman's monthly menstrual cycle. Closely linked with women's biological cycle are also certain sociological taboos directly intertwined with their communities' "green spirituality". Indirectly, this traditionally gave women power over their sexuality, including choosing and determining when children could be conceived, when they could be weaned off the breast, and also how to grow their families. Some of the lunar months have also adopted fe/male principles from the nomenclature used to define them, naturally embedding nature and the ecosystem in managing human affairs and the elements.

Systems, institutions and places that rendered certain trees, forests, rivers, mountains, caves, snakes, animals, birds and reptiles that some communities traditionally considered sacred were disrupted and desecrated. The ripple effects are evident in the rampant destruction of the environment evident in most post-independence resettled areas (Maathai, 2010; Harrison, 2006). The human factor therefore becomes indispensable in managing issues to do with the environment. Yet, 'Euro-modern' scientific approaches to environmental management seem to be insensitive to these indigenous cultural and indigenous scientific realities.

Contradictions Surrounding African Farm Land, Black Labour, and Ecological Preservation: The Case of Olive Schreiner's *Trooper Peter Halket of Mashonaland* (1897), Doris Lessing's *The Grass is Singing* (1950) and Pauline Henson's *Case Closed* (2003)

This section takes into account the polyphonic voices characterising the contradictions of conquest, denigrated humanity of the Black person, productivity, and ecological preservation in three White female-authored narratives, interrogating the status accorded the Black against the background of present day discourses of eco-criticism and ecology activism. My discussion on the ecological preservation using literature as a case study follows the sequential order in the selected texts' publication dates.

Trooper Peter Halket of Mashonaland that opens this section is a story given by a first person narrator bearing the same name. Trooper Peter Halket joins Cecil John Rhodes' privately owned BSAC in search of fortune, especially land that troopers earned as rewards for successful raids and plunder against the indigenous populations of Mashonaland and Matebeleland. On one such mission, Trooper Peter Halket gets lost and finds himself alone at night on a hill. Peter experiences an epiphany that changed his life. As he was striving to keep himself warm using a wooden fire on that lonely hill, Peter gets an anonymous visitor who admits to being a Jew, but never on a similar mission as the rest of Peter's party. His was a mission to win souls. Peter retells the strange Jewish male intruder how their company had recently decimated a village, mowing down people indiscriminately. Peter further recounts how they blew up a cave to smoke out any surviving fugitives. The cave had been sanctuary for survivors of the raids, especially the displaced women and children. The Jew informs Peter that one such very old woman had just passed on after helping another woman to give birth. The new mother had vanished blending with the environment following the treks of her kith and kin.

Like Conrad's (2007) Kurtz in *Heart of Darkness* who displays human skulls as trophies for his conquest of the African during his elephant ivory hunting escapades, Peter similarly boasts of displays of rows of male human skulls looking like corn rows during their raids of conquest in Mashonaland. He also testifies of carrying away the villagers' grain and burning the surplus that they could not carry as a way of smoking out any remnant survivors. The young woman who had been assisted to give birth intuitively blends with nature and keeps away from the eye of the raiders. Peter boasts about how he once owned two such industrious female servants whose labour in his garden earned him money and fame among his counterparts. Peter boasts that for the six months that he stayed with them, he never paid a dime for their services and labour. The two women later vanish with all his bullets while he was away on Ndebele raids. Using the Biblical 2 Kings metaphor of King Ahab murdering Naboth for his ancestral land heritage, the Jewish companion questioned Peter why they would continue allowing the Ahabs of their day to continue murdering, robbing and dispossessing the Naboths of their day with impunity. At the end of the epiphany, Peter vows to go back to England and preach against the violent killings and raids to dispossess and displace Africans from their land. This is contrary to the motto that had drawn him to Africa: making a fortune using African land and free labour. Peculiar to note in Peter's narrative is how the late female fugitive women managed to blend so well with nature. Peter also marvels at his two Shona female servants' ambidexterity at work and acquisition of his language. Olive Schreiner uses Peter's testimony to raise awareness about the barbaric bloody conquest, land dispossession and colonisation spear-headed by Cecil John Rhodes who "prefers land to a nigger".

Olive Schreiner's narrative that uses Peter Halket as the voice exposes the hypocrisy in preaching ecological preservation when conquest itself was a dispossessive and violent act that dislodged indigenous populations from secure environments where they used their own epistemologies to preserve nature. Populations were left vulnerable and exposed to new unfamiliar territories where they could further be displaced without any warning, being hunted down like animals of the wild. What authority would one have to talk about ecological activism under such circumstances? Eric Harrison's autobiographical *Jambanja* (2006) written more than a century later, similarly projects a Rhodesian south-eastern Lowveld ready for white purchase, occupation and settlement without any regard for the indigenous population. Manase (2016: 126) exposes a post-2000 white Zimbabwean ecological activism and advocacy that decries post-2000 Zimbabwe's failure to strive for an all-inclusive redefinition of access to land. Manase (2016: 126) further comments on Meryl Johnson's ecological activism at the height of the post-2000 land occupations arguing that "[t]he advocacy maps the counter discourses and pro-environmental practices seeking to eradicate the ecologically destructive ones… and the horrible disruption of the farms' ecological balance, can only be viewed as destructive practices deserving condemnation". Without trivialising the nobility of ecological activism, when read side by side by a critical reader, Olive Schreiner and Eric Harrison's narratives create a debacle regarding an understanding of what ecological activism really is and who the beneficiaries are and why. It is difficult to appreciate, understand and think about ecological activism in abstractions to some simple-minded people like me when certain demographic groups are continuous targets of exclusion from accessing primary subsistence resources such as land.

Doris Lessing's *The Grass is Singing*, as a case study, elaborates my point more clearly. The narrative opens with a newspaper article reporting the murder of Mary Turner, wife to Dick Turner, a commercial farmer in the Ngesi area of Southern Rhodesia. "The houseboy, who has been arrested, has confessed to the crime. No motive has been discovered. It is thought he was in search of valuables" (Lessing, 1950: 9). The story opens a Pandora's Box for a reader and critic examining issues of ecological activism, conceptualisations of the humanity of the Blacks and their place in the conservation scheme, particularly their right to subsistence in comparison to the pre-eminence given to conservation of animals in post-2000 Zimbabwe. Lessing's narrative takes further the zoological treatment, minus the rights, that the conquered Blacks are subjected to. In Lessing's novel, the "niggers" stay at a corner of the farm in an overcrowded compound where their dwellings sprout like natural growths from the earth. Dick Turner, a Rhodesian failed farmer in the narrative, cannot afford buying "niggers" at five pounds a head any longer and would have to depend on voluntary labour (*Ibid*: 170).

The third person narrator in the same narrative lays bare nuances about Mary Turner, Dick Turner's wife's disregard for blacks' physical, psychological, spiritual, emotional, cultural and environmental securities. The depictions are not far from commonly-held societal beliefs, principles, philosophy, vision and motto. After she sjamboks one of the male labourers, she does not see anything wrong treating "him as it was natural to her to treat natives" (Lessing, 1950: 175): "It made her furious to think that this black animal had the right to complain against her, against the behaviour of a white woman" (*Ibid*: 147). "[T]hey should not be taught to read and write: they should be taught the dignity of labour and general usefulness to the white man" (*Ibid*: 191), "a machine without a soul" (*Ibid*: 188). If Mary Turner "disliked native men, she loathed the women. She hated the exposed fleshiness of them…Their babies hanging on to them like leeches…they were alien and primitive creatures with ugly desires she could not bear to think about" (*Ibid*: 115-116), "chattering evil-smelling creatures" (*Ibid*: 117). Worse off than their male counterparts, the Black female are dismissed as insolent and indolent, and deserving no attention at all in the world of the White commercial farm. Yet, their lives as human beings matter. In African cosmology, female fecundity and productivity as well as participation in sustaining livelihoods are celebrated, making them co-players in issues of survival and eco-preservation. Silencing them, as does the white voices in Lessing's narrative, denies them agency on matters that directly affect their continued existence and collective survival.

Further, in the same narrative, Charlie Slatter, another commercial farmer and Dick Turner's neighbour, boasts of owning a sjambok first to use on the "nigger" before buying a plough. He later annexes Dick's farm after he psychological breaks down at his wife's demise. Charlie Slatter unashamedly admits to having dongas on the farm and he continues taking more without taking any conservation measures. The larger the land Charlie Slatter clears for commercial tobacco production, the higher the income returns and proceeds. Silence from authorities implies that ecological balance and environmental preservation were under control. Nevertheless, it is evident that both the land and the male "nigger" labourer principally constitute the hen that lays the golden egg. Yet, ironically, he does not care about how the same hen survives. As evidenced from post-2000 White writing, eco-criticism has only begun to raise concerns against this exploitative legacy at a time that there are new political players on the land. As noted elsewhere in the discussion, the cash economy and private ownership of the environment accounts for the environmental carnage that we witnessed today.

Ironically, even on Black-owned commercial farms, the status of the labourer remains pathetic. Yet, awareness campaigns for ecological conservation continue bombarding the press. Henson's *Case Closed* (2003) depicts the tragic "cycle of poverty" haunting the Black labourer. Magosvongwe (2013: 162) argues that "[t]he text exposes the affluence, comfort and security of the farmhouse that the new African landed-gentry enjoy in post- independence Zimbabwe against the insecurity, poverty and malleable existence of the compound-sheltered farm-labourers. The indigenous commercial farmer, if he follows the direction of his predecessors on the farms, "replace[s] one form of exploitation by another, more ruthless [in] form" (Abrahams, 2000: 377). The struggle on the farm frontier becomes more complex as labourers have to deal with bigoted Black farm-owners like George Shamba. Shamba claims not to interfere "in [his] workers' private lives" (Henson, 2003: 95) on account that he is not his "brother's keeper" (*Ibid*)."

"For the black farm labourer the farm is a lived irony. It is a familiar but perverted territory. Although the farm is situated in a familiar territory, it remains external to the Black man's nature because it is organised for purposes outside his indigenous philosophy" (Chirere, 2004 cited in Magosvongwe, 2013: 165). Shamba's murky Mavhuradonha Farm symbolises the unbroken legacy of settler farm self-aggrandizement and hollow material accumulation at the expense of the impoverished and marginalised. In addition to dealing in illicit emerald deals, Shamba also conceals arms caches on his farm for trans-border arms deals that he uses to expand his economic empire. When he is eventually uncovered and arrested, Shamba's case is closed and dropped on account of his connections with the powerful political elite. "Apparently, it is not considered to be in the national interest to prosecute Mr Shamba, he is – and I quote – too valuable an example of indigenous success. His prosecution would be counter-productive to the good of the nation as a whole" (Henson, 2003: 142). Similarly, once 'national interest' is adopted on issues where ecological conservation principles have been violated, the cases are never followed through. The Chinese-owned China Town to the west of Harare is one such case whereby Environmental Managing Authority (EMA) was silenced after it raised concerns about the wetland being unsuitable for construction.

Thus, ecological activism that does not address the root causes, perpetuates the problem and makes it even more complex because of the subterranean negativity about the dispossessed and marginalised Black majority lives generally. The human factor aspect can never be ignored to perpetuity if the desired ecological balance is to be achieved and sustained. The 'innocent victim' trump card in contemporary ecological activism supporting reinstatement of minority clique privileges on former commercial farms and wildlife conservancies can only hold for a fleeting moment.

Contemporary Black Literary Voices on Black Women and Eco-criticism: Selected Short Stories from Memory Chirere's *Somewhere in this Country* (2006)

In this section I use short stories to bring in contrastive and polyphonic voices that speak to eco-criticism and the new land resettlements. Contrary to White-authored writings against an avalanche of Black presence on former commercial White farms, the present analysis focuses on Chirere's exploration of land as an allegory of renewal and how it effects wholeness of formerly dispossessed and marginalised people. In fact, their coming onto these 'new' lands is in itself psycho-spiritual healing and injects more purposeful existence. Not in any specific order, stories to be examined include "Suburb"; "Somewhere"; "Maize"; "A roof to repair"; "Signs" and "Sitting carelessly", as already indicated. In

"Maize" as in Ngugi's *The River Between* (1965), Chirere symbolically recuperates the myth of man and woman's bonding with the land and nature and the view that land is both spiritual anchor and heritage. Magosvongwe (2013: 181) observes that "Somewhere" and "Maize" dramatise this peculiar aspect of Shona philosophy. "Maize" and "Watching" in which man and woman resettle on land that they now perceive as their own, show land as a signifier of restoration of harmony between man and nature. The stories thus explore presuppositions "of a stable identity associated with landownership and land as a signifier of loss whose recovery would imply the recovery of an identity" (Ogude, 1999: 46). To then launch an outcry against this re-established union that had been dislodged and fractured by colonial land policies in the name of ecological preservation implies continual privileging of Western hegemony.

The opening paragraphs of "Maize" show a woman "satisfied that she had come here and this beneath her feet was her land, soil. Her own virgin earth where one could dig and dig without striking rock. Here where ... one's soul crept into a hole and rested like some kind of veldt bird that develops a camouflaged nest on the ground" (Chirere, 2006: 63), implying serenity arising from re-connecting with the land. "[I]t [also] speaks about human presence and settlement" (*Ibid*: 65). "She was too tired to go across the acres of grass and bushes to acquaint more with her new neighbours" (*Ibid*: 63). She feels completeness at becoming one with nature on the land that she can call her own. In this regard, issues surrounding ecological activism bring in new challenges and complexities relating to the formerly dispossessed and marginalised people's "relationship" with 'their' land. The woman's union with nature is fully consummated at the arrival of a male companion who initially claims to be seeking shelter from a rain storm. The man congratulates the woman for getting "this portion here... on [her] own" (*Ibid*). "These people say it is too late in the season to give me acres. Ah, how I wish I had my own acre (*Ibid*), showing the satisfaction that the ordinary beneficiaries of land restoration have with land redistribution after years of land dispossession. That the land is "virgin" also gives picture of land lying idle, perhaps kept for speculation purposes while millions scavenge for a living in over-crowded and over-used communal lands.

As in real life, influx of Blacks seeking resettlement on new lands, a major factor undergirding post-2000 internal migration (Potts: 2011) has seen new communities of people from different "places of origin and even mannerisms" (Chirere, 2006: 63) being established. "Watching" (Chirere, 2006: 44-46) that shows a couple freshly settled at the edge of a linear village similarly alludes to this phenomenon. Land-resettlement witnesses people discarding colonial land policies that distorted the Africans' social reality. Ironically, it is partly establishment of these settlements that some sections of society associate with environmental and ecological degradation. "Sitting Carelessly" (Chirere, 2006: 76-79) depicts Pempani of Malawian origin who is now persona non grata since the occupation of his former White boss' farm: "By the road. I come from a place by a road" (Chirere, 2006: 77). The displaced women and children are worse off victims. Homelessness and squatting for former mine and farm labourers have become commonplace in post-2000 Zimbabwe yet ecological and human rights activists focus more on the plight of animals and forests that have been disturbed by Black presence at land occupations. In fact, crises of this nature became rampant on a wide scale with colonial conquest in 1897, further heightened by land donations to White war veterans of the 1918 World War 1 and 1945 World War 2 (Hanlon, Manjengwa and Smart, 2013). Contradictions and approaches to resolving these ecological issues therefore demand careful thought and futuristic planning.

That "Maize" ends with the myth of creation dramatised by the romantic embrace between the resettled woman and the man from Madziwa shows Chirere legitimising renewal and recreation through new claims to land ownership. Magosvongwe (2008: 306) observes that "Maize" also depicts the bliss of ownership and creativity that come with the privilege of subjectivity in freed space(s). Land/the new environment in "Maize" symbolises the "larger than life character which provides not only the physical context within which the lives of the other characters can be worked out, but also a force they can identify with" (Gikandi in Killam, 1984: 237).

273

"Somewhere" explores the psycho-spiritual and environmental securities that homeland provides. The unquenchable yearning for spiritual reconnection with home mentally destabilises the old man to a point of suffering an incurable illness. As soon as the drivers reach the precincts of "the old man's boyhood territory" (Chirere, 2006: 32) —"this panorama of hills, valleys, forests… " (*Ibid*: 33)— he miraculously recovers and comes to be: "Olelele-e-e! Muchekawakasungabeta!"(*Ibid*: 31. The old man shouts his totemic praise name hoisting himself up and gazing excitedly at the greying hills in the distance. Repeated exclamations of "Muchekawakasungabeta" (*Ibid*: 32) which is his totemic identity speak of spiritual re-connectedness, aspects that ecological activists may not readily appreciate. Yet, these demand enquiry and attention for sustainable ecological preservation: "Maybe the brothers wondered less and less why a man developed fully separate from all this, since distant boyhood, would not only die to see this but actually go to it" (*Ibid*: 33). The old man often mentioned some hills even in sleep. "There was a need to identify these hills somewhere in this country and have him [the old man] see them as soon as possible" (*Ibid*: 31). The observation confirms Ndlovu's (2010: 118) argument that among Zimbabweans, especially those who feel de-personalised by the Diaspora, home is a value-laden phenomenon intricately woven with the concept of land and belonging.

To buttress the foregoing subterranean narrative in Chirere's story, Feris and Moitui (in Bennett, 2011: 212) observe that relationships in the homestead are centred on ritual relationships among the living and their ancestors. From the domestic level, this connectivity extends to the sphere of polity where it is directed towards reinforcing the political authority of kings, chiefs and other traditional leaders. Chenjerai Hove's *Bones* (1988) traces this aspect, linking the Second Chimurenga to the legendary Nehanda's prophecy about repossessing land. Nehanda's spirit is reported to have been instrumental towards re-igniting the quest for repossessing the stolen lands, a quest that culminated in the Third Chimurenga that partly accounts for the post-2000 ecological activism.

Nevertheless, complications notwithstanding, the major difference between rural and urban resettlements appears to be that those in the countryside seem to be endorsed by the establishment on the basis that they are "a clear demonstration that the Government has delayed in redistributing land" (Chari, 2010: 137, citing the President). These resettlements are viewed as the pursuit of the liberation struggle — an expression of "a struggle that cannot be corrected by the trespass law, but by the equitable and just land distribution" (Ibid). Similar self-initiated settlements by ordinary marginalised people in the urban areas suffer violence at the hands of the authorities as evidenced by the Operation Murambatsvina of 2005 and other post 2015 demolitions of 'illegal structures' by local authorities. Tagwira's *The Uncertainty of Hope* and Chikwava's *Harare North*, depict the resulting trauma —a tactical political blunder by a leadership that alienates itself from the marginalised majority's genuine need for land for housing development. The myriad contradictions make ecological preservation and management more problematic as approaches appear elitist to a lay person.

"Suburb" in the same collection appears to be a compromise to the extremities in Chikwava and Tagwira's novels. Set on the fringes of the city, Suburb casts a divergent picture about the forced and violent removals of the ordinary urban-dwellers from their newly-founded havens and land. Like Petina Gappah's "An Elegy for Easterly", hapless urban- dwellers become residents of a settlement/suburb of shacks and survive the wrath of Operation Murambatsvina. Epitomised in Martha Mupengo's double tragedy, Black women suffer most at the scourge of these ecological and environmental disruptions. Martha dies during the demolitions of their shacks while giving birth at the Easterly Farm settlement.

"Suburb" challenges stereotypes of insensitive elitist urban local authorities and re-invents a narrative about settlements like White Cliff, Harare South, Sally Mugabe Heights and Hatcliffe on the outskirts of Harare that survived the swoop of Operation Murambatsvina. By naming the settlement "Suburb", the writer tacitly endorses its safety and continued existence. "When asked, as it often occurred, from where and when he had come, [the founder] said he was 'from all the corners'" (Chirere, 2006: 10) — "Everyone who is literate and who can afford papers knows the history of this country closely and must know who the old man was" (*Ibid*: 11).

Symbolically, "Suburb" begs that ecological activism that is divorced from people's lived realities and historicity of the liberation struggle risk blighting their own success.

Furthermore, despite challenges of patronage and corruption, in the event that government abdicates responsibility, ex-fighters have emerged the vanguard championing struggles against people's stagnation in impoverishment and homelessness. Hanlon *et al* (2013: 22) submit: "Veterans have extra social and political standing, which gives them additional authority and certain privileges—although there are also accusations that some …have abused their special standing." However, despite the ex-combatants' redemptive role in settling issues of urban accommodation and resettlement in general, Chirere's "Suburb" must not be misconstrued as championing disregard for city by-laws as the latter indeed exacerbates environmental degradation and ferments general disease outbreaks if immediate service provision is not set up.

Chirere's (2000) "A Roof to Repair" explores different layers of treachery concerning land and ecological preservation. It examines illegal gold panning by an unemployed ex-combatant, Saizi and others. Saizi's mother, Marwei, has been deserted by her husband who is roaming the commercial farms escaping his inability to sustain the family. Symbolically, farms represent escapism: "You can go to the farms and stay there forever" (Chirere, 2006: 56). The farm in this regard typifies betrayal. The farm becomes the antithesis of African fatherhood. Marwei's pottery alone cannot sustain the family. Nevertheless, from an African-centred ecological perspective, her talent can be viewed in a very positive light. Marwei looks to the earth as sacred because it is the epicentre to her creation, as inspiration and source of the clay that accord her space to show her creativity. This rootedness in nature and use of nature provides the anchor for her existence. Feris and Moitui (in Bennett, 2011: 202) observe that in ATR, the minerals in the earth, the rivers, mountains and oceans are all [potentially] sacred objects which the spirits intermittently use to communicate their will on one's life. Successful ecological activism can therefore not be seen to be divorced from a people's spirituality and moral geography.

276

After returning from the war Saizi takes to gold panning to earn a living. Political liberation without material and economic liberation becomes what Mandaza (2001) surmises as a crown without jewels, making the ex-combatants' joblessness a more scathing mockery. Ruminating over the war in song gives strength to Saizi's "tired body and tired mind" (Chirere, 2006: 58). His workmates taunt his liberation war credentials of Liberator and Comrade, mocking him that he moved from liberator to destitute gold-panner and always with the law behind him. He is forced to reflect on the "days of fresh hope" (Chirere, 2006: 58) in the independence euphoria. The scathing irony is that exploitation of mineral wealth by the formerly dispossessed and marginalised masses could transform lives if a Government committed to its peoples' economic well-being would not only repeal the Mining and Minerals Act, but also create conditions, including making provisions for easy access to equipment, capital and tools by the formerly excluded who would want to venture into mining. The struggle for economic liberation rages on. "It is not over. It has changed only. It is here with us. We only chopped its tail but its head is well" (Chirere, 2006: 59). The systems remain intact. Unequal access to the country's major resources has been barely touched. Alluvial panning and sale of gold on the "black market" are illegal (Scoones *et al*, 2010: 175). Like the old man in "Suburb", Saizi disregards surrendering to the violence of African exclusion that perpetuates social injustices that independence promised to redress. Several other short stories and narratives explore post-2000 land issues that inadvertently affect demographic distribution and their impact on ecological balance that ecological activism perceives to be facing real threat. The patterns take different forms, but not without serious contradictions that demand careful thinking through for holistic and more sustainable and all-embracing practicable approaches to be achieved.

Conclusion

My chapter has played around with the ironies characterising ecological activism in Africa. The chapter has analysed post-2000 Zimbabwean White writing and its ecological activism thrust from its soft underbelly, forcing readers to acknowledge and interrogate some of the root causes of the ecological carnage that post-2000 Zimbabwe must deal with. It concludes that patronising ecological activism that absolves certain sections of the society from taking responsibility for ecological damage that post-2000 Zimbabwe must fight and win smirks at hypocrisy. These are symptoms of an 'unsettled land' (Alexander, 2006) that is internally fraught with self-defeating tensions and conflicts. Further, using literary depictions spanning for over a century beginning 1897 till post-2000 as reference points, the chapter also argues that a-historical approaches that downplay the historical realities that created conditions that nurtured and ferment the current ecological challenges will only yield partial solutions that perpetuate the ecological problems. Ecological activism that foregrounds material interests of one section of society whilst downplaying the correction of historical injustices or imbalances and denouncing self-renewal of communities through more equitable redistribution of resources threatens tearing communities apart. Zimbabwe's solutions to post-2000 ecological challenges lay in holistic solutions to the country's perennial land reclamation question and transparent management of the resources. White commercial farmers' apprehension about land restitution, redistribution and attendant despondency alone does not constitute an ecological crisis of the magnitude that White ecological activism projects portray. This does not in any way insinuate that ecological balance needs to be safeguarded.

In addition, activism that puts the life of animals above that of human beings, Black labourers and the formerly dispossessed, excluded marginalised majority sadly testifies of insensitivity about the plight of other human beings, bringing into question the sincerity of such undertakings and the undergirding agendas. For example, whose paradise has been plundered? From Schreiner's 1897 narrative of the BSAC plunder in Mashonaland, to Catherine Buckle's *African Tears,* whose tears must be remembered by our ecological activists? Harrison (2006) whose autobiographical writing commends Meryl Johnson for animal preservation activism at the height of the land reclamations and occupations, ironically puts animal life above that of the labour that had catapulted them into the wealth that they are now fighting to defend in their activism. The differential human worth using whatever formulae and justification also further polarises society on issues such as ecological preservation that require collectivism across all communities. Finally, while efforts to protect wild animals and the environment in post-2000 Zimbabwe are commendable, the depictions in the selected literary texts used in support for sensitivity to the human condition, insinuate that if basic human subsistence needs are not given serious consideration, efforts to achieve ecological balance will just remain a mere pipe dream. Africa's worst tragedy has been her amnesiac memory. Lucifer Mandengu in Charles Mungoshi's *Waiting For the Rain* (1975) ironically suffers from such amnesia when he laments his birth and ancestral heritage as a biological mistake, forgetting the humanly-orchestrated conditions that have made his existential background so pathetic.

Ecological disasters playing out on resettled farms are a reflection of chickens coming home to roost. Competing and partisan ideologies on matters to do with distribution of resources are therefore retrogressive in the long term. More inclusive approaches that embrace the heterogeneous perceptions about land (Manase, 2016: 136), its uses and its conservation is what will salvage the country from the current carnage and move it forward. Finally, ecological activism that does not embrace humankind's complex material, physical, emotional, psychological, intellectual and spiritual being may not produce the desired ecological balance, thereby calling for more holistic strategies when dealing with issues about ecology and environmental management. As Ferres and Moitui (2011) rightly argue, in addition to embracing religious consciousness and its interdependence with the natural environment, the dilemma to address ecological and environmental 'crises' must be taken as everyone's matter of concern as well as matter of fact.

References

Abrahams, P. (2000) *The Black Experience in the 20th Century.* Bloomington: Indiana University Press.

Adjibolosso, S. (2017) 'The Human Factor Foundation of Action'. Paper Presented at the University of Zimbabwe Research Week Closing Ceremony on Friday 28th July. Harare: University of Zimbabwe Great Hall.

Alexander, J. (2006) *The Unsettled Land: State-making and the Politics of Land in Zimbabwe 1893-2003*. Oxford: James Currey/ Harare: Weaver Press. Barclay, P. (2010) *Zimbabwe, Years of Hope and Despair*. London: Bloomsbury Publishing.

Barker, J. (2007) *Paradise Plundered: The Story of a Zimbabwean Farm*. Harare: Jim Barker.

Chari, T. (2010) 'Salience and Silence: Representation of the Zimbabwean Crisis in the Local Press'. *African Identities, Vol. 8* (2), (pp.131-150).

Chikwava, B. (2009) *Harare North*. Harare: Weaver Press.

Chirere, M. (2006) *Somewhere in this Country*. Pretoria: UNISA Press.

Chung, F. (2006) *Re-Living the Second Chimurenga: Memories from Zimbabwe's Liberation Struggle*. Stockholm: The Nordic Africa Institute: Weaver Press.

Conrad, J. (2007) *Heart of Darkness*. London: Vintage Books.

Ferris, L. and Moitui, C. (2011) 'Towards Harmony between African Traditional Religion and Environmental Law'. In Bennett, T. W. (Ed.) *Traditional African Religion in South African Law*. Cape Town: UCT Press. (pp. 200-222).

Gappah, P. (2009) *An Elegy for Easterly*. Harare: Weaver Press.

Gikandi, S. (1984) 'The Growth of the East African Novel'. In Killam, G. D. (Ed.) *The Writing of East and Central Africa*. London: Heinemann. (pp. 231-246).

Hanlon, J., Manjengwa, J. & Smart, T. (2013) *Zimbabwe Takes Back Its Land*. Johannesburg: Jacana.

Harrison, E. (2006) *Jambanja*. Harare: Maioio Publishers.

Henson, P. (2003) *Case Closed: A Detective Story Set in Zimbabwe*. Gweru: Mambo Press.

Hove, C. (1992) *Bones*. Harare: Baobab Books.

Hughes, M. D. (2010) *Whiteness in Zimbabwe: Race, Landscape, and the Problem of Belonging*. New York: Palgrave Macmillan.

Kanengoni, A. (1997) *Echoing Silences*. Harare: Baobab Books.

Kincaid, J. (1988) *A Small Place*. New York: Farrar, Straus and Giroux.

Lan, D. (1986) *Guns and Rain: Guerrillas and Spirit Mediums in Zimbabwe*. Berkeley and Los Angeles: University of California Press.

Lessing, D. (1950) *The Grass is Singing*. London: Heinemann African Writers Series.

Lyons, T. (2004) *Guns and Guerrilla Girls*. Africa World Press, Inc.

Maathai, W. (2010) *The Challenge for Africa*. London: Arrow Books.

Mafongoya, P., Jiri, O., Mubaya, C., Gwenzi, J., and Mafongoya, O. (2016) 'The Role of Indigenous Knowledge Systems in Climate Change, Prediction, Adaptation and Mitigation in Sub-Saharan Africa'. In Magosvongwe, R., Mlambo, O. & Ndlovu, E. (Eds.) *Africa's Intangible Heritage and Land*. Harare. University of Zimbabwe Publishers.

Magosvongwe, R. (2013) 'Land and Identity in Zimbabwean Fiction Writings in English from 2000-2010: A Critical Analysis'. Unpublished DPhil Thesis. University of Cape Town.

Magosvongwe, R. (2008) 'Contrasting Discourses of Emancipation and Empowerment in Selected Albums by Hosiah Chipanga and Fungisai Zvakavapano'. *Muziki, Journal of Music Research in Africa*. Vol. 5 (8). (pp.75-91).

Mandaza, I. (2001) 'Southern African Identity: A Critical Assessment'. In Bekker,S. *Shifting African Identities: Volume II in the Series Identity? Theory, Politics, History* Pretoria: Human Sciences Research Council. (pp. 133-152).

Mangudya, J. (2017) Paper on Zimbabwe's Dollarized Economy Presented at a University of Zimbabwe's Business and the Media Symposium. Llewellyn Lecture Theatre. 12th July 2017.

Manase, I. (2016) *White Narratives: The Depiction of Post-2000 Land Invasions in Zimbabwe*. Pretoria: UNISA Press, African Humanities Program

Mungoshi, C. (1975) *Waiting for the Rain*. London: Heinemann Educational Books.

Ndlovu, T. (2010) 'Where is my Home? Rethinking Person, Family, Ethnicity and Home under Increased Transnational Migration by Zimbabweans'. *African Identities, Vol. 8*(2), (pp.117-130).

Ogude, J. (1999) *Ngugi's Novels and African History: Narrating the Nation.* London: Pluto Press.

Pilossof, R. (2012) *The Unbearable Whiteness of Being: Farmers' Voices from Zimbabwe.* Cape Town: UCT Press.

Potts, D. (2011) *Circular Migration in Zimbabwe & Contemporary Sub-Saharan Africa.* Cape Town: UCT Press/James Currey.

Primorac, R. (2006) *The Place of Tears: The Novel and Politics in Zimbabwe.* London/New York: Tauris Academic Studies.

Ramose, M. B. (2005) *African Philosophy through Ubuntu.* Harare: Mond Book Publishers.

Raftopoulos, B. (2009) 'The Crisis in Zimabwe, 1998-2008'. In Raftopoulos, B. & Mlambo, A. (Eds.) *Becoming Zimbabwe.* Harare: Weaver Press. (pp. 201-232).

Rogers, D. (2010) *A Memoir of Mischief and Mayhem on a Family Farm in Africa: The Last Resort.* New York: Three Rivers Press.

Scoones, I. (2010) *Zimbabwe's Land Reform: Myths and Realities.* Woodbridge: James Currey.

Schreiner, O. (1897) *Trooper Peter Halket of Mashonaland.* London: T Fisher Unwin.

Tagwira, V. (2006) *The Uncertainty of Hope.* Harare: Weaver Press.

Taringa, N. T. and Bishau, D. (2016) 'Shona Traditional Religions Dark Green Spirituality: An indispensable Intangible Heritage for Sustainable Land Reforms in Zimbabwe'. In Magosvongwe, R., Mlambo, O. & Ndlovu, E. (Eds.) *Africa's Intangible Heritage and Land.* Harare: University of Zimbabwe Publications. (pp. 52-66).

Vambe, L. (1972) *An Ill-fated People.* Gweru: Mambo Press.

Wa Thiongo, Ngugi. (1965) *The River Between.* London: Heinemann.

Chapter Eleven

"Decolonising" and Democratising Pedagogical Translation in Foreign Language Teaching: The Role of Mediation as Strategy

Okom Emmanuel Otegwu

Introduction

Translation has, for long, been used as a tool in foreign language teaching and learning contexts. However, it has generated considerable controversy as methodologies have evolved towards more active communicative approaches. The communicative approach, which arose in the seventies, has become synonymous with the development of functional language skills in authentic communicative situations, and is firmly centered on the learner (Semistraitis, 2006). It has been typically pitted against the traditional "grammar-translation" teaching method, which has been critiqued for its text-centeredness, decontextualised study of language and disregard for the development of oral communicative skills. Despite the wide criticism the grammar-translation method has suffered (and, by extension, the use of translation in language teaching), translation that is integrated meaningfully in foreign language learning holds multiple possibilities that are advantageous to language acquisition. It builds a pedagogical bridge back to the mother tongue (L1) as the language of spontaneous, natural reference, allowing for reflexive comparisons (Cuq & Gruca, 2005: 402). It thus draws attention to important metalinguistic understanding of the functional and structural aspects of language. It may facilitate the end goal of successful communication, in conveying an intended meaning and producing an accurate and appropriate segment of discourse (Chiţu, 2014: 201–211). In addition, pedagogical translation can help learners enhance their analytical and problem-solving skills which are essential in everyday life as well as in most working fields.

This chapter takes as its point of departure the premise that translation -as a form of mediation between languages- is an inevitable human activity in a globalised world where bi-multilingual and multicultural settings are the norm. Furthermore, it is an activity with multiple possibilities, which should be tailored to the context and needs of learners and grounded in a post-modern teaching and learning paradigm. However it is imperative to note that postmodernism is not designed to really decolonise foundational African materialities principally because postmodernism is antifoundationalist and it denies the existence of realities, authenticity and [African] human essence. The latter has shown us that no single method of teaching can guarantee effective language learning hence the need for adaptability and openness with important guiding principles. Some of the features of postmodern language education, as theorised by Finch (2006), include: student-centered learning; collaborative, autonomous learning; learning language through popular culture, post-colonialism (including the use of diverse variants of one language, regional dialects and pronunciations) and the recognition of the relativity and subjectivity of language use and acquisition, shaped by affective, social and cultural filters. Postmodernism as based on constructivist principles of knowledge promotes the pragmatic over the theoretical, rejecting the principle of "expertise"; accepts interaction between the "knower and the non-knower" as a form of co-construction, and not the mere transmission of knowledge from an individual to another. This paradigm significantly underscores postmodern democratic teaching and learning which means that each actor in the classroom situation is free to express their individual opinion for collective consideration, understanding and decision-making. Indeed, language and methodological prescriptiveness and uniformity often diminish rather than enhance language acquisition, as they aggravate and/or create existing asymmetrical power relations which are manifest in the colonial ideologies of language legitimacy and ownership. Furthermore, theory and practice ought to be inter-related at all times in the language classroom situation. Postmodernism is connected to the "postmethod" in that it accepts a diversity of strategies which place emphasis on knowledge construction and situation-based decisions (Fahim and Pishghadam, 2011: 42).

This chapter seeks to explore the ways in which pedagogical translation may be diversified and integrated meaningfully within the project of multilingualism, democracy and global citizenship. We aim to demonstrate this through the use of mediation as a teaching and learning strategy. Preparing students to be "glocal" citizens of the world, being , sensitive and open to both local and global languages and cultures has become a crucial objective in language education, particularly in multilingual and multicultural societies like Nigeria, where tensions and sensitivities around race, ethnicity and language are rife. Global developments call for the preparation of students to face challenges of migration and mobility, social inequality or environmental destruction (Cates, 2005; Georgiou, 2009). It stands to reason that acquiring an intercultural competence is part and parcel of this process, as, to quote Georgiou (2009) citing Humboldt (1836: 60), learning to express oneself in words other than one's own is 'to acquire a new standpoint in our world-view'

Translation, as denoted by its prefix, fundamentally means carrying something across, etymologically derived from the Latin "transferre" or Greek "metapherein" (Leornadi, 2010: 65). Catford (1965: 20) simply defines translation as the "replacement of textual material in one language (source language) by equivalent textual material in another language (target language)". Translation is however much more than this: while its primary purpose is to provide semantic equivalence between the source language and target language it also, significantly involves cross-cultural communication. Rendering an exact equivalence is one of the major challenges of translation, given distinct grammars with their unique metaphorical and idiomatic nature. The success of translation for foreign language speakers in real communicative situations and in the foreign language classroom serves the more immediate purposes of language acquisition and communication. To this end, in this chapter, we conceptualise mediation as a concept and pedagogical tool, and argue that translation - itself is a form of mediation between languages- , requires further mediation to facilitate effective learning in foreign language classroom settings. The chapter further contextualises the notion of "decolonisation", as a means of decentring learning strategy within the language classroom and proposes a working concept of mediation as a teaching and learning strategy. It provides a brief critique of teaching methodologies, from the grammar translation method to the post method, and a framework for rethinking pedagogical translation through mediation, as a collaborative, "decolonised" and democratic classroom practice.

Relationship between Mediation with Postmodernism, Post-method, Globalisation and Democratisation

Vygotsky (1978) considers language as an instrument of mediation and a symbolic tool that allows human beings to mediate between their minds and the outside world. According to Braescu (2010), the genesis of pedagogical mediation within the framework of sociocultural theory is premised on knowledge construction through interactions characterised by creativity, diversity, investigation and the exchange of learning. These kinds of constructivist interactions find their place in the framework of the postmethod and postmodernism.

Mediation as a teaching, strategy facilitates communication, intercomprehension and intercultural competence and recognises that the presence of two different languages is imperative in the learning situation. The use of multidirectional, interactive mediating strategies as per the Common European Framework of Reference for Languages (2001) may remedy, if not overturn, traditional teaching methodologies which are arguably indicative of "colonised" models, both in content and approach. This is further illustrated in the democratic values and practices which are activated through mediation viz. negotiating meaning, inter-subjectivity/inter-culturality, and task-based learning such as summarising a text to arrive at a precise meaning of the said document before any translation is done. It would not be an exaggeration to qualify the traditional teaching of translation as a "colonised" model, as it is dominated by the teacher – as expert and holder of knowledge, and the text – as representative of a canon and of "high culture"- to the detriment of the learner. Democratisation of teaching and learning requires decentring the process of teaching and learning, and letting learners of heterogeneous levels be provided with the opportunities and freedom to learn and discover things by themselves. The advocates (Iloanya, 2017:257-260) for democratisation of teaching and learning postulate that learners "should have access to shared learning responsibilities, self-regulated learning processes, avenues for formative feedback to be given to their teachers and dynamic peer-to-peer interactions which permit collaborative and cooperative learning". Indeed, the traditional approach which focuses solely on translation, that is, written production and comprehension (Davies, 2004:3), is divorced from real life communicative situations, and is decontextualised. Furthermore, traditional pedagogical translation as the sole means of teaching and learning a foreign language is upheld by the bias of word by word equivalence and disempowers learners from making their own individual and collective language choices in building meaning in a collaborative way.

"Decolonising" the Language Classroom?

In the era of globalisation, human mobility and rapidly growing technology, geographical, linguistic and cultural borders have become increasingly blurred because of the widespread use of the internet, the rise of complex social formations due to immigration and integration. It is also quite possible that they become blurred due to coercive, colonising, authoritarian global matrices of power that cascade to Africa and the rest of the global south. Yet epistemic frames of reference and the power relations they bring to bear have been slow to shift in the sense of difficulties persistent in the application of teaching strategies. And so, half a century after the end of [formal] colonialism, calls for the "decolonisation" of educational models and institutions are ubiquitous. For example in South Africa, the Fees Must Fall Movement signals a new politically conscious generation who does not accept the status quo and is agitating for structural change in the education sector. Decolonisation is a useful notion in the field of language education, functioning as a broad framework to reconsider existing approaches and to propose more progressive, inclusive means of foreign language teaching using translation. In the field of language teaching and policy, decolonisation has generally been advocated to promote, develop and adopt a diversity of African indigenous languages rather than the sole language of the colonisers (Batchelor, 2009). There are yet difficulties to recognising decolonisation in the teaching of languages. For instance, the negative attitudes towards indigenous languages by African elites are part of challenges to implementing language policy, for example the Kenya Education Commission Report known as the Ominde Report claimed that it would be a "grave misuse of public funds to translate textbooks and supplementary books into "Kiswahili" and that it would not be possible to use this language because it would require adaptation to unaccustomed scientific uses" (Muthwii and Kioko, 2004: 66).

In the field of translation pedagogy, decolonisation firstly suggests adapting and constructing discourses in harmony with local (indigenous) contexts and realities. As such, any meaningful process involving the decolonisation of foreign language teaching requires a fundamental shift from the concept of a uniform method to the concept of postmethod which is dynamic, diversified and individualised. This entails a transformation of teachers' beliefs, reasoning and cognition into strategic principles that might empower "teachers to theorise from their own practice and practice what they have theorized" (Ahmadian and Rad, 2014: 593).

Critical pedagogy aims at dismantling a traditional teacher–centered pedagogy to establishing a more democratic and comprehensive teacher learner relationship. This implies a student-centered learning. Students need to also be disaggregated as they are of different levels and not homogeneous. This is a pedagogy which deviates from the grammar-translation model. It is however important to note that there is no simple or fail-safe formula to guide teachers (McGregor, 2012). What is the strategy to be considered? A strategy is conceptualised as the calculation or manipulation of power relationships that becomes possible as soon as a subject with will and power (academic institutions, learners, business, an army, a city) can be isolated (de Certeau, 1984: 35). On the other hand tactic depends on time and "must constantly manipulate events in order to turn them into opportunities." (de Certeau, 1984: xiii). Tactic moreover deals with carrying out the objectives laid out in strategy, accurately and efficiently.

The term strategy, in the language learning sense, has come to be applied to the conscious decisions and attitudes made by foreign language speakers or teachers in the process of learning or using the language. Strategies can differ in nature, from planning the organisation of one's learning (a metacognitive learning strategy) through using mnemonic devices to learning vocabulary (cognitive learning strategies), to rehearsing what one expects to say (a performance strategy), to bolstering one's self-confidence for a language task by means of "self-talk" (an affective strategy) (Andrew, 1998). Strategies thus refer to planned techniques which the learner may follow as a guide to acquire knowledge when given the opportunity and motivational aptitude to put the language into use (Rubin, 1975:43). The multiple strategies also require a variety of dynamic and meaningful tactics for any appropriate language learning.

Effective teaching strategy however requires that teachers provide a variety of activities to meet the needs of different learning styles, so that students will at least select the ones that appeal to them. This is a pragmatic approach and it seems feasible since classroom situations vary according to learners and the environment (Hussein, 2009).

Diversification is also synonymous with the diversity of student profiles, cultural, linguistic or otherwise. The classroom diversification paradigm implies students' learning needs as resources that are developed to the extent that their capabilities and limitations allow for it in the various domains of human growth (e.g. cognitive, social, emotional, physical, aesthetic). Thus, classroom diversification presumes that the more students' learning needs in a classroom are related to one another by the kinds of technology and resources available for them to use, the more there are chances for effective learning in the classroom situation. This may results in higher overall levels of learning productivity across all students (Lopez, 2007).

As regards the teacher-learner relationship, there is need for inter-subjectivity, which infers shared cognition and consensus in the shaping of ideas and relations in the classroom situation in order to

289

foster foreign language teaching/learning. This allows for democratizsation, which according to Iloanya (2017:257-276) advocates for equal opportunity in the classroom. There is no single model of pedagogy or class organisation that characterises student-centred learning. Students may work individually or in small groups in learning centres. While learner-centred approaches may involve independent work, there is a common perception that learning is facilitated by interaction with other learners. Bruner (1996:84) links constructivism and cooperative/collaborative learning and expression of student-centred learning in his claim that learning should be 'participatory, proactive, communal, collaborative and given over to the construction of meanings (Laury-Brady, 2004).

This further means that the learner and the teacher have equal access to appropriate learning tools, such that any barriers that may hinder students' participation in teaching and learning sessions are done away with, thereby breaking with traditional lecture method. The process thus allows for decentring student-teacher's free participation in developing the nature, creation and transmission of knowledge. Within this paradigm, the learner is the target in the learning process while the teacher plays the role of a facilitator rather than dominating the teaching and learning processes. Students, in the translation or language class are allowed to make their voices heard, rather than be subdued as passive listeners, who should be diligent and obedient. It is nonetheless important to have a brief analytical view of translation as a method and cross examine its position in the language teaching and learning didactics.

Overview of Pedagogical Translation

Generally, translation is a long-standing method in the teaching of foreign or second languages. Long before grammar-translation method (GTM) arose in the 19th Century in Europe there had been an emphasis on grammar since the 16th Century in classical language teaching (Maichia, 2008). The grammar-translation method aims at writing accurately, translating into foreign languages and memorisation of vocabulary as well as teaching of literature (Rivers, 1981). Soon the GTM began to lose advocates as theorists started finding faults with the lack of oral communication. In spite of the severe attacks, the grammar-translation method is still widely practiced. Liu (1969) argues that grammar plays a vital role in communicative language as learners are consciously aware of the form and structure of the target language. The grammar-translation method was followed by the direct method, synonymous with the "natural method" which adopts naturalistic principles of language acquisition, meaning that second language learning is presumed to follow similar patterns of first language learning through direct association with persons or objects, avoiding any translation (Marquos-Aguado and Becerra, 2013). It is however, difficult to transfer the prevailing conditions of a native language into a classroom setting. Soon the direct method metamorphosed into audio-lingualism. The audio lingual method was introduced during the Second World War to respond to the needs of the American Army so as to enable them to understand and speak other languages as native speakers. The method is built through a process of "mechanical habit formation", while developing the language skills in the target language with no resort to translation in language teaching (Richards and Rodgers, 2003:50). Subsequently, the communicative approach in language teaching emerged in the 1970s and 1980s (Richards, 2006); Rivers, 1981), and signified a shift of emphasis from the mechanical practice of language patterns to task-based learning for effective language use. The approach emphasises interaction as a form of interpersonal activity within society (Rivers, 1981). This shift was a landmark in L2 teaching, pointing towards a concrete democratisation of the classroom, where authentic interactions are required for a fairer mode of discussions and free learning. The communicative approach received criticism as it proved effective for smaller classes but problematic for larger groups. Smaller classes are best for optimal interaction, although large classes may be subdivided into manageable small sizes for the purpose of mediating interactional activities. When at a point each small group presents their work to the general large class, there is a tendency of greater numbers of students learning from each other at the same time.

This dilemma has opened the way for the use of mediation in the classroom (Ahmadian and Rad, 2014). The action-oriented principle and task-based approach have their roots in the decentred CEFR (Common European Framework of Reference for Languages), with Vygotskyan (1978) constructivism and sociocultural theory in language teaching as they involve mediating and interactive activities in the classroom situation. Language as a communicative task is seen as bringing about an outcome through creation of meanings in a real-world activities and the assessment of tasks (Skehan, 1998: 173). Ellis (2003:16) explains a task as a work plan that requires learners to process language pragmatically in order to achieve an outcome that can be evaluated in terms of appropriate content. Task-based instruction is relevant at all times since learning itself is a form of activity.

Although each method was used at a time, it was replaced as in a relay in the quest to find a more effective alternative method in language acquisition. The postmethod, however, contributes to the debate on the democratisation and "decolonisation" of teaching and learning models. Karamaravadivelu (2006:161) characterises postmethod pedagogy as being (i) generated by practitioners on the ground (ii) sensitive to local needs, wants and situations (iii) based on the lived experience of both learners and teachers. The postmethod is further informed by three-dimensional pedagogic parameters, viz. that there should be a practical relationship between theory and practice. Secondly, the postmethod premised on linguistic, social, cultural, political and educational factors infers that the method should be sensitive to a particular group of teachers and learners with set goals within a particular institutional context and sociocultural milieu. Lastly, this method aims at motivating learners in a classroom situation for personal and social transformation.

Tosun (2009) argued in favour of the postmethod as derived from the concept of "globalization and postmodernism or rather the postmethod condition" and besides Kumaravavadivelu (2006), suggests that modern pedagogy should be flexible as it takes into account macrostructures (social, cultural, historical and political) that may influence, modify and correlate with the microstructures of the classroom situation.

From the above discourse on the various methods and methodologies, translation has a limited place for which there is a need for rethink. However, the source language or first language, as a reference system, helps to eliminate misunderstandings in the process of the foreign language learning. Mediating through the first language with translation puts the learner into an active problem-solving situation thereby improving learner's understanding of the target language (Liu, 1969). Going by these explanations, it would require selective activities to be able to pass across the message for which integrating mediation in the teaching of foreign language would be appropriate.

Mediation as a Language Teaching and Learning Concept

To what extent can the use of mediation contribute to a better teaching of translation in order to facilitate learner's comprehension in language learning? In this section, we intend to clarify the claims of mediation in order to apply it to the field of language learning and teaching. Precisely, Pym's (2002; 1) perspective of "linguistic mediation" covers everything that can happen when languages are in contact with the impulse for communication across their boundaries". When we learn the language of the other, that is a form of mediation, so is recourse to pidgin or a lingua Franca. Mediation involves a conversation in several languages as in the use of passive knowledge of the other's tongue or the various forms of code-switching. In brief each mediating activity is aimed at increasing or developing the competence of the leaners.

According to Stathopoulou (2015), the notion of mediation in translation studies refers to the bridge between languages and cultures and more concretely, to the intervention of participants involved in translation exercise from the source text. In this sense, Hatim and Mason (1990:242) refer to mediation as "the extent to which text producers and receivers feed their own (appropriate) beliefs into their processing of a given text." According to the Council of Europe (2001:14) mediating is one of the basic aims of foreign language acquisition and takes the forms of interactional language activities, whereby learners work in groups while processing an existing text. Processing a given text is certainly not restricted to a particular professional; rather it is deemed as a linguistic exercise.

Examples of mediating techniques or activities are summarising, restructuring, rewording, reformulation, clarification, role play and paraphrasing. All these activities aim at clarifying meanings of texts in the context of language learning. Stathopoulou (2015) is of the view that mediation is rather a form of communication that cuts across linguistic and cultural boundaries through the translator's mediating. The understanding of mediation would suggest relevant different types of language activities performed through teacher or learner or tools in a language class that help learners to have implicit meanings of a message or text or concepts for effective learning of the language. This might be through explanation in mother tongue, storytelling, role play, and reformulation and translation between the writer and reader and also between the cultures of composition and reception.

Written mediation involves the exact translation of legal or scientific texts, literary translation, summarising gist while using any working languages in translation. This written mediation can also be referred to as "para-translation" activities that give learners ample opportunities to comprehend the message in a given language. Much as these activities represent language courses on their own, they play the role of mediation for the translation to serve as an effective tool in language learning. The mediating activities can be carried out concurrently or simultaneously in the learning process. Moll (2000:257) explains the centrality of mediation to learning signifying that human beings interact with their worlds primarily through mediational means via cultural artefacts, tools and symbols, including language. These instruments play crucial roles in the formation of human intellectual capacities.

Functions and Potentialities of Mediation in Foreign Language Teaching/Learning

Despite the proliferation of theories, their classifications and counter criticisms in translation and L2 pedagogy, translation has continued to be used as a tool for language teaching. However the traditional approach of read and translate texts still predominates and needs to be reconsidered with the integration of mediation. But mediation through humanoid robots according to Nhemachena, (2017:15) is invariably taking employment away from human beings leaving them without human security and with depleted human "development" opportunities. Scholars are however discussing alternatives as Nhemachena (2017) notes that the non-formal sectors will offer solace for those whose jobs are taken over by the humanoid robots. In the event, mediation through humanoid robots technology needs direct human supervision and monitoring. Similarly, mediation through machine translation cannot replace human translation when it requires idiomatic expressions and poetic writing that may require human logical reasoning. There is this feeling that robots remain at the services and directives of humans (Nhemachena, 2017).

That Nigerian universities are yet to practically embrace the machine aided translation for the purpose of using translation as a tool for foreign language teaching and learning, perhaps due to lack of a practical guide and sensitisation for diversified and dynamic strategies pertaining to pedagogical translation. Thus Serbessa (2006:129-130) opined that the traditional "chalk and talk "(or marker and white board) lecture approach with students as passive recipients of knowledge is no longer appropriate for today's generation. Although the traditional lecture approach may appear to have some merits, we content that this approach cannot compete with the wide range of mediating approaches and strategies that may be employed to encourage students' participation.

In this regard, mediation as a strategy for interaction and task-based learning is a big step towards more democratic and collaborative modes of learning. In order to ascertain the extent to which, if at all mediation is applied in foreign language teaching and learning a study was carried out in the Nigeria French Language Village (NFLV), Inter-university Centre Badagry, Lagos. Here, certificate and diploma French programmes are run for Nigerian learners. The French Village serves as a year abroad centre particularly for the undergraduate learners of French language from Nigerian universities and Colleges of Education. This is the centre where students undergo French language immersion programme. The French Village is further mandated by the federal government to ensure that Nigerians speak French as it has been declared the second official language besides English. French language is the medium of instruction in French Village "Ici on parle français" (Here we speak French).

In terms of our study, five translation lecturers were observed in classroom situations. Generally the lessons centre on such topics as "Introduction aux procédés élémentaires de la traduction", "Faux–amis", "Les temps verbaux" as well as short passages for translation in class. From the observations, it was firstly obvious that the seating arrangements do not allow teachers to employ much interactive learning. Front to back seating arrangements encourage unidirectional teacher-student communication. This further discourages students from talking among themselves for most of the time learners focus their attention on the instructor. Mediating activities require small working groups or teams for proper interactions which were barely employed. It is envisaged that the large size of classes would have allowed for the formation of small interactive groups of learners, but with the seating arrangements in a typical class of 40 students or more, very few students speak out to respond to questions.

In the choice of method, communicative approach was generally adopted. In the process techniques of translation were explained to the students. Sentences covering the different tenses were written on the board for the students to translate. Short and simple texts were also given to students to translate. During the class observations on translation, individual participation was encouraged, somehow, directly and indirectly or unconsciously some mediating activities for example paraphrasing and reformulation were employed in the two thirds of the classes observed. Nonetheless, the conscious use of mediating activities within interactive teams of learners would have been more advantageous in the language classes. As relates to translation, generally the teachers adopted the contrastive linguistic approach of Vinay Darbelnet (1958) using techniques of translation principally classified into direct and indirect procedures of translation for teaching language. Since language communication is not only at the linguistic level but cross-cultural as such it would pay off better if the practices and exercises are cushioned with mediating interactional activities so that the class does not adopt, by default, the usual traditional read and translate texts.

Generally, collaborative learning and task-based learning are useful when students of different levels of proficiency seek to help one another in the class. The fast learners in small groups can perform the scaffolding role, taking the place of a teacher and contributing useful information to increase other learners' competence and performance. This becomes more evident as students perform activities in small groups in writing, rewriting, editing, summarising and reformulating. Rezvani and Bigdeli (2012) referring to Stark (2005) state that with these activities the learners create opportunities for collaborative learning. These activities are what the Council of Europe (2001) affirms as mediating activities being ancillary to translation. Though important as they assume a creative role, these activities are not consciously emphasised in a didactic translation class for the furtherance of foreign language learning. Cooperative learning increases the tempo of communication and social skills. Translation teaching is not just giving texts to students to translate nor just forming different groups that are not performing. It is all about creating a conducive learning environment where each participant will be fairly engaged in a rewarding task going through a process for a fruitful end product. The language teacher can therefore create working groups for proper processing of translation texts for the purpose of foreign language learning. As such Davies (2005) frowns at the imposition of the teacher's answer as the only one, rather it should serve as a guide. Through small interactive group activities, even introverts are motivated to participate and learn freely in the class.

Mediation is thus to be applied as an interpersonal activity focusing on the interpretation and representation of meanings that may take place in the communicative space between writers and readers (Stathopoulou, 2014). The interpersonal activity refers to the participants' potential to establish and maintain social relationships and have interpersonal encounters and its outcome is measured in terms of the personal rapport created in the classroom. Interpersonal activity and communication treat the classroom as a microcosm of society, built within a larger society having its rules and role relationships. The classroom community presents different contexts for different participants who bring different social realities with them. The interpersonal activity goes with interactional textual activity proposed by (Kumaravadivelu, 2006) and it refers to the linguistic realisation that creates logical written or spoken texts that enable foreign language learners to understand the message as intended.

Translation activities assuming the role of mediating activities and collaborative learning are of particular advantage in foreign language learning, thus Kaye (2009) stipulates that translation in groups can encourage learners to discuss the meaning and use of language at the deepest possible levels as they work through the process of understanding and then looking for equivalents in another language which also infers translanguaging. Translation as a real-life activity is increasingly important with on line information, thereby encouraging distance language learning and intensifying classroom learning. Computers and the internet are some basic instruments within the concept of transhumanism which is an intellectual and cultural movement supporting the use of technology to improve human mental and physical characteristics and psychological capacities. However transhumanism is also antihumanism in the sense that it is postanthropocentric and thus it diminishes human sovereignty and autonomy as it elevates the machines. It is often used as a synonym for "human enhancement" (Bostrom, 2003). With computer and internet sharing common information with different learners, sharing similar ideas, all point to diversification and democratic learning in the face of globalisation.

Discussion of differences and similarities during the translation process helps learners understand the interaction of the two languages and the interferences caused by their first language. It also helps learners appreciate the strengths and weaknesses of the source and target languages, for example in the comparison of idiomatic and metaphoric expressions. The collaborative learning through texts is what we regard as working together around the texts to achieve the maximum benefit of language learning. Translating different parts of the texts, learners bring examples of their own mother tongue for discussions also by sharing email materials or google translation compared to manual translation.

Learning a foreign language infers empowering oneself with intellectual instruments for confronting the real and the unknown, as well as personal enrichment through knowledge of other cultures and other views of the world. We are all the same moving toward an age where everyone will be able to translate, for various reasons including language learning, just as everyone can sing (some better than others, some for fun, some of course for money or as a profession, learning but all with the basic capacity). Therefore translation should be taught from the practical point of view for communicative reasons.

Conclusion

Effective language teaching and learning suggests the application of combined and appropriate strategies or approaches in order to meet the challenges and demands of the present generation of learners with new technologies, and ever evolving learning environments. The bid is to practically find innovative means of making learners be creative and motivated in the learning process. This is where the role of mediating activities is advocated in foreign language learning through the democratic and interactive classroom situation.

Instructor's need is to translate the knowledge into effective classroom practice, and such knowledge might require further development and investigation. The aim is not necessarily to instruct the teachers how to teach but to sensitise them to the need and concerns of employing interactional mediating activities with translation which we believe will accelerate the learners' understanding and communicative competence through language acquisition in the evolving globalisation. However it is imperative to note that just as globalisation challenges the sovereignty of some nation states and regions, the use of technology including posthuman robotic technology also challenges the autonomy and sovereignty of human beings in Africa. In this sense, it challenges the very autonomy and individualised learning that it purports to enhance because the human beings can become cyborgs or appendages of machines or technology.

References

Ahmadian, M. and Erfan Rad, S. (2014) Postmethod Era and Glocalized Language Curriculum Development: A Fresh Burden on Language Teachers. *Journal of Language Teaching & Research*, 5(3).

Andrew, C.D. (1998) *Strategies in Learning and Using a Second Language*. London and New York: Longman.

Batchelor, K. (2014) *Decolonizing Translation: Francophone African Novels in English Translation*. Routledge.

Bostrom, N. (1999) Transhumanism and Posthumanism http://www.thenanoage.com/trnashumanism.posthumanism.ht m #poshhuman

Bostrom, N. (2003) Transhumanist Values [in *Ethical Issues for the 21st Century*, ed. Frederick Adams (Philosophical Documentation Center Press, 2003); reprinted in *Review of Contemporary Philosophy*, Vol. 4, May (2005)] [pdf] *www.nickbostrom.com*

Brady, L.I. (2004) Towards Optimal Student Engagement in Teacher Education. *The Australian Journal of Teacher Education*.

Catford, J. A. (1965) *A Linguistic Theory of Translation*. London: Oxford University Press.

Cates, K. (2005) Teaching for a Better World: Language Education in Japan. In *Osler, A., Starkey, H. 2005. Citizenship and Language Learning: International Perspectives*. Stoke on Trent: Trebtham Books: 59-73.

Chesterman, A. (2016) *Memes of Translation: The Spread of Ideas in Translation Theory* (Vol. 123). John Benjamins Publishing Company.

Chiţu, R E. (2015) Intercultural Dimension in Language the Function of Pedagogical Translation npissh.ro/ro/wp-content/uploads/sites/2/2015/12.

Council of Europe (2001) *Common European Framework of Reference* .on line *http://www.coe.int/t/dg4/education/elp/elp-reg/cefr_EN.asp* European Language Portfolio.

Cuq, J. P. and Gruca, I. (2002) *Cours de didactique du français langue étrangère*. Grenoble: Presses universitaires de Grenoble.

Cyr, P., and Germain, C. G. (1996) *Les stratégies d'apprentissage*. Québec: CLE international.

Davies, M. G. (2004) *Multiple Voices in the Translation Classroom: Activities, Tasks and Projects* (Vol. 54). John Benjamins Publishing.

de Certeau, M. (1984) *The Practice of Everyday Life*. Berkeley CA: University of California Press.

Ellis, R. (1992) *Second Language Acquisition and Language Pedagogy*. Clevelon: Multilingual Matters Ltd.

Ewards, C. & Willis, J. (eds) (2005) Teachers Exploring Tasks in English Language Teaching pp40-468 New York; Anthony Roweb Ltd. Chippenham and Eastourne.

Fahim, M. and Pishghadam, R. (2011). Postmodernism and English Language Teaching. Iranian Journal of Applied Language Studies, 1(2): 27-54.

Finch, A.E. (2006). The Postmodern Language Teacher: The Future of Task-based Teaching. *Studies in British and American Language and Literature, 78*:221-248.

Georgiou, M. (2009). Language Learning for Global Citizenship: the Intercultural and Political Dimensions of Foreign Language Education. In *Intercultural Education: Paideia, Polity, Demoi, Proceedings of the International Conference Co-organised by the International Association for Intercultural Education (IAIE) and the Hellenic Migration Policy Institute (IMEPO), Under the Aegis of UNESCO.*

Güngör, M. A., & Demirbas, M. N. (2011) Application of Cognitive and Socio-Cultural Theories in CALL. *iJET, 6*(2): 33-36.

Hatim, B., & Mason, I. (1990). *The Translator as Communicator*. London: Routledge.

Hussein, N. (2009) Eclecticism and Language Learning *Al- Fatih Journal*. No .39 April

Iloanya, J. (2017). Democratisation of Teaching and Learning: a Tool for the Implementation of the Tuning Approach in Higher Education?. *Tuning Journal for Higher Education, 4*(2): 257-276

Kaye. P. (2009) Translation Activities in the Language Classroom www.teachingenglish.org.uk/article/**translation.**

Kumaravadivelu, B. (2006) *Understanding Language Teaching: From Method to Post method.* Routledge.

Lantolf, J. P. (2000) *Sociocultural Theory and Second Language Learning.* Oxford University Press.

Leonardi, V. (2010) *The Role of Pedagogical Translation in Second Language Acquisition: From Theory to Practice.* Peter Lang.

Liu, Q.X. and Shi, J.F. (2007) An Analysis of Language Teaching Approaches and Methods--Effectiveness and Weakness. *Online Submission,* 4(1):69-71.

Littlewood, W. (2007) Communicative and Task-based Language Teaching in East Asian Classrooms. *Language Teaching,* 40(3):243-249.

Lopez, O.S. (2007). Classroom Diversification: A Strategic View of Educational Productivity. *Review of Educational Research,* 77(1): 28-80.

Machida, S. (2011) Translation in Teaching a Foreign (second) Language: a Methodological Perspective. *Journal of Language Teaching and Research,* 2(4): 740-7.

Marqués Aguado, T., & Solís-Becerra, J. A. (2013) An Overview of Translation in Language Teaching Methods: Implications for EFL in Secondary Education in the Region of Murcia. In *Revista de Lingüística y Lenguas Aplicadas* (Vol. 8, (1): 38-48). Editorial Universitat Politècnica de València.

Mawere, M. (ed.) (2017). *Underdevelopment, Development and the Future of Africa.* Bamenda: Langaa RPCIG.

Moghaddam, A. A. and Rahman, A. (2012) Three of Concepts: Modernism, Postmodernism and Globalization. *Elixir Social Sciences,* 43: 6643-6649.

Moll, L. C. (2000) Inspired by Vygotsky: Ethnographic Experiments in Education.

Vygotskiperspectives on Literacy Research: Constructing Meaning through Collaborative Inquiry: 256-268.

Muthwii, M.J. and Kioko, A.N. (eds.,) (2004) *New Language Bearings in Africa: A Fresh Quest.* Multilingual Matters.

Nhemachena, A. (2017) Hearing the Footfalls of Humanoid Robots: Technoscience, (Un-)employment and the Future of "Development" in Twenty-First Century Africa, in Mawere, M. (ed.,) *Underdevelopment, Development and the Future of Africa*. Bamenda: Langaa RPCIG.

Nieto, C. H. (2007) Applications of Vygotskyan Concept of Mediation in SLA. *Colombian Applied Linguistics Journal*, (9): 213-228.

Nigeria French Language Village (2016), *Quarterly Bulletin*. Badagry.

Nilsson, P. (2008). Recognizing the Needs-Student Teachers Learning to Teach from Teaching. *Nordina: Nordic Studies in Science Education*, 4(1):92-107.

Pym, A. (2004) January. Localization and the Training of Linguistic Mediators for the Third Millennium. In *FORUM. Revue internationale d'interprétation et de traduction/International Journal of Interpretation and Translation* (Vol. 2, No. 1, pp. 125-135). John Benjamins Publishing Company.

Stark, P. (2005) Integrating Task-based Learning into Business English Programme.

Rezvani, R. and Bigdeli, R.A. (2012) A New Direction in Translation Pedagogy: Task-based Translation Teaching: 638-643.

Richards, J.C. and Rodgers, T.S. (2014). *Approaches and Methods in Language Teaching*. Cambridge University Press.

Richards, J. C. (2005) *Communicative Language Teaching Today*. SEAMEO Regional Language Centre.

Rivers, W. M. (1981) *Teaching Foreign-language Skills*. Chicago: University of Chicago Press.

Rubin, J. (1975). What the 'Good Language Learner' Can Teach Us, TESOL Quarterly, 9, 41-51.

Sayuki, M. (2008) A Step Forward to Using Translation to Teach a Foreign/Second Language, *Electronic Journal of Foreign Language Teaching* Vol. 5, (1): 140–155 http://e-flt.nus.edu.sg/.

Sekhan, P. (1998) *A Cognitive Approach to Language Learning*. Oxford: Oxford University Press.

Semistraitis, V. (2006) Peculiarities of the Communicative Approach in Teaching English.

http://webdoc.sub.gwdg.de/edoc/ia/eese/artic26/linas/3_200 6.html.

Serbessa, D. D. (2006) Tension between Traditional and Modern Teaching-learning Approaches in Ethiopian Primary Schools. *Journal of International Cooperation in Education*, 9(1):123-140.

Stathopoulou, M. (2013) Investigating Mediation as Translanguaging Practice in a Testing Context: Towards the Development of Levelled Mediation Descriptors. In *the Proceedings of the International Conference" Language Testing in Europe: Time for a New Framework*.

Thompson, I. (2013) The Mediation of Learning in the Zone of Proximal Development through a Co-constructed Writing Activity. *Research in the Teaching of English*: 247-276. Cambridge.

Tosun, B.C. (2009). A New Challenge in the Methodology of the Post-Method Era. *Journal of Language and Linguistic Studies*, 5(2): 1.

Vinay, J.-P. et Darbelnet, J. (1958). Stylistique comparée du français et de l'anglais. Paris: Didier.

Von Humboldt, W. (1836/1988) *On Language*. Cambridge: Cambridge University Pres

Vygotsky, L. S. (eds.) (1978) *Mind in Society: The Development of Higher Psychological Processes*. Harvard University Press.

Vygotsky, L. S. (1980) *Mind in Society: The Development of Higher Psychological Processes*. Harvard.

Yu, Y., & Wang, B. (2009) A Study of Language Learning Strategy use in the Context of EFL Curriculum and Pedagogy Reform in China. *Asia Pacific Journal of Education*, 29(4): 457-46.

Chapter Twelve

The Literary Constructions of the Metaphysical in the African Milieu

Coletta Kandemiri & Nelson Mlambo

Introduction

The natural world is the physical world consisting of visible matter. However in the 18th century some European thinkers conflated God with nature (see Evensky, 2005) such that for them nature has become the polite word for God. For purposes of this chapter nature is not conflated with God or with Eurocentric notions of immanence of God in matter. The metaphysical world is the invisible world which is believed to exist, is understood to be mutually and intermittently connected to the natural world, from an African worldview. However, access to the metaphysical, despite its invisible attributes, can be made possible through the qualitative dimension of fiction and its apt ability to represent the un-representable. This chapter explores the representation of the metaphysical phenomenon in *The Other Presence,* a novel by Nyathi (2008) and further probes the supernatural phenomena as connected to the social world, the African personhood and the environment. The metaphysical is not visible to the naked human eye but somehow influences human lives directly and indirectly. It is a power that operates within its own spheres and is directly linked to human beings and their environment. Thus, human beings talk of 'spiritual realms' which are the spaces occupied by these bodiless (astral) supernatural forces, whose presence can only be felt by the unusual manifestations that become interpretable. In some African cultures and traditions, the metaphysical is acknowledged and forms part of those groups' values. Traditional African values refer to a composite set of principles, knowledge and beliefs that are held in high esteem in particular African societies and that may be regarded as the guidelines for human behaviour (Blake, 1993). The traditional African values include the sense of community life, good human relations, sacredness of the religion, time, respect for hierarchy, authority and elders, as well as sense of language and proverbs (Emeka, 2012). Thus the metaphysical is embedded in the value of sense of the sacredness of religion in some of these particular African groups. This chapter reveals that some African cultural groups conjugate these metaphysical aspects as part of their life. In the novel *The Other Presence* (Nyathi, 2008), what we see is the metaphorisation of human life such that the metaphysical is brought out through the manifestations in whirlwinds and creatures to which spirits intermittently attach themselves. The chapter is a qualitative desktop research framed by the metaphysical theory together with the African worldview theory as the sub-theory. This chapter seeks to explore the fictionalisation of the metaphysical or supernatural phenomena as related to the social world and the behaviours of people within the social world. The probing is done by referring to the way the metaphysical is portrayed in the novel *The Other Presence* (2008) by Francis Sifiso Nyathi.

The term metaphysical refers to "the intangible, the supernatural, the mystical that concurs with the concrete, the metaphorical" (*Oxford Advanced Learner's Oxford Dictionary* 2010: 931). The terms metaphysical and supernatural are therefore used synonymously in this present exploration. The metaphysical is not visible to the naked ordinary human eye but may influence human lives directly and indirectly. It is a power that operates within its own spheres and is directly linked to human beings and the universe. Thus, human beings talk of 'spiritual realms' which are the spaces occupied by these astral, supernatural forces whose presence may only be felt by unusual manifestations that become interpretable.

The presence of the metaphysical may manifest in different ways, anywhere and anyhow, with some of the prevalent manifestations being easily identified and properly handled as well as managed by human beings. Of much interest is the way the metaphysical powers exhibit their presence to human beings. The metaphysical in its invisible state forms part of human existence. The coexistence creates commotion and order (as in the cosmological and not necessarily cosmo-chaos as it were) on the part of human beings as the human beings try to come to terms with the invisibles.

In some African cultures and traditions, the metaphysical or the supernatural is acknowledged and it forms part of the African values of those particular groups. Traditional African values refer to a composite set of principles, knowledge and beliefs that are held in high esteem in African societies and that are regarded as the guidelines for human behaviour (Blake, 1993). The traditional African values include the sense of community life (including *ubuntuism*), good human relations, sacredness of religion and religious rites, shrines and places, time, respect for authority and elders, as well as sense of language and proverbs (Emeka, 2012). The metaphysical is embedded in the value of sense of the sacredness of religion. This gives rise to the question of what religion is.

Africans are often associated with African concepts of ethnic identity and culture. Many believe in supernatural beings and the supernatural in as much as it relates to the African personhood. African religious systems seek to explain the persistence of evil and suffering, as much of the suffering that people encounter is believed to be caused by the supernatural. For much of what happens in the African context, whether good or bad, there is always a reason behind (Mbiti, 1989).

In some parts of Africa, the supernatural can be manipulated by human beings for both good and evil uses. This is in agreement with Mbiti (1989:75) who stresses the fact that the spirit world of the African people is densely populated with spirit beings, spirits and the living dead or the spirits of the ancestors. And in such a world, there are human beings who have the powers to communicate with, or rather have access to these spirits. People like herbalists and traditional healers (as opposed to the western view of witchdoctors) are meant to join forces with the supernatural so that they are guided on medicines that help the people in their communities to curb some, if not all, kinds of illnesses. The problem arises when these herbalists and traditional healers defy the intended operations by using the same powers to manipulate roots, herbs and spiritual powers that in turn harm other people. This now becomes the evil manipulation of the supernatural and it includes acts such as witchcraft, sorcery and harmful magic which are the very aspects that are troubling contemporary African communities and have been troubling the African past as well. A literary examination of the novel *The Other Presence* (Nyathi, 2008) in this chapter therefore seeks to demonstrate Achebe's concept of "the novelist as a teacher" where the author portrays and validates the ever-presence of the metaphysical in Kwena village, driving home the fact that the metaphysical can take any form.

Defining the Metaphysical and Discussing the Theoretical Framework

The natural world is the physical world which is visible to the human eye. This is the world in which human beings, animals, water bodies, physical landforms and other physical features are found. This natural world is easy to discuss as it is physically present and is visible. On the other hand, the metaphysical is defined as events, forces or powers that cannot be explained by laws of science; the metaphysical is rather attributed to gods or magic (*Oxford Advanced Learner's Dictionary*, 2010:1499). In this study, the terms metaphysical and supernatural are used synonymously referring to the invisible but existing presence. *Webster's New World Dictionary* (2015) defines the metaphysical as existing or occurring outside the normal experience or knowledge of man. It is not explainable by the known forces or laws of nature but it involves the spiritual and Godly realms. There currently appears to be no empirical evidence to this phenomenon since its explanation is beyond the known laws of science. However, the qualitative facet of life, the "unsayable" and "unsaid" is concretised through fiction and made more present and more felt to the society through story telling as what Nyathi (2008) does. Through fiction therefore, that is derived from the everyday realities of life of a people and as a way of rendering the truth in metaphorical ways, the metaphysical or the supernatural can thus be made more pronounced and as such it may be defined as the hidden element that makes the natural and supernatural formation complete. Story telling therefore, being part of African culture and as a way of articulating the "unsayable" helps us to grasp that which can elude quantification and 'empiricisation', and by so saying this helps us in understanding the representation and analysis of the metaphysical in the novel *The Other Presence* (Nyathi, 2008).

The attribute of the supernatural, that of being above the laws of science, limits human beings from learning and knowing more about the metaphysical phenomenon. However, much has been written and said around the globe on different aspects pertaining to the metaphysical, giving mixed viewpoints on the nature of the supernatural even though it is reasonably a challenge to argue convincingly for the existence of invisible objects. This attribute can, however, be made accessible through the qualitative dimensions of fiction and its apt ability to present the un-presentable.

This exploration employs the metaphysics theory as the overarching theory and adopts the African World View Theory as the sub-theory since the primary text *The Other Presence* (2008), is from Africa and written from an Afrocentric perspective. The metaphysics theory, according to the *Stanford Encyclopaedia of Philosophy* (2015), looks at the ways in which anything that is, can be spoken about or thought to be this appears incomplete. The supernatural is something that is talked about and people have a way of distinguishing the supernatural as well as acknowledging it.

Also the *Encyclopaedia of Black Studies* (2007) notes that the African worldview theory is a combination of the classical and contemporary, continental and diasporic Africa, overarching perspectives on human experience and the natural and phenomenal world. It is differentiated from the worldviews of other people in so far as it is rooted in and grows out of African history and culture. African people's beliefs about God, nature, and major life rituals (such as birth, puberty, adulthood, marriage, and death) exhibit enough commonalities to warrant being called an African worldview. According to Rabaka (2007), these commonalities in many areas of the life-worlds and lived experiences of African people render interminable philosophical disputes and semantic discussions as to whether there exists a general or universal African worldview utterly unnecessary and unrewarding. One can thus know the African worldview by knowing what tasks are performed by a discussion of it.

The metaphysical is present all over the world but the way it is perceived and comprehended differs from continent to continent and from society to society, as the human species perceives culture and religion differently, and it has different cultural and historical backgrounds. The African Worldview Theory is also preferable for this chapter in that both the supernatural and the natural aspects are incorporated in the theory. The supernatural element is evident in *The Other Presence* (Nyathi, 2008) as the story is set in Africa and it depicts a specific African people's ways of life (people of Kwena village). The text, though a micro-sample, mirrors the typical day-to-day living of some Namibian people and African people as well and it renders the African Worldview Theory apt to this exploration as it is rooted in African sensibilities and grows out of the vicissitudes of African history. This chapter, therefore, explores the presentation of the metaphysical in the context of the African Worldview Theory through Nyathi's (2008) novel.

The Metaphysical in the Novel *the Other Presence*

The Other Presence (Nyathi, 2008) opens with the mourning village members gathered at Ma Simanga's homestead, to bury yet another child from the same homestead. Elder Sinvula is being suspected to be responsible for the death of Akapelwa, who happens to be his late brother's son. As a group of mourners go to the hospital to collect the body of the deceased Akapelwa, on their way back they encounter strange happenings. First a whirlwind threatens to disturb the mourners. Secondly, a member of the village, Chuma, is attacked by a snake and is rescued by Elder Sinvula. At the grave site, again the whirlwind reappears and it is 'calmed' by Elder Neo. Then a mysterious, dead-like vulture falls from the sky, landing on Akapelwa's casket, as well as, an owl is seen up the tree in broad day light. Elder Neo, in a trance like that of a possessed person, openly warns Ma Simanga to desist from collecting bones and eccentric roots which seem to be bringing about the 'strange' happenings to her homestead. Doctor Castro ends the story by encouraging all the villagers to be tested for HIV and AIDS. Throughout the novel (*The Other Presence* 2008) Nyathi provides yet another dimension which showcases the manifestations and representations of the metaphysical. The metaphysical in *The Other Presence* (Nyathi, 2008) is mainly concerned with sorcery, witchcraft, accusations and suspicions, superstitions and forebodings.

The Natural Phenomena and the Metaphysical

In Chapter 1, the opening lines describe a whirlwind which is a disturbance to the serene and funereal atmosphere of Akapelwa's wake, thus causing mourners to panic. The whirlwind is threatening and portends a calamity such that its appearance is believed, in Kwena village, to be signalling something untoward, something which is yet to be known and foreboding a sense of death and disquiet given the fact that the villagers are gathered because of death;

> The tree at the centre of the village swung towards the west. The whirlwind beat its way through the thickets of the forest as it forced its path towards the compound. Dust flew high into the heavens and slowly started taking the natural space of the clouds. Pieces of dead wood, grass and leafage lifted high up and faded into the blue sky. One could vividly see the ugly specks these titbits and debris of nature were creating in the sky. It was not a pleasant sight (Nyathi, 2008:1)

Whirlwinds are a common sight especially in the open African terrains, but the one that is being described in the above quotation appears not to be normal. The fact that the villagers are gathered at a funeral, and the whirlwind seems to be targeting particularly the compound where they are gathered, is a cause for trepidation. There is a perturbation as this particular type of whirlwind signals the presence of the metaphysical, noted by the way the villagers react to its manifestation. The villagers are able to discern that this is not any other ordinary type of whirlwind but an omen that seeks to reveal something and also to cause havoc if it is not curtailed; whilst some of the villagers seem to be able to explain, predict and to some extent rebuke, calm down, divert and or control some of these metaphysical situations as we see in Elder Neo. This is corroborated by Maluleke (2012:3) who observes that the values and beliefs held by members

311

of a community are reflected in their traditional cultural practices and in this case what we see is a community that is bound by its sense of beliefs and practices as they all see the "unpleasantness" borne out of this natural phenomenon. Thus, the whirlwind is pronounced as eccentric and as something that carries engrained metaphysical characteristics which are a feature of the Kwena people' beliefs.

"Conjugation" of the Spiritual and Natural Worlds

The presence of the whirlwind threatening to disturb the mourners at Ma Simanga's compound requires a spiritual and supernatural remedy in order to prevent a possible devastation. One of the elders of the village, Elder Neo, is vested with "the power of [his] ancestors that function in [his] voice" (Nyathi, 2008:2) which enable him to communicate with the spiritual world. This is noted by the way he commands the whirlwind when he says;

> Find your path to your haven of peace and leave the children of life in their already troubled cradle. We seek serenity from you and not another spell of anguish. I implore you to pardon us of our infirmities. Please find your path where your legs suit your walk and not where your fangs will consume our creation. (Nyathi, 2008:2)

The whirlwind responds to elder Neo's command by remaining still for a while and then moving rapidly into the forest. The scenario is a typical exhibition of the supernatural at work. The extra-mundane, as asserted by Onyedinma and Kanayo (2013) that of the relationship which exists between human beings and the spiritual world, is evident in this instance. As such, elder Neo is able to instruct the whirlwind to go away and not disturb the mourners. Moreover, Elder Neo further explains that this apt ability, one which is of a Biblical nature where Jesus calms down the storm is also and has also been evident in Africa since Neo's ancestors "... commanded the dead and living long before you and I called this forsaken earth" (Nyathi, 2008: 2). Neo's response and explanation therefore shows that the power of the supernatural and the human ability to intervene when natural disasters strike is not new to Africa but it is something which has been practiced for generations for the good of mankind. There what is critical to the present generation is to find out 'where the rain began to beat us', how Africans derailed and lost such life giving interconnections between the natural and the supernatural. Moreover, noteworthy is that the supernatural powers that Elder Neo possesses are not for his own use for personal aggrandisement but in a show of humility he warns other villages that "Do not tempt me into bragging about the strength and powers of the elders of the unknowable world, elder Dube; since when have the living boasted superiority over the dead?" (Nyathi, 2008:3). What comes out here is that indeed there is a spiritual world that has "the strength and powers" which is a reality for the Kwena people. This spiritual world is inhabited by the "elders" who have departed the present physical world and they operate in the physical world through vessels like Elder Neo and such vessels act in humility for the good of the society at large. Thus, the African worldview is functional in this scenario where the metaphysical is exhibiting itself, and the African people reacting to the phenomenon, thus buttressing the relationship between the natural and supernatural worlds.

The forebodings that are represented in *The Other Presence* (Nyathi, 2008) may be interpreted as premonitions that entail Elder Sinvula to be vigilant and to be prepared. However, the issue of premonitions is somehow subjective, depending on how different cultural groups perceive the concept of superstition. In the specific African context of the Kwena people, superstitions may be marked as part of cultural beliefs as fictional writers incorporate them into their works like *The Other Presence* (Nyathi, 2008), a literary work reflecting the lives and realities faced by the Kwena as a metaphorical representation of an African microcosm .

In *The Other Presence* (Nyathi, 2008:32), Sinvula embarks on a quest to find out what had caused Akapelwa, his nephew's death and on his way he encounters black cats mating and also an owl. This encounter instils fear and induces anger in Sinvula as the creatures he meets are culturally concomitant to the supernatural world that portends an evil omen, as evident from the text:

It was difficult to tell whether elder Sinvula was in a state of confusion or insanity. His fears of these strange happenings had now changed to anger. He was angry at his failure to understand what was actually happening to him, seeing all these strange creatures that were traditional omens of witchcraft. He was not sure whether to throw questions to his ancestors or simply call on the powers of the heavens. (Nyathi, 2008:32)

The metaphysical has peculiar ways of presenting itself to human beings. It could be that the spiritual world may be trying to communicate something to elder Sinvula by making him see these strange happenings on his way to the hospital. However, the persistent question is always about the difficulties to argue for something that is not visible to the human eye, which makes it difficult to point at exactly what the premonitions mean or represent, or maybe they are not even linked to the spiritual world at all.

Elder Sinvula is being suspected to be a wizard, and being responsible for Akapelwa's death, as well as all the misfortunes befalling Ma Simanga's compound as presented in Chapter Four of the novel *The Other Presence* (Nyathi, 2008). The belief that somebody or some force is behind the lives of people is prevalent in most African societies, hence the acceptance and belief in the existence of the metaphysical. In Africa, the supernatural can be manipulated by human beings for both good and evil uses (Mbiti 1989) and consequently from this perspective, elder Sinvula is being indicted. Everything that happens in the Kwena context ought to be a reason for it; hence the death of Akapelwa is being blamed on elder Sinvula. Mbiti (1989:75) stresses the fact that the spirit world of the African people is very densely populated with spirit beings, spirits and the living dead or the spirits of the ancestors, which Nyathi (2008) alludes to in the title of the novel as some "presence". It is these spirits that callous human beings manipulate for self-aggrandisement and as such elder Sinvula is wrongfully accused to be one of those who use the evil powers to harm other people.

In Chapter Seventeen, the convoy of mourners from the morgue encounter two whirlwinds which are moving towards the convoy (Nyathi, 2008:87). This raises apprehension as noted by the way Neo says to his elderly companions, "What is the matter with the other world today? Whirlwinds during morning time like this could not be a signal of peace" (Nyathi, 2008:87). The 'other world' being referred to is the spiritual world and the language used here is something that is understood by all the people around, which demonstrates that it is a part of their culture and belief system and not something alien to the villagers. The whirlwinds in this scenario are believed to be a form of communication from the spiritual world, an extra-mundane of a top-down nature as asserted by Onyedinma and Kanayo (2013), where the supernatural world communicates to the human beings. The metaphysical, though invisible, makes itself visible to the mourners through the strange and fierce whirlwinds. In the novel, up until now it has not been clearly established as to what might be the possible cause of the mishaps that the mourners are encountering, but elderly characters like Elder Neo and Situmbeko can rationally sense that something is wrong as they interpret the message communicated by the spiritual world.

Natural phenomena like the whirlwind and natural animals, birds as well as humans are used in the manifestations of the metaphysical. A whirlwind may be seen as a natural occurrence, but in this case in the context of the novel *The Other Presence* (Nyathi, 2008), together with the owl, vulture, black cats and the snake, they connote the influence of the metaphysical from an African (as represented by the Kwena village) point of view. The wind and the creatures maintain their natural appearance as they are known to be, but they are believed to be under the influence of the metaphysical powers which control them as a means of communicating to the Kwena people.

Mediums

Moreover, Elder Neo may possibly be described as a 'medium' and a go-between, connecting the physical and the spiritual world, considering the role that he plays in *The Other Presence* (Nyathi, 2008). A medium is one who links the human beings with the spiritual world and ancestors. There is a belief among some African people that ordinary human beings cannot speak directly to God as God is considered as the Supreme Highest being and, therefore, not an equal. Thus, there should be a medium to serves as a link between human beings and the ancestors who in turn serve also as a medium between the human medium and God. A typical representative of the presence of the metaphysical is presented as elder Neo communicates with the whirlwind where it reads:

> Upon noticing the imminent chaos that could be caused by the winds, elder Neo stepped out of the vehicle and pulled out his knife and pointed it to the heavens. In an artistic manner, the shinning and brandishing knife cut across in the lifting dust as Neo uttered those ferocious, yet instructive, words to the void of the whirlwinds. "Go back to anthills of troubled souls, you restless spirits of a lesser breed," commanded Neo (Nyathi, 2008:88).

The winds made their "presence" known as they have found their way and are moving in the direction in which another unusual occurrence is witnessed when Chuma is attacked by a python (Nyathi, 2008:89). However, Chuma is rescued by Elder Sinvula who kills the snake by piercing through the head of the serpent with a knife (Nyathi, 2008:90). From there, the convoy proceeds to Ma Simanga's compound where the villagers witness yet another appalling revelation of the metaphysical. Villagers gathered at the graveside, pending burial events taking place, and awaiting the entombment of Akapelwa, but they are startled by some kinds of petrifying creatures:

> Their eyes were fixed on a bird that had strangely fallen from the skies onto the casket. It was a dead vulture. It looked like something that had died a long time ago. A few moments after its fall, an owl landed on a huge tree whose branch hung just above the casket (Nyathi, 2008:103).

This dead-like vulture and owl are believed to be some omens of witchcraft and their presence usually beckons the existence and interaction of the supernatural and the natural worlds. Witchcraft can be classified under the occult. Montenegro (2008:1) defines the occult as "an underlying supernatural worldview supporting various

316

practices that are designed to access information or power through reading hidden meanings, or through contact with supernatural beings or forces". The revelation of the vulture and the owl, to a certain extent carries a hidden meaning and, according to Mashau (2007), it may also be referred to as mysterious. However, through Nyathi's use of foreshadowing and flashbacks, the meaning and reason for such an 'unusual' manifestation is still to be revealed as the story draws to an end.

The medium, Elder Neo, vested with the powers of connecting with the spiritual world, challenges 'the dead like vulture and the owl' and commands the spirit in the creatures by condemning it to the sculls of darkness where it belonged (Nyathi, 2008:103). The spirit in the creatures responds to Elder Neo's directive instantly without wavering. There is thus a discernible interaction between the natural world and the spiritual world, such that though the spirits are not visible, their materialisation is made apparent:

> The vulture that looked dead at first now blinked its eyes and lifted itself onto its limbs. It pranced a little on the casket and flapped its wings loudly before taking off. It lifted itself into the air and flew towards the forest. The owl that had all along been looking from the branch hooted again and took off as well and followed the vulture (Nyathi, 2008:103).

This all happens after elder Neo has angrily commanded these vile creatures. Thus characters such as elder Neo who are bestowed with powers that allow them to interact with naturally with their own society and also with the spiritual world, are important linkages between the physical and the spiritual world from an African perspective. They regulate the relationship between the natural and spiritual worlds by reproving what may be deemed bad and evil, at the same time advocating what may be perceived and valued as good. Acts such as witchcraft, are alleged to disturb and counterculture some of the African cultural tenets such as communalism, harmonious and egalitarian existence, and yet to an alien mind that has not sought to understand them, these are criticised as they are understood as simply the use evil magic powers.

317

Though Elder Sinvula is being falsely accused of instigating the calamities that have befallen Ma Simanga, characters like Elder Neo intercede and regulate such situations. In *The Other Presence* (Nyathi, 2008), the manifestations of the metaphysical may be related mostly to activities affiliated to occultic practices such as witchcraft. The problem therefore is to figure out who may possibly be responsible for these strange happenings as they carry and maintain attributes of the occult. Igwe (2004) asserts that witchcraft is believed to cause epileptic fits, excessive weight gain, accidents, infertility, and miscarriages, among other mishaps. The strange happenings in *The Other Presence* (Nyathi, 2008) may as well thus be attributable to some forms of witchcraft.

Witchcraft draws its powers from the spiritual world and as such, it can only be reversed by a character that also has a spiritual link like a medium. Thus Elder Neo as a medium is able to instruct the strange whirlwinds to move away from the gathered mourners as well as driving the spirit that is lodged in the strange creatures. As a medium, Elder Neo "was the only one running the show" (Nyathi, 2008:103), implying that he became the only character who could deal with the spiritual problem that was at hand. Towards the end of the novel Elder Neo identifies the culprit responsible for all the strange happenings such as the whirlwinds and the dead-like vulture, as evidenced from the novel where it reads:

> When Neo's eyes finally caught Ma Simanga's, it was clear that one of them had some explanation to do about the strange ordeal that they had just witnessed. Then Neo disengaged his eyes and winked. He looked around the gathering and then back to MaSimanga. "Give none blame but your own self that has caused your misery. Your endless travels and collection of eccentric roots and bones from strangers have opened a portal of misery into your compound." (Nyathi, 2008:103)

It has come to light that Ma Simanga is responsible for the whirlwinds that have been attempting to disturb the mourners on a number of occasions. The knowledge of her secretive life of collecting eccentric roots and bones has been exposed by the powers of the medium that is linked to the spiritual world. This in itself resonates to the values and beliefs attached to African cultural groups. Maluleke (2012:3) asserts that traditional cultural practices reflect the values and beliefs held by members of a community for periods often spanning for generations. These beliefs and values shape a community's way of conduct amongst themselves, their environment and with the supernatural world. A sense of community and being humane are considered as great values of traditional African life. It can thus be concluded that Ma Simanga is a typical example representing how humans manipulate the metaphysical for self-aggrandisement.

Discussion of the Textual Analysis

From the foregoing it appears that the metaphysical forms part of life of some African cultural groups, as substantiated by the manifestations of the supernatural in *The Other Presence* (Nyathi, 2008). Thus through the novel, the metaphysical is integrated in the African worldview theory. Through the fictional representation of the metaphysical in *The Other Presence* (Nyathi, 2008), the mutual interconnectedness of the African cultural groups and the spiritual world is fortified. Somehow, the metaphysical from an African perspective, leans on the African dichotomy notably from the good and evil binary attached to it. From the novel, it is evident that the spiritual world may be a force of good and it may also be a bad force.

In *The Other Presence* (Nyathi, 2008), the presence of the medium, elder Neo, presents a crucial figure that represents the good side of the supernatural world as he helps in solving the enigma behind the mysterious manifestations, witnessed in the text. Elder Neo points at Ma Simanga, exposing her and advising her to desist from collecting bones and eccentric roots, which are believed to be linked to, and are the point of attraction for the evil spirits haunting her homestead and the lives of the villagers of Kwena.

The presence of modernity and the exposure to foreign religions, such as Christianity (as represented by Reverend Guiseb) slowly melts away the traditional African culture and religion and by implication Nyathi seems to suggest that this is the 'point where rain began to beat us'. The melting away entails the separation of African

319

people from their cultural ways which enable them to interact with the supernatural world. Therefore the further the African people drift away from their African footing and anchoring, the more calamities they encounter, which globalisation, modernity and or even Christianity may never be able to address or attempt to provide solutions for. Eventually African people lose their Africanness and plunge them into problems as their life is directly and mutually connected to the spiritual world, and as they are spiritual problems, they require spiritual attention.

Conclusion

This chapter therefore argues that the natural world is the physical world which is visible to the human eye, and as such it is easy to discuss or make reference to. On the other hand, the metaphysical world, which is invisible but is believed to exist, is understood to be mutually connected to the natural world from an African worldview, especially as presented by Nyathi (2008) through the novel *The Other Presence*. Thus, access to the metaphysical, despite its invisible attribute, was made possible through the qualitative dimension of fiction and its apt ability to represent the un-presentable.

Through the fictional work of *The Other Presence* (Nyathi, 2008) the invisible, which is the supernatural is made visible. The text represents typical African social settings including the presence and manifestations of the supernatural. The text revealed occasions on which the supernatural world, through the spirits visiting the natural world therefore manifest in a top-down manner. Moreover, the novel also presented how the natural world of live human beings consult the supernatural world for different reasons which represents a bottom-up approach. Thus the metaphysical/supernatural is successfully and convincingly represented in a qualitative manner in *The Other Presence* (Nyathi, 2008).

References

Blake, C. (1993) Traditional African Values and the Right to Communicate, *African Media Review* 7(3).

Emeka, A.T. (2012) African Cultural Values, Retrieved from http://www.emeka.at/

Maluleke, M. J. (2012) Culture, Tradition, Custom, Law and Gender Equality, *P E R / P E L Journal* 15(1), Retrieved from http://dx.doi.org/10.4314/pelj.v15i1.1

Mashau, T. D. (2007) Occultism in African Context: A Case for the Vhavenda Speaking People of the Limpopo Province, *In Die Skriflig* 41(4), 637-653.

Mbiti, S.J. (1990) *African Religions and Philosophy,* London: Heinemann.

Mbiti, J. S. (1989) *African Religions and Philosophy*, (2nd ed.), Ibadan: Heinemann Educational Books Nigeria Ltd.

Montenegro, M. (2008) Witnessing to People in the Occult. *Christian Research Journal* 31(5) Retrieved from http://www.equip.org

Nyathi, S. F. (2008) *The Other Presence*, Windhoek: The African Publishers cc.

Onyedinma. E. E., and Kanayo, N. L. (2013) 'Understanding human relations in African traditional religious context in the face of globalization: Nigerian perspectives', *American International Journal of Contemporary Research* 3(2).

Oxford Advanced Learner's Dictionary, (2010), New York: Oxford University Press.

Rabaka, R. (2007). Another African Worldview, *Encyclopedia of Black Studies,* Retrieved from http://knowledge.sagepub.com

Stanford Encyclopaedia of Philosophy (2015), Retrieved from http://www.iep.utm.edu/